First World War

and Army of Occupation

War Diary

France, Belgium and Germany

9 DIVISION
Headquarters, Branches and Services
General Staff
1 May 1914 - 6 June 1917

WO95/1739

The Naval & Military Press Ltd
www.nmarchive.com
Published in association with The National Archives

Published by

The Naval & Military Press Ltd

Unit 10 Ridgewood Industrial Park,

Uckfield, East Sussex,

TN22 5QE England

Tel: +44 (0) 1825 749494

www.naval-military-press.com

www.nmarchive.com

This diary has been reprinted in facsimile from the original. Any imperfections are inevitably reproduced and the quality may fall short of modern type and cartographic standards.

© Crown Copyright
Images reproduced by permission of The National Archives, London, England, 2015.

Contents

Miscellaneous	C Form Messages And Signals.		
Miscellaneous	A Form Messages And Signals.		
Miscellaneous	C Form Messages And Signals.		
Miscellaneous	C Form (Original) Messages And Signals.		
Miscellaneous	A Form Messages And Signals		
Miscellaneous	C Form Messages And Signals		
Miscellaneous	A Form Messages And Signals		
Miscellaneous	G. 813.		
Miscellaneous	S. A. Bde	05/05/1917	05/05/1917
Operation(al) Order(s)	9th Division Order No. 129	08/05/1917	08/05/1917
Miscellaneous	Amendment No. 1 To 9th Division O.O. 130	09/05/1917	09/05/1917
Operation(al) Order(s)	9th (Scottish) Division Operation Order No 130		
Miscellaneous	March Table To Accompany 9th Division Order No. 130		
Miscellaneous	26 D Bde	16/05/1917	16/05/1917
Operation(al) Order(s)	9th Division Order No. 131.	25/05/1917	25/05/1917
Miscellaneous	Movement Table To Accompany 9th Division Order No. 131 dated 25/5/17	25/05/1917	25/05/1917
Miscellaneous	Casualties From 28/4/17 to 11/5/17		
Map			
Map	Map 2		
Miscellaneous	Narrative of Events		
Miscellaneous	Part 1 Events Prior To May 3rd.		
Map			
Miscellaneous	Map I		
Miscellaneous	Events Prior To May 3rd		
Miscellaneous	Part II Plan And Disposition For May 3rd		
Miscellaneous	Plan And Disposition For Operation On May 3rd		
Miscellaneous	Part III Events On May 3rd		
Miscellaneous	Events On May 3rd.		
Miscellaneous	Appendices		
Miscellaneous	Index To Appendices.		
Miscellaneous	Account of The Battle On May 3rd 1917 26th Infantry Brigade.		
Miscellaneous	27th Infantry Brigade. Report On The Attack On 3rd May 1917		
Miscellaneous	Casualties From 28/4/17 To 11/5/17		
Heading	General Staff 9th (Scottish) Division War Diary for May 3rd 1917 With Appendices		
War Diary	Railway Cutting St. Laurent Blangy	03/05/1917	03/05/1917
Miscellaneous	C Form Messages And Signals.		
Miscellaneous	A Form Messages And Signals.		
Miscellaneous	C Form Messages And Signals.		
Miscellaneous	A Form Messages And Signals.		
Miscellaneous	C Form Messages And Signals.		
Miscellaneous	A Form Messages And Signals.		
Miscellaneous			
Miscellaneous	A Form Messages And Signals.		
Miscellaneous	C Form Messages And Signals.		
Miscellaneous	A Form Messages And Signals.		
Miscellaneous	C Form Messages And Signals.		
Miscellaneous	A Form Messages And Signals.		
Miscellaneous	C Form Messages And Signals.		
Miscellaneous	C Form (Duplicate) Messages And Signals.		
Miscellaneous	A Form Messages And Signals.		
Miscellaneous			

Miscellaneous	C Form Messages And Signals.		
Miscellaneous	C Form (Original) Messages And Signals.		
Miscellaneous	A Form Messages And Signals.		
Miscellaneous	C Form (Duplicate). Messages And Signals.		
Miscellaneous	A Form Messages And Signals.		
Miscellaneous	C Form Messages And Signals.		
Miscellaneous	A Form Messages And Signals.		
Heading	9th Division War Diary		
War Diary	Etrun	09/04/1917	12/04/1917
War Diary	St Nicholas	12/04/1917	12/04/1917
War Diary	Etrun	12/04/1917	12/04/1917
War Diary	St Nicholas	12/04/1917	12/04/1917
War Diary	Railway Cutting St. Laurent Blangy	03/05/1917	03/05/1917
War Diary	St Nicholas	05/06/1917	06/06/1917
Heading	General Staff 9th (Scottish) Division War Diary June 5th/6th 1917		
Miscellaneous	Cover For Documents. Nature of Enclosures.		
War Diary	St Nicholas	05/06/1917	06/06/1917
Miscellaneous	A Form Messages And Signals. App. 1		
Miscellaneous	A Form Messages And Signals. App. 2		
Miscellaneous	A Form Messages And Signals. App 3		
Miscellaneous	A Form Messages And Signals. App 4		
Miscellaneous	A Form Messages And Signals. App. 5		
Miscellaneous	A Form Messages And Signals. App 6		
Miscellaneous	C Form Messages And Signals. App 7		
Miscellaneous	C Form Messages And Signals. App 8		
Miscellaneous	C Form Messages And Signals. App 9		
Miscellaneous	C Form Messages And Signals.		
Miscellaneous	C Form Messages And Signals. Appx 10		
Miscellaneous	C Form Messages And Signals.		
Miscellaneous	A Form Messages And Signals. Appx 12		
Miscellaneous	A Form Messages And Signals.		
Miscellaneous	9th (Scottish) Division Defence Scheme (Provisional)		
Miscellaneous	9th (Scottish) Division Defence Scheme (Provisional)	01/06/1917	01/06/1917
Miscellaneous	Appendices May 1917		
Miscellaneous	Cover For Documents. Nature of Enclosures.		
Miscellaneous			
Miscellaneous	A Form Messages And Signals.		
Miscellaneous	C Form (Original) Messages And Signals.		
Miscellaneous	A Form Messages And Signals.		
Miscellaneous	C Form Messages And Signals.		
Miscellaneous	A Form Messages And Signals.		
Miscellaneous	17th Corps 15th Division 34th Division 4th Division		
Miscellaneous	A Form Messages And Signals.		
Miscellaneous	XVII Corps. 4th Division		
Miscellaneous	A Form Messages And Signals.		
Miscellaneous	C Form Messages And Signals.		
Miscellaneous	A Form Messages And Signals.		
Miscellaneous	C Form Messages And Signals.		
Miscellaneous	A Form Messages And Signals.		
Miscellaneous	C Form Messages And Signals.		
Miscellaneous	A Form Messages And Signals.		
Miscellaneous	C Form Messages And Signals.		
Miscellaneous	A Form Messages And Signals.		
Miscellaneous	C Form Messages And Signals.		
Miscellaneous	A Form Messages And Signals.		

Miscellaneous	C Form Messages And Signals.		
Miscellaneous	A Form Messages And Signals.		
Miscellaneous	C Form Messages And Signals.		
Miscellaneous	A Form Messages And Signals.		
Miscellaneous	C Form Messages And Signals.		
Miscellaneous	17th Corps. No. G. 410		
Miscellaneous	C Form Messages And Signals.		
Miscellaneous	A Form Messages And Signals.		
Miscellaneous	C Form Messages And Signals.		
Miscellaneous	A Form Messages And Signals.		
Miscellaneous	C Form Messages And Signals.		
Miscellaneous	C Form (Duplicate) Messages And Signals.		
Miscellaneous	C Form Messages And Signals.		
Miscellaneous	A Form Messages And Signals.		
Miscellaneous	C Form (Duplicate) Messages And Signals.		
Miscellaneous	A Form Messages And Signals.		
Miscellaneous	17th Corps. 15th Division. 34th Division 51st Division		
Miscellaneous	A Form Messages And Signals.		
Miscellaneous	Messages And Signals.		
Miscellaneous	C Form Messages And Signals.		
Miscellaneous	15th Division. 34th Division.		
Miscellaneous	C Form Messages And Signals.		
Miscellaneous	26th Brigade. 27th Brigade. S.A. Brigade "Q"		
Miscellaneous	C Form Messages And Signals.		
Miscellaneous	C Form (Duplicate) Messages And Signals.		
Miscellaneous	C Form Messages And Signals.		
Miscellaneous	26th Brigade. 27th Brigade. S.A. Brigade		
Miscellaneous	C Form Messages And Signals.		
Miscellaneous	26th Brigade. 27th Brigade. S.A. Brigade.		
Miscellaneous	A Form Messages And Signals.		
Miscellaneous	Messages And Signals.		
Miscellaneous	Appendices 12-4-17		
Miscellaneous	A Form Messages And Signals.		
Miscellaneous	Messages And Signals.		
Miscellaneous	A Form Messages And Signals.		
Miscellaneous	C Form Messages And Signals.		
Miscellaneous	17th Corps. No. G. 492		
Miscellaneous	27th Brigade S.A. Brigade. No. G.499	12/04/1917	12/04/1917
Miscellaneous	C Form Messages And Signals.		
Miscellaneous	XVII Corps. 26th Brigade. S.A. Brigade. C.R.A.	12/04/1917	12/04/1917
Miscellaneous	C Form Messages And Signals.		
Miscellaneous	26th Brigade S.A. Brigade. No. G.495	12/04/1917	12/04/1917
Miscellaneous	26th Brigade. 27th Brigade. S.A. Brigade 197 M.G. Coy. C.R.A. C.R.E.	12/04/1917	12/04/1917
Miscellaneous	C Form Messages And Signals.		

9TH DIVISION

GEN. STAFF

MAY 1917.

9TH (SCOTTISH) DIVISION

NARRATIVE OF EVENTS

MAY 3RD 1917

GENERAL STAFF.
9TH (SCOTTISH) DIVISION

W. 15517—M. 141. 250,000. 1/16. L. S. & Co. Forms/W 3091/2.

Army Form W. 3091.

Cover for Documents.

Nature of Enclosures.

Notes, or Letters written.

NARRATIVE OF EVENTS

P A R T 1.

E V E N T S P R I O R T O M A Y 3 R D.

PART 1.

EVENTS PRIOR TO MAY 3RD.

1. The 9th Division (less Artillery, R.E. and Pioneers) was relieved from the battle front by 51st Division on April 14th/15th.

2. On completion of relief the Divisional H.Q. were established at HERMAVILLE, but later moved to OHELERS, the Brigades being distributed :-

26th Infantry Brigade BAILLEUL-AUX-CORNAILLES
27th Infantry Brigade PENIN
S.A. Infantry Brigade MONCHY BRETON

3. On April 28th orders were received for 9th Division to relieve 37th Division in the Left Sector of the Corps front on nights 28th/29th and 29th/30th April.

4. Owing to lack of reinforcements it had been decided to leave the 1st South African Brigade in the MONCHY BRETON Area.

5. G.O.C. 9th Division assumed command of Left Sector at 10 a.m. on April 30th.

6. A Brigade (52nd) of 17th Division was placed at disposal of G.O.C. 9th Division on evening of May 2nd.

P A R T   11.

P L A N A N D D I S P O S I T I O N F O R

M A Y 3 R D.

PART 11.

PLAN AND DISPOSITION FOR OPERATION ON MAY 3RD.

1. The Division was to take part in an offensive in co-operation with 4th Division (17th Corps) on right and 31st Division (X111 Corps) on Left on May 3rd.

The first and fifth Armies were also attacking.

A message was received at Divisional H.Q. on evening of May 2nd that tomorrow's battle would be the biggest the British Army had ever taken part in.

2. The Division was attacking with 26th Infantry Brigade on the Right and 27th Infantry Brigade on the Left, the 52nd Brigade 17th Division being placed at the disposal of G.O.C. as a reserve.

The Divisional objective being the capture of the line WEED - WHY and WEAK trenches and the BIACHE - GAVRELLE road from its junction with WEAK trench to junction with BANK at I.2.a.5.8.

3. The Artillery barrage was to open at ZERO (3.45 a.m.) 200 yards east of our front trench for 4 minutes, and from there move forward. A Machine Gun barrage was to move 400 yards in advance of the Artillery barrage.

4. On the objective being reached consolidation was to be at once begun. Patrols were also to be pushed out to regain touch with the enemy and capture any hostile batteries that might be within reach.

5. The 26th Infantry Brigade was disposed for attack:-

5th Cameron Hrs	Right Assaulting Battalion
8th Black Watch	Left Assaulting Battalion
10th A.& S. Hrs.	Support
7th Seaforth Hrs.	Brigade Reserve.

6..........

6. The 27th Infantry Brigade was disposed as follows :-

9th Scottish Rifles	Right Assaulting Battalion
6th K.O.S.B.	Left Assaulting Battalion
11th Royal Scots	Support Battalion
12th Royal Scots	Brigade Reserve

7. The 52nd Infantry Brigade (17th Division)

9th Northumberland Fusiliers 10th Lancashire Fusiliers	BROWN LINE
9th West Riding Regiment 12th Manchester Regiment	BLUE LINE RAILWAY CUTTING

....
____

P A R T 111.

E V E N T S O N M A Y 3 R D.

PART 111.

EVENTS ON MAY 3RD.

1. ZERO hour was at 3.45 a.m. at which hour our artillery barrage opened and the attacking wave of Infantry advanced.

2. At this early hour it was quite dark and the attacking troops lost direction almost immediately. The enemy who appeared to be ready for our attack opened heavy machine gun fire almost at once from trenches and shell holes, which were closer to our front line than had been expected and which had consequently missed the barrage.

3. 5th Cameron Hrs., who were on the Right of the 26th Infantry Brigade's attack were drawn off by hostile lights being sent up from short lengths of trenches echeloned ~~on~~ in depth swung to their Right and crossed the front of the 2nd Essex Regiment (4th Division) who in the darkness mistook them for enemy and fired on them.

4. The 8th Black Watch on the Left of the ~~27~~ 26th Infantry Brigade also lost cohesion and as far as could be ascertained only a few isolated groups of men ever reached the enemy's front trench.

The two supporting companies of 10th A.& S. Hrs. kept straight on and apparently passed the left flank of the 5th Cameron Hrs. and they also came under heavy enfilade machine gun fire from the direction of the RAILWAY EMBANKMENT and CHEMICAL WORKS.

5. The 9th Scottish Rifles on the right of 27th Infantry Brigade failed to pick up the lamp to guide their left and in spite of compass bearings the two assaulting companies swung to their right and some of the men on the

right.........

swung to such an extent as to mistake the front line of 28th Brigade for the German line and advanced on it firing from the hip. The remainder of these companies struck GUNNER earlier than was intended. Only one wounded officer of these companies returned and reported that this trench was quite undamaged by artillery fire and was occupied by the enemy at about one man per yard. The Left Company probably crossed WHIP trench, but nothing is known of it, or the Right Company, both of which appear to have pressed on. The supporting companies as they advanced came under hostile machine gun fire and dug themselves in 200 yards or so beyond CORK trench.

6. The 11th Royal Scots, supporting battalion, seeing nothing in the dark, pushed up, as ordered, the two companies for the occupation of WISH and WHIP trenches, but these became involved with the rear of the Scottish Rifles who were held up by machine gun fire. Part of these companies dug themselves in with the Scottish Rifles, the remainder were withdrawn to CUBA. The rear two companies also halted in CUBA.

7. On the Left the situation at once became involved. Shortly after the attack began O.C. 6th K.O.S.B., supporting company telephoned back from WIT trench that as the assaulting companies had left that trench and gone on to WOMBLE, he himself was following them to occupy WOMBLE according to his orders.

8. From this it would appear clear that three companies of 6th K.O.S.B. crossed WIT trench and carried on towards their objective.

9. Later the O.C. 9th Scottish Rifles and Major HAMILTON (90th Field Coy. R.E.) not knowing that the rear part of the Scottish Rifles had been held

up moved across to the right of K.O.S.B. in WISH and on arrival there saw one party of about 50 Germans enter WIT near its South end and one further North, both these parties were taken to be prisoners sent back by Scottish Rifles and K.O.S.B's. An officer and 2 men were actually sent to bring the right party in; all three were hit. On receiving this report it was realised that WIT trench was re-occupied, or at any rate occupied, and that the enemy now interposed between the three companies of K.O.S.B's and the remainder of the Brigade.

10. At 4.15 am F.O.O. reported that there had been no hostile lights for last ten minutes, but there was heavy machine gun fire from South Bank of River SCARPE, the hostile barrage had commenced about three minutes after ZERO.

11. At 5.50 a.m. General KENNEDY reported verbally that he was unable to give definite information yet, but from reports of wounded it appeared that our assaulting troops were all back in our front line; the casualties being caused by machine gun fire from the Right.

12. At 6.12 am General KENNEDY reported that there was an officer of the 5th Cameron Hrs with about 40 men consolid-ating in CUTHBERT trench, but he appeared to be isolated. This party was later withdrawn.

13. At 6.17 am a report was received from 27th Infantry Brigade stating that hostile barrage was heavy in front of CUBA. Right Battalion (Scottish Rifles) at 5.10 am reported they had no definite news but thought battalion was making progress. Left Battalion (K.O.S.B) at 4.40 am reported battalion and Right of 31st Division had reached WIT trench, but was not in touch with Right.

14. At 6.30 am the 52nd Brigade (17th Division) which had been placed at disposal of G.O.C. 9th Division and had spent night in ST. NICHOLAS, moved two battalions to BROWN LINE and two battalions to BLUE LINE.

15. Consequent on these reports from 26th and 27th Infantry Brigades, H.Q. XVll Corps and Divisions on flanks were informed that reports indicated attack of our Right Brigade had failed with loss. Left Brigade believed to have made a little progress, but no definite information.

16. At 6.50 am General KENNEDY (26th Inf. Bde) reported that the cause of the trouble was machine guns in the Embankment, he thought between CUPID and COST. In the meanwhile he had ordered the Artillery to bring back the barrage to CUTHBERT but not South of CASH or North of grid line between I.7 and I.1.

17. Contact aeroplanes reported at 7 am that there were no flares shown in advance of our original front line.

18. At 7 am 31st Division, on our left, reported very heavy hostile barrage. The attack on OPPY had apparently failed. Right and Left Battalions had suffered heavily during assembly which appeared to have disorganised the attack.

19. At 7.20 am F.O.O. 32nd Bde. R.F.A. reported that WOBBLE trench had been captured and that patrols were out 600 or 700 yards in front of SQUARE WOOD. Slow progress in centre.

20. Enquiry was then made of 27th Inf. Bde regarding above report of F.O.O. The Brigade Major replied that he had no information to confirm this. The Germans were

reported......

reported to be still in WIT trench (which is West of WOBBLE) firing on our troops in our original front line.

21. At 7.45 am information was received from XVll Corps that 4th Division had been ordered not to renew their attack. Artillery fire was being brought back. The Heavy Artillery to fire on CANDY, CYPRUS, and CARROT trenches and on ROEUX where more than 400 yards from our line.

22. At 7.45 am General MAXWELL (27th Inf. Bde) reported that three companies of Left Battalion (6th K.O.S.B) were beyond WIT trench somewhere, one company and three M.G's still in our front trench. WIT trench appeared to be occupied by Germans along its whole length on our front and also to the North of us. The Brigade of 31st Division on his Left did not know position of its troops in front. The situation on the Right was that 9th Scottish Rifles had got about three companies in the "BLUE" beyond WISH trench and perhaps beyond WIT trench. There was at one time nobody in lower portion of WISH trench. Behind in CORK trench there was a conglomeration of men who were the remainder of the Scottish Rifles trickled back and some of the two companies 11th Royal Scots, who were to have occupied WISH and WIT trenches, behind the Scottish Rifles, ~~more~~ NONE of these two companies got forward. In CUBA trench there were six platoons 11th Royal Scots and one machine gun in action and one knocked out. There were two platoons of 11th Royal Scots in shell holes in front of 8th Black Watch's left, all the Black Watch were back in CUBA. Three companies of his reserve battalion (12th Royal Scots) were still in FAMPOUX line (GREEN line)

General MAXWELL had ordered artillery to keep intermittent bombardment on WIT trench. The right of 27th Brigade was entirely swept by enemy holding ground in front of 26th Brigade. General MAXWELL did not propose to make any effort to get into WIT trench for the time being, as it would be hopeless till southern part is cleared and until 31st Division take their part.

23. At 7.50 am 31st Division reported that they were unable to make any progress and that their Right Brigade was back on defensive in original front line. About twenty minutes later 31st Division reported that enemy was counter attacking along whole front of their Right Brigade in force and had taken the WINDMILL at GAVRELLE, two battalions from Divisional Reserve had been sent up in support.

24. At 8.39 am orders were received from XVll Corps that general attack was not to be pressed for the present. All local successes of 4th Division were to be exploited to the full with a view to capturing CEMETERY, CORONA trench CHEMICAL WORKS and buildings North of Railway. 9th Division was to continue bombardment of points which had held up their attack. Heavy Artillery was to bombard ROEUX, CARROT, CYRRUS and CANDY trenches and Railway East of CUPID. The above order was repeated to 26th and 27th Infantry Brigades and C.R.A.

25. At 9.10 am the H.Q. XVll Corps were informed that attack of Right Brigade had failed and that original line was now held. Three companies of each leading Battalions of the Left Brigade appeared to have crossed WIT trench, but WIT trench was now occupied by Germans.

Consequently these companies which passed WIT

trench......

trench were for the present cut off. It was not intended to attack WIT trench till higher ground to south can be secured, meanwhile original front line was held.

26. At 9.50 am a report was received from XV11 Corps H.A. that our men had been seen in SQUARE WOOD. 27th Infantry Brigade and 31st Division were informed.

27. At request of 27th Infantry Brigade arrangements were made with 17th Corps for an aeroplane to reconnoitre area round WOBBLE trench and SQUARE WOOD and call for flares to ascertain if possible if any of our men were there or not. The aeroplane flew over the area at 11.40 am and called for flares, but none were shown. Apparently there were no troops British or German in WOBBLE trench, but visibility was bad, owing to smoke. The aeroplane had been fired on by hostile machine guns from West end of WEED trench.

28. General KENNEDY (26th Infantry Brigade) reported at 11.15 am that the approximate strength of his Brigade was :-

8th Black Watch	205
7th Seaforth Hrs.	intact
5th Camerons	143
10th A.& S. Hrs.	300

29. At 12.50 pm orders were issued for 27th Infantry Brigade to assault WIT trench between cross roads (WISH cross roads I.2.c.) and northern boundary of 9th Division

at.........

I.1.b.7.8 at an hour to be notified later. WHIP and WIT trenches and WOBBLE trench N. of I.2.a.5.8 were to be intensely bombarded from ZERO hour. At Zero plus 2 minutes the artillery fire was to lift off the portion of the trench to be assaulted. A smoke barrage was to be placed South of the WISH cross roads to conceal the advance from the high ground to south.

Units were notified later that the hour of assault would be 8 p.m.

30. At 1.25 p.m. touch was re-established with 31st Division S.E. of GAVRELLE in our original line.

31. 4th Division reported at 5.55 p.m. that they were holding original front line with exception of posts near ROEUX Station (I.13.central) in some enclosures and buildings near CHATEAU and possibly in CHEMICAL WORKS. Enemy had been advancing into CORONA trench. Situation in CLOVER trench was not clear. The enemy had made several strong counter attacks. One Company, Rifle Brigade(4th Division) and one company (9th Division) had been sent to clear up situation.

32. At 6.50 pm orders were issued for one Field Company R.E. and two companies 9th Seaforth Hrs. (Pioneers) to be at the disposal of each Brigade on night May3rd/4th. for work in clearing the front line and communication trenches. Connection between WISH trench and BRICKFIELD in CUBA to be made by the construction of intermediate strong points which can be subsequently connected by a continuous trench

33. At 7.35 pm orders were received from XVll Corps for Divisions to consolidate and improve positions held. Touch was to be kept with the enemy by means of patrols.

These instructions were repeated to all concerned.

34. At 8 p.m. two companies 12th Royal Scots attacked WIT trench. The trench was strongly held and the Royal Scots in their attack came under very heavy machine gun fire from WIT trench just as they crossed the RIDGE before reaching the trench. Those of the Royal Scots who got in were ejected.

35. The attack enabled a good many K.O.S.B's to return to our lines.

APPENDICES.

I N D E X   T O   A P P E N D I C E S.

=*

APPENDIX 1.

ACCOUNT OF THE BATTLE ON MAY 3RD ,1917.

26th INFANTRY BRIGADE.

1. The assembly was carried out in good order, and was completed by 3 a.m.

The brigade formed up for attack as ordered in Brigade Order No. 111.

2. The barrage opened at ZERO, but appeared to be ragged, especially on the right flank, and some casualties were sustained in the assaulting battalions from our own artillery.

3. Owing to the darkness at Zero, direction was soon lost and there was no cohesion in the attack. The enemy appeared ready for our attack and opened heavy machine gun fire almost at once, from trenches and shell holes, which were closer to our front line than had been expected, and which had been missed by the barrage. Opposite the right flank of the attack, the enemy lights were sent up from his short lengths of trenches "echeloned" in depth, and this caused the 5th Cameron Highlanders to mistake them for the enemy front line and to swing to their right, and cross the front of the 2nd ESSEX Regiment. This caused the latter Regiment to shoot at the 5th Cameron Highlanders who also sustained heavy casualties from enemy Machine Gun fire.

The 2 Supporting Companies, 10th Argyll and Sutherland Highlanders kept straight on and apparently passed the left flank of the 5th Cameron Highlanders,

Highlanders ....

Highlanders, and they also came under Heavy enfilade Machine Gun fire from the direction of the RAILWAY EMBANKMENT and the CHEMICAL WORKS.

The 8th Black Watch on the left also lost cohesion, and as far as is known, only a few isolated groups of men ever reached the enemy front line. So great was the confusion owing to the intensity of the darkness, that the right Battalions of the 27th. Brigade actually mistook our own front line for the German line, and advanced on it firing from the hip. This accounts for the fact that so many men of the 27th Brigade eventually got into our trenches.

4. The German Machine Guns caused heavy casualties, and caused the attackers to return to our front line. Here a second attack was organised and a gallant attempt was made to capture the German front line, but it failed, and by this time, our barrage had almost, if not quite reached its final limit. The remnants of the assaulting Battalions were driven back by heavy Machine Gun fire, to our own trenches, which were at once organised for defence against counter-attack.

5. When the enemy discovered that our attack had been repulsed, his Artillery fire, which had been both intense and accurate, slackened down, and his snipers, lying scattered all over the ground in shell holes, became extremely active, and caused casualties.

6/..............

6. Owing to the fact that so few Officers were left from any of the assaulting Companies, it is impossible to collect any accurate accounts of what really took place, but in the opinion of those who are still with their Battalions, the failure was caused by the darkness and our unprepared state for a night attack.

==*=*=*=*=*=*=*=*=*=*

OBSERVATIONS ON THE ATTACK.

Assembly was easily carried out, and no interference from Hostile Artillery.

All ranks are agreed that the hour of ZERO was too early and that the darkness caused the attack to lose all direction and cohesion.

No attack on a large scale has been done by this Division at night, for a very long time, and it was not expected that such an operation was contemplated. Sufficient care and thought had not, therefore, been given to working out the necessary details to ensure the success of an attack in the dark. Had longer notice of the change of the ZERO hour been given, it would still have been possible to lay out tapes and provide phosphorescent boards, taking careful compass bearings etc., the plan of attack would have been entirely altered, so as to ensure touch being kept from front to rear. I should have made successive advances on the "Leap Frog" system instead of going straight through.

I was only informed at 2 pm. that the ZERO hour had been changed - the alteration of 20 minutes having the effect of changing the whole character of the attack from a daylight to a night attack.

It.................

It is not necessary for troops to know the hour of ZERO, but it is absolutely necessary that they should know some days beforehand if it is to be by day or by night.

All arrangements had been made for daylight observation and transmission of reports. From my Headquarters it was possible to see the whole field of operations, but owing to the dark, this was not used and it was most difficult to follow the progress of the attack.

. . . .

THE ADVANCE.

The difficulty was accentuated in the dark by the fact that on the right flank the 4th Division front line was some 200 yards behind my Brigade and the line from there gradually ran back. The result was that as the men advanced, the enemy Very Lights appeared on their right flank, and the whole attack of the 5th Cameron Highlanders swung round in that direction. The 10th Argyll and Sutherland Highlanders supporting companies kept direction better, and went right through the gap left between the Cameron Highlanders and the Black Watch. They were, ofcourse, a long way behind the barrage, but went right over CHARLIE

and ....

CUTHBERT trenches until they came under very heavy Machine Gun fire from all sides, and bombing counter-attacks from vicinity of GAVRELLE - PLOUVAIN road. Most of them appear to have got into shell holes, and are gradually making their way back, 68 having come in at night, but I fear the remainder are killed or prisoners.

The Black Watch attack was repulsed by machine gun and rifle fire, and bombs. They made a second attack and drove the enemy out of CHARLIE and CUTHBERT, killing a good many, but were unable to remain, owing to very heavy enfilade fire from Machine Guns in the EMBANKMENT and CHEMICAL WORKS.

The whole attack was eventually withdrawn to the original front line, and the defehce re-organised. This was rendered very difficult by 3 enemy aeroplanes who flew constantly up and down the line at a very low altitude, firing at our men. One was eventually brought down with Machine Gun fire, but the boldness of the enemy aeroplanes, which has noticeably increased lately, was quite unprecedented as far as the experience of this Brigade goes.

<u>ENEMY TACTICS.</u>

The enemy did not appear to be in his trenches, but occupying shell holes everywhere with a very great number of machine guhs, used both for frontal fire with his advanced troops, and also from the flanks.

He appeared to be quite ready for our attack as he opened at onee with his Artillery barrage, and machine gun and rifle fire. His artillery barrage was negligible as far as "stopping" the advance goes.

His Infantry used their rifles well and supplemented it with the bomb at close quarters.

The machine guns however, are the real defence and are handled with great skill.

The 10th Argyll and Sutherland Highlanders who got near the embankment say they had guns on top of the embankment and others at the foot, and echeloned back in shell holes. It would seem, therefore, that he is usihg his machine gun as a very mobile weapon, though the rapidity with which certain grazing fire is brought to bear on certain zones, seems to show that he must have a certain number of guns in permanent positions firing on barrage lines.

OUR TACTICS.

It is difficult to write about these without

appearing.................

appearing to critisise ,but I think the following points may be worth consideration.

We have, with the very limited opportunities of training which can be allowed to troops engaged in trench and active warfare, been able to concentrate on one form of attack - the organised trench attack. This has been perfected, but neither Officers or men know any other. The fighting has, at present, got into the advanced stage when we cannot rely on complete artillery preparation or "Protection". The enemy's position is nebulous and constantly changing - he is constantly producing awkward little situations for us, his local Commanders appear to act with skill and determination, encroaching on us constantly with bombing attacks forming little pockets of snipers or Machine Guns in unexpected places, not waiting in definite lines of trenches, to be barraged by our Artillery. Against this, we are using the same tactics as in the first phase. The barrage, I think, should now be shrapnel, but all ground in vicinity of enemy trenches, should be constantly searched at night, to get the enemy in his shell holes.

More smoke still is required to blind his Machine Guns, and gas, if possible.

Known bad pockets should be passed round, a feint or holding attack being made against such places. The actual position of the Machine Guns is not the bad pocket, but the place where the

bullets...............

bullets from that gun sweep. We are apt to avoid the place where the Machine Guns are, and attempt to brush past in the Zone where they kill.

As far as Infantry are concerned, if the first organised attack is held up and they lose their barrage, there is a tendency to think that nothing more can be done. It certainly is no good launching a fresh attack or sacrificing more troops against Machine Guns in position, but I think the Infantry of the old army, who were taught the old Infantry advance by alternate rushes, supported by their own rifle and machine gun fire, who knew how to fight a battle of localities and tactical points, would gain much ground, even when the original attack has become disorganised, and would be constantly putting the enemy at a disadvantage. An extended wave gets into shell holes in pairs etc., without leadership, and it is lost. I think each extended line wants a pivot of troops in close formation, in close support.

We appear to be suffering from:-

(1) Want of leadership, which can in some way be corrected by less extended formation and more practice for Officers and N.C.O'S handling and leading men.

(2) Want of initiative, which can in some way be remedied by fuller explanation of the general situation, and the encouragement and direction of local

enterprises during the lulls in main operations.

(3) Want of elasticity and scope in training and formations.

(4) Want of training of rank and file.

APPENDIX 2. 11.

27th INFANTRY BRIGADE.

REPORT ON THE ATTACK ON 3RD MAY, 1917.

1. Objective of Brigade, as shewn on plan. As it would not be possible to discover and pick up the small features i.e. road track, WEAK and WHY Trenches, assaulting Battalions were directed to halt behind the protective barrage and as soon as there was light enough to see the above, to occupy the line made by them and dig in.

2. Distribution of Brigade at ZERO.

9th Scottish Rifles, right assaulting Battalion formed up in CORK and CUBA. (echeloned behind the right of Left assaulting Battalion which occupied a more advanced trench), right on BRIQUETERIE in touch with 26th Brigade.

6th K.O.S.B., left assaulting Battalion, formed up in WISH Trench, OLIVE and CIVIC, with left in touch with 93rd Brigade of 31st Division.

Support Battalion.	11th Royal Scots in CANDIA.
Brigade Reserve.	12th Royal Scots in German third system trenches.
27th M.G. Company.	1 section with each Assaulting Battalion. Half Section with Support Battalion. 1 section to remain in North portion of WISH. Half section to remain in South portion of WISH, and in WHIP when reached and passed by the attack of the Right Battalion.
Stokes Battery.	To remain in third system till required, the ammunition being dumped in WISH.
28th Machine Gun Coy.	Was employed under the Division for barrage fire during the attack, but was subsequently attached to this Brigade.

3.

3. Orders for Brigade Action at ZERO. (3-45 a.m.)

Right Battalion. (Scottish Rifles) with two Companies in front line, each in two waves, and two in close support in columns of platoon, to leave their front trenches at Zero and, moving with their left on a lamp placed as a guide to it on the extremity of the K.O.S.B. right, to get level with the latter Battalion and push on with it when the barrage straightened out and crept eastwards. Support Company to dig a second line left on road as a support to front line.

Left Battalion. (K.O.S.B.) with two companies in front line and one in support was to leave the fourth company in reserve in front trench. Right of Battalion on a due East bearing, left on road track in touch with 93rd Brigade of 31st. Division. Assaulting Companies to leave WISH Trench at ZERO to get under the barrage. Support Company to occupy WOBBLE as a second lime to the new one to be occupied.

Support Battalion. (11th Royal Scots) two companies to occupy WISH and WHIP Trenches. Two Companies to stand fast in CUBA prepared to fill a gap if one occurred between Brigade right and 26th. Brigade left.

Reserve Battalion. (12th Royal Scots) to remain

in....................

in German third system as Brigade Reserve.

4. Narrative.

At Zero, 5-45 a.m. it was just possible to see some 40 to 50 Yards along a white path or track: otherwise it was dark and direction except with compass impossible. The advance of this Brigade was at an oblique angle to the front held.

At ZERO, the right Battalion got clear of its trenches the lamp to guide the left was not picked up and in spite of compass bearings the two assaulting companies swung up their left shoulders, so that instead of going due East they moved S.S.E. the right thereby striking CUTHBERT trench earlier than intended. Only one wounded Officer of these Companies returned and reports that this trench was quite undamaged by Artillery Fire and was occupied by the enemy at about 1 man per yard. Some killing was done in this trench, the Officer himself (a very good one) shooting three Germans. The left Company probably crossed WHIP, but nothing is known of it or the right company, both of which appear to have pressed on. The supporting Companies as they advanced came under Machine Gun fire and dug themselves in 200 Yards or so beyond CORK Trench, right on the bank.

The right Company of the 26th Brigade lost direction to the left at ZERO and was mixed up with the rear companies of the Scottish Rifles.

The...............

The Supporting Battalion 11th Royal Scots seeing nothing in the dark pushed up, as ordered, the two Companies for the occupation of WISH and WHIP trenches, but these became involved with the rear of the Scottish Rifles held up by Machine Gun fire. Some dug in with the Scottish Rifles, the remainder were withdrawn to CUBA.

The rear two Companies also halted in CUBA.

On the left the situation was, and still is, involved.

Shortly after the attack began, O.C., 6th K.O.S.B. Supporting Company telephoned back from WIT Trench that as the Assaulting Companies had left that trench and gone on to WOBBLE, he himself was following them to occupy WOBBLE according to his orders.

It seemed absolutely clear from this that three K.O.S.B. Companies had crossed WIT, and carried on towards the objective. O.C.,K.O.S.B. reported, somewhat later, that Scottish Rifles on right and 26th Brigade on Scottish Rifles right were held up, and he therefore was sending a platoon to block South end of WIT to protect his right.

Later again, O.C. Scottish Rifles and Major HAMILTON R.E. not knowing that the rear part of the Scottish Rifles had been held up moved across to K.O.S.B. right (in WISH) and on arrival there saw one party of about 50 Germans enter WIT near its South end and one further North: they took both these parties to be prisoners sent back by Scottish Rifles and K.O.S.B.

and.............

and actually sent an Officer and two men to bring the right party in. All three were hit by some other enemy. On receiving this report verbally from Major HAMILTON I realized that WIT was re-occupied, or at any rate occupied and that the enemy now interposed between us and three companies of K.O.S.B.

Enquiry from the Brigade on my left elicited the fact that it had not reached WIT at all and had no hope of doing so. I accordingly asked for Artillery fire on that part of WIT opposite my front in the hope of clearing the Germans out, and this fire was kept on, first for a considerable period, and then intermittently during the morning.

No news came back from the K.O.S.B. and the only possible information of them was that received from the artillery that some of our men were seen in SQUARE WOOD.

This situation did not change all day.

Unwilling to leave troops, which had got on, unsupported and cut off, I decided to attack WIT Trench with the object of holding it during the night to allow K.O.S.B. to return under cover of darkness to our lines instead of into German hands.

At 8 p.m. therefore while there was still good light, one and a half companies from the Reserve Battalion (12th Royal Scots) were ordered to make the attack, covered on each flank by artillery fire and Machine Gun barrage to obscure the view of enemy Machine Guns. These flank barrages to continue till

darkness...........

darkness set in. An Officer patrol was, after the capture of WIT, to go out and find K.O.S.B's.

At 8 p.m. Artillery opened for one minute on WIT, and the 6 platoons attacked.

For long (nearly an hour) it was thought that they had succeeded, but as no report came back, but only a few wounded men it was realised that it had failed. M.G. fire from the right appears to have swept the 200 yards of "No Man's Land" with such effect that of about 150 who started no less than 120 were casualties of whom 80 are missing.

As a result of the attack however, a considerable number of K.O.S.B's came in, mostly from the right half of the attack front. Included amongst these was Captain TILTMAN Commanding the Right Assaulting Company K.O.S.B. He reported that until he returned to our lines and learnt we were attacking WIT, he thought he was in front of WOBBLE. Not only did he cross a trench, a poor one, in the morning which he took to be WIT, but he re-crossed it again and halted in it on coming back when our 8 p.m. attack began. The only explanation is that he took the small sections of trench about 80 yards beyond our front line for WIT.

But this, though apparently the truth as regards the Right Assaulting Company, could not apply to the Left Company and the Support Company, in front of which there is no such subsidiary line between their starting trench and WIT itself. The only conclusion to be drawn therefore is that WIT trench opposite our Left was either unoccupied or over-run by the K.O.S.B's. left assaulting Company and Support Company and must have been re-occupied after they passed beyond. The message from the Support Company Commander already referred to makes it perfectly clear that a trench was crossed, and as there is no semblence of one, even by the latest air photographs, except WIT, it must have been WIT that this

K.O.S.B. crossed. How far they advanced beyond will now never be known, as the whole of them have disappeared. But whatever the truth, I should under similar circumstances act no differently again, and I believe the G.O.C. would not have me act differently. Troops which press on deserve to be supported in every way, and those which have the confidence that they will be so supported, and that they will be assisted if they get into trouble will go further than those who have not this confidence.

The alternative of clearing WIT with the reserve battalion much earlier in the day presented itself to me, but had to be rejected, for with Brigades held up in their original front lines both on right and left, it would have resulted in nothing but the inevitable loss of any such troops sent on the mission. To wait for the approach of darkness was, I think, the only chance.

I regret that the casualties suffered by the Brigade are heavy. Of an approximate number of 2,200 bayonets when the Brigade went into action, 38 officers and 912 other ranks ~~and~~ are killed, wounded and missing.

If however the attack was unsuccesful and casualties heavy, I sbbmit that an enemy which cannot take advantage of a successful defence by counter attack is one that is either ignorant of war or has little stomach for it. The Germans are not ignorant of war; counter attack, to their credit, was almost their religion. A satisfactory conclusion can there be drawn from their absolute failure to strike back on May 3rd.

An interesting incident occurred at 1 am on night of 2nd/3rd May. While the support battalion was forming up in CANDIA trench an enemy aeroplane, flying low, fired tracer bullets along it and then signalled with a light.

This was immediately followed by coloured lights sent up from the enemy"s front line, and a few minutes later a heavy artillery barrage fell on CANDIA and CUBA positions for about 20 minutes. Just previous to Zero the enemy again bombarded these two trenches.

I shall submit, later, names of officers, N.C.Os and men whose services I desire to bring to the notice of the G.O.C.

9TH DIV

G.S.

MAY, 1917

War Diary

+

appendices

July 14th – July 29th
both inclusive

(4497) W. 4884/M680 250,000 8/16 McA. & W., Ltd. (Est. 279) Forms/W 3091/3.

Army Form W. 3091.

Cover for Documents.

Nature of Enclosures.

Notes, or Letters written.

Instructions regarding War Diaries and Intelligence Summaries are contained in F. S. Regs., Part II. and the Staff Manual respectively. Title pages will be prepared in manuscript.

WAR DIARY
or
INTELLIGENCE SUMMARY.

(Erase heading not required.)

Army Form C. 2118.

Place	Date	Hour	Summary of Events and Information	Remarks and references to Appendices
RAILWAY CUTTING (St LAURENT – BLANGY)	1st	10 am	G.O.C. 4th Division took over command of ~~left~~ Right Division front on our right	
		2 pm	G.O.C. Corps held a conference at H.Q. 9th Division	
		4 pm	G.O.C. 9th Division held a conference at Divisional Headquarters for Brigade commanders, C.R.A., C.R.E.	
		10 pm	9th Division Order No 127 for movement of 52nd Infantry Brigade (17th Division) on May 3rd this brigade has been allotted as a Divisional reserve.	App 1
			Preliminary Instructions No 1 for Operations on May 3rd issued.	App 2
			Weather fine and warm	

M.H.

Instructions regarding War Diaries and Intelligence Summaries are contained in F. S. Regs., Part II. and the Staff Manual respectively. Title pages will be prepared in manuscript.

WAR DIARY
or
INTELLIGENCE SUMMARY.
(Erase heading not required.)

Army Form C. 2118.

Place	Date	Hour	Summary of Events and Information	Remarks and references to Appendices
RAILWAY CUTTING ST LAUREN-BLANGY	2nd	2pm	9th Division Operation Order No 128 for operations on May 3rd issued.	App
			Preliminary instructions No 2 for operations on May 3rd issued.	App 4

A5834 Wt. W4973/M687 750,000 8/16 D. D. & L. Ltd. Forms/C.2118/13.

Instructions regarding War Diaries and Intelligence Summaries are contained in F. S. Regs., Par. II. and the Staff Manual respectively. Title pages will be prepared in manuscript.

WAR DIARY
or
INTELLIGENCE SUMMARY.
(Erase heading not required.)

Army Form C. 2118.

Place	Date	Hour	Summary of Events and Information	Remarks and references to Appendices
RAILWAY CUTTING	3rd May	3.45am	ZERO hour, our artillery put down barrage and assaulting Infantry advanced.	
ST.LAURENT BLANGY	1917	4.4am	A message timed 3.30 am was received from 27th Infantry Brigade reporting that movement into assembly area was complete.	App 5
		4.10am	32nd Bde. R.F.A. reported that enemy was putting down heavy barrage all along our front line. The same Brigade reported heavy rifle and machine gun fire on our front about half an hour later.	App 6.7
		4.15am	F.O.O. reported that there had been no hostile lights for last ten minutes. Heavy M.G. fire from south of RIVER. Enemy barrage commenced about 3 minutes after ZERO.	App 8
		4.55 am	Report from 32nd Bde. R.F.A. (timed 4.35) stated that hostile lights were going up further East.	App 9
		4.55 am	General KENNEDY (26th Inf. Bde) reported that his Brigade observer reported that enemy's Very Lights were being sent up from much further EAST. Hostile barrage had slackened considerably. A certain amount of M.G. fire from RIGHT. It was still too dark for observation.	
		5.3 am	31st Division (on our LEFT) reported our barrage opened at 3.45 am. Enemy appeared slow in replying. Enemy barrage on Right Brigade commenced 10 minutes after ZERO. Coloured lights now ceased.	App 10
		5.15 am	Following report (G.755) was sent to 17th Corps and repeated to 4th and 31st Divisions. Reports that at 4.55 am state that light was not good for observation. Hostile Very Lights being sent up further EAST. Barrage now decreased.	App 11
		5.20 am	A report was received from 4th Division (on our Right) that their Right Brigade was getting on well. Left Company Somerset Light Infantry had got into ROEUX. Right Company was held up.	
		5.50 am	General KENNEDY (26th Inf. Bde) reported that he was unable to give definite information yet, but from reports of wounded it appeared that our assaulting troops were all back in our front line, The casualties being caused by M.G. fire from Right.	

A6945 Wt. W11422/M1160 350,000 12/16 D. D. & L. Forms/C./2118/14.

Instructions regarding War Diaries and Intelligence Summaries are contained in F. S. Regs., Par. II, and the Staff Manual respectively. Title pages will be prepared in manuscript.

WAR DIARY
or
INTELLIGENCE SUMMARY.
(Erase heading not required.)

Army Form C. 2118.

Place	Date	Hour	Summary of Events and Information	Remarks and references to Appendices
RAILWAY CUTTING ST LAURENT BLANGY	3rd May	6.12.	General KENNEDY (26th Inf. Bde) reported an officer of 5th Camerons in CUTHBERT trench, consolidating, has about 40 men with him but appeared to be isolated.	
		6.17am	27th Inf. Bde reported telephone communications forward of old German 3rd system broken. Enemy's barrage reported heavy in front of CUBA. Right Battalion at 5.10 am had reported no definite news but think Battalion is getting on. Left Battalion at 4.40 am reported Battalion and right of 31st Division had reached WIT trench, but was not in touch on Right.	12
		6.20am	XVII Corps and Divisions on flanks informed that reports indicate attack of Right Brigade has failed with loss. Left Brigade believed to have made a little progress, but no definite information.	13
		6.50am	52nd Bde. R.F.A. reported that CUTHBERT trench was now evacuated by our Infantry.	14
		6.50am	32nd Bde. R.F.A. reported that WOBBLE trench had been captured, and advance continued 700 to 800 yards in direction of SQUARE WOOD.	15
		6.50 am	General KENNEDY (26th Inf. Bde) reported that cause of the trouble was machine guns in EMBANKMENT, he thought between CUPID and COST. He had told the artillery to bring back barrage to CUTHBERT, but not South of CASH or North of grid line between I.7 and I.1.	
		7.0 am	Map dropped by contact aeroplane showed no flares in advance of our original front line.	
		7.0am	31st Division reported very heavy hostile barrage. Germans putting up many lights, white breaking into two red balls. Attack on OPPY apparently failed. Right and Left Battalions suffered heavily during assembly, which seems to be disorganised the attack.	16
		7.20am	~~32nd~~ 52nd Bde. R.F.A. reported that WOBBLE trench had been captured. Patrols out 600 or 700 yards in front of SQUARE WOOD. Slow progress in centre. On enquiry being made Brigade Major 27th Inf. Bde. stated message from F.O.O. regarding capture of WOBBLE trench had been repeated to him. He had no information to confirm this. Germans were reported to be still in WIT trench (West of WOBBLE) firing on our troops in our original front line.	17

Army Form C. 2118.

WAR DIARY
or
INTELLIGENCE SUMMARY.
(Erase heading not required.)

Instructions regarding War Diaries and Intelligence Summaries are contained in F. S. Regs., Par. II, and the Staff Manual respectively. Title pages will be prepared in manuscript.

Place	Date	Hour	Summary of Events and Information	Remarks and references to Appendices
RAILWAY CUTTING ST LAURENT BLANGY	3rd May	7.45am	B.G., G.S. XVll Corps informed G.S.O.1 that he had told 4th Division not to renew their attack, Artillery fire was being brought back. The Heavy Artillery to fire on CANDY, CYPRUS, and CARROT trenches and on ROEUX where more than 400 yards from our line.	
		7.45am	General MAXWELL (27th Inf. Bde) reported that three companies of Left Battalion (6th K.O.S.B) are beyond WIT trench somewhere. WIT trench appears to be occupied by the Germans. It is occupied all along its length, and also occupied to North of us. Brigade on his Left does not know where its people are. One company and three machine guns still in old front line. The situation on the right was that 9th Scottish Rifles had got three companies at least, half of this, or three companies in the "BLUE" beyond WISH and perhaps WIT. There was at one time nobody in lower portion of WISH. Behind in CORK trench a conglomeration of men who are the remainder of the Scottish Rifles trickled back, and some of the two companies of the 11th Royal Scots, who were to have taken WISH and WIT trenches, behind the Scottish Rifles. None of these two companies got forward. In CUBA there are 6 platoons 11th Royal Scots and one machine gun in action and one knocked out. Two platoons of the 11th Royal Scots in shell holes in front of 8th Black Watch's Left, all the Black Watch are in CUBA. Three companies of Reserve Battalion (12th Royal Scots) still in the GREEN LINE. Have asked F.O.O. to keep intermittent bombardment on WIT. Our right is entirely swept by enemy, who are holding 26th Inf. Bde's Area. That he did not propose to make any effort to get into WIT for the time being because Lt-Col. SMYTHE (O.C. Left Battn.) reports it would be hopeless to do this until Southern part is cleared and from his own point of view until Brigade on Left takes their part of WIT trench.	
		7.50am	31st Division reported that they had been able to make no progress, and that Right Brigade was back on defensive in original front trench.	18
		8.10 am	31st Division reported enemy was counter-attacking whole front of their Right Brigade in force and had taken the MILL at GAVRELLE, Two Battalions from Divisional Reserve had been sent up in support.	19

Instructions regarding War Diaries and Intelligence Summaries are contained in F. S. Regs., Part II. and the Staff Manual respectively. Title pages will be prepared in manuscript.

WAR DIARY
or
INTELLIGENCE SUMMARY.
(Erase heading not required.)

Army Form C. 2118.

Place	Date	Hour	Summary of Events and Information	Remarks and references to Appendices
RAILWAY CUTTING ST.LAURENT BLANGY	3rd. May	8.39am	Orders received from XVII Corps that general attack was not to be pressed for present. All local successes of 4th Division to be exploited to full, with a view of capturing CEMETERY, CORONA trench, CHEMICAL WORKS, and buildings North of RAILWAY. 9th Division to continue bombardment of points which held up their attack. Heavy Artillery was to bombard ROEUX, CARROT, CYPRUS, and CANDY trenches and RAILWAY East of CUPID. The above order was repeated to 26th and 27th Inf. Bdes and C.R.A.	
		9.10am	The following report was sent to the XVII Corps:- Right Brigade attack has failed and original front line is now held. Left Brigade, three companies of each of the two leading battalions appear to have crossed WIT trench, but WIT trench is now occupied by Germans, Consequently the companies which passed WIT trench are for the present cut off. It is not intended to attack WIT trench till higher ground to south can be secured, which is out of the question at present. Meanwhile original front line is held.	
		9.50am	Report received from Corps H.A. through Liaison Officer that our men are in SQUARE WOOD. G.S.O.1 informed 27th Inf. Bde and 31st Division and inquired about 31st Division's barrage going on to SQUARE WOOD. 31st Division were also informed as to situation as far as we knew it.	
		10.5am	27th Inf. Bde. reported that on hearing that 93rd Inf. Bde, on their left, was being counter attacked, General MAXWELL had ordered up one company of Reserve battalion to CIDER trench and was keeping artillery on to WIT trench. 28th M.G. Coy has 8 guns now barraging the ground beyond our objective in the direction of WAIT trench and SQUARE WOOD, the other 8 are barraging all the high ground East of CUTHBERT so as to protect the Right and rear of 27th Inf. Bde troops in the direction of WOBBLE, otherwise no change. 27th Inf. Bde unable to do more on its front until high ground on right is taken as it commands their area. 93rd Inf. Bde. are in their front line and have no intention of reoccupying WIT, which will make it difficult for 27th Inf. Bde to do so although it is important for them to get rid of the enemy interposing between their advance men and original front line.	

Army Form C. 2118.

Instructions regarding War Diaries and Intelligence Summaries are contained in F. S. Regs., Part II. and the Staff Manual respectively. Title pages will be prepared in manuscript.

WAR DIARY
or
INTELLIGENCE SUMMARY.
(Erase heading not required.)

Place	Date	Hour	Summary of Events and Information	Remarks and references to Appendices
RAILWAY CUTTING ST.LAURENT BLANGY	3rd May	10.5am	27th Inf. Bde were informed that Major HAMILTON (90th Field Coy.R.E.) had reported that the Germans were on Hill 80 N.W. of GAVRELLE. General MAXWELL replied that the Germans were towards HILL 80.	
		10.10am	27th Inf. Bde asked if an aeroplane could be sent to reconnoitre area of WOBBLE trench to ascertain if possible whether our men are there or not.	23
		10.10am	G.O.C. reported situation verbally to G.O.C. 17th Corps. Our infantry seen in SQUARE WOOD, WIT trench occupied by Germans who came in to it from the North. WIT trench cannot be retaken unless ground is retaken on right, and also unless the Right Brigade of 31st Division could attack on our Left. 31st Division were unable to do this, were only just managing to hold their original line. Smoke was required on right of 27th Inf. Bde.	
		10.50am	XVII Corps were asked if an aeroplane could be sent to reconnoitre the area of WOBBLE trench and SQUARE WOOD to ascertain if possible whether our men are there or not.	24
		10.25am	27th Inf. Bde were asked if they were in touch with 31st Division on their Left, the Brigade replied that their Left troops could see troops on Right of 31st Division in original trench. This information was repeated to H.Q. XVII Corps.	
		10.46am	31st Division reported that they were holding Eastern edge of GAVRELLE to RAILWAY. The WINDMILL had changed hands three times. They were then organising a new attack on it. Apparently their Left Brigade was checked in their advance in OPPY WOOD which enabled the enemy to counter attack exposed left flank of Right Brigade and roll it up.	25
		10.54am	Information received from 17th Corps that an aeroplane was being sent to call for "flares" and reconnoitre area WOBBLE trench and SQUARE WOOD to ascertain if possible if our men were there or not. 27th Inf. Brigade were informed.	26

A6945 Wt. W11422/M1160 350,000 12/16 D. D. & L. Forms/C./2118/14.

Army Form C. 2118.

Instructions regarding War Diaries and Intelligence Summaries are contained in F. S. Regs., Par. II, and the Staff Manual respectively. Title pages will be prepared in manuscript.

WAR DIARY
or
INTELLIGENCE SUMMARY.
(Erase heading not required.)

Place	Date	Hour	Summary of Events and Information	Remarks and references to Appendices
RAILWAY CUTTING ST LAURENT BLANGY	3rd May	11.15am	General KENNEDY (26th Inf. Bde) reported that the approximate strength of his Brigade was now as follows:-	
			8th Black Watch 205 7th Seaforths Hrs. intact 5th Cameron Hrs. 143 10th A. & S. Hrs. 300	
		11.45am	26th Inf. Bde were informed that 4th Division had some men dug in on road West of CHEMICAL WORKS. They were going to push along CORONA trench and try and take the CEMETERY.	
		12.20pm	Instructions were sent to 27th Inf. Bde to establish connection with 31st Division, and to report when touch had been gained.	
		12.40pm	XVll Corps reported that contact patrol aeroplanes would fly along Corps front and call for flares at 2 pm, paying special attention to CHEMICAL WORKS.	28
		12.45pm	XVll Corps reported that contact aeroplane called for flares at 11.40 and 11.50 am but none were shown. Apparently there were no troops British or German in WOBBLE trench, but visibility bad owing to smoke. Aeroplane was fired on by hostile machine guns from West end of WEED trench.	
		12.50pm	26th Inf. Bde reported that units in the front trenches state that CHILI trench was being heavily shelled by 4.2 and 5.9 howitzers from N.E., counter battery action required. The necessary arrangements were made made accordingly with Heavy Artillery.	

A6945 Wt. W11422/M1160 350,000 12/16 D. D. & L. Forms/C./2118/14.

Army Form C. 2118.

Instructions regarding War Diaries and Intelligence Summaries are contained in F. S. Regs., Par. II, and the Staff Manual respectively. Title pages will be prepared in manuscript.

WAR DIARY
or
INTELLIGENCE SUMMARY.
(Erase heading not required.)

Place	Date	Hour	Summary of Events and Information	Remarks and references to Appendices
RAILWAY CUTTING ST. LAURENT BLANGY	3rd May	12.50	9th Division message G.771 was issued, this ordered 27th Infantry Brigade to assault WIT trench between cross roads I.2.c. and northern boundary of 9th Division at I.1.b.7.8 at an hour to be notified later. WHIP and WIT trenches and WOBBLE trench N. of I.2.a.5.8 will be intensely bombarded from ZERO hour. At ZERO plus 2 minutes the artillery fire will lift off the portion of the trench to be assaulted. A smoke barrage will be placed South of the cross roads in I.2.c. and conceal the advance from the high ground on south.	29
		1.25	31st Division reported that their right was now in touch with our left (27th Inf. Bde) S.E. of GAVRELLE.	30
		1.27	The above information was reported to 27th Inf. Bde.	31
		2.0	27th Inf. Bde reported that 6th K.O.S.B. were now in touch with 15th West Yorkshire Regt (31st Division)	32
		3.6	31st Division reported that enemy had been seen in valley N.E. of GAVRELLE (C.19.b.) preparing for another attack on GAVRELLE WINDMILL. Artillery was engaging him. The above information was repeated to 27th Inf. Bde.	33 & 34
		3.6	Instructions from XV11 Corps artillery for support of attack by 27th Inf. Bde were received.	
		3.28.	F.O.O. 52nd Brigade reported at 2.57 pm white lights were being sent up from CUBA trench I.7.a.3.3. It was ascertained later that these lights were sent up by our troops as our artillery was shooting short.	35
		3.30	31st Division reported that they had recaptured WINDMILL at GAVRELLE.	36
		4 pm	All concerned were notified that ZERO hour for attack by 27th Inf. Bde would be 8 p.m.	37

Army Form C. 2118.

Instructions regarding War Diaries and Intelligence Summaries are contained in F. S. Regs., Par. II, and the Staff Manual respectively. Title pages will be prepared in manuscript.

WAR DIARY
or
INTELLIGENCE SUMMARY.
(Erase heading not required.)

Place	Date	Hour	Summary of Events and Information	Remarks and references to Appendices
RAILWAY CUTTING ST. LAURENT BLANGY	3rd May	5.55	4th Division reported that they were holding original front line with axception of posts at I.13.central in some enclosures and buildings near CHATEAU and possibly in CHEMICAL WORKS. Enemy have been advancing into CORONA trench. Situation in CLOVER trench not clear. Enemy had made several strong counter attacks. One company Rifle Brigade and one company 9th Division have been sent to clear up situation.	
		6.50	Orders were issued for one Field Company R.E. and two companies Pioneers to be at disposal of each Brigade tonight for work in clearing front line and communication trenches. O.C. 9th Seaforths to arrange to place one additional company at disposal of each Brigade for the purpose. Connection between WISH trench and the BRICKFIELD in CUBA to be made by the construction of intermediate strong points which can be subsequently connected by a continuous trench.	
		7,35	Orders received from XV11 Corps for Divisions to consolidate and improve the positions held. Touch to be kept with the enemy by means of patrols. The above order was repeated to C.R.A., C.R.E. 26th and 27th Infantry Brigades.	
		8.0pm	27th Bde attacked WIT trench with 12th Royal Scots (two companies)	
		9.15	General MAXWELL reported verbally that both companies got into the trench. The right company was knocked out by hostile machine gun fire after getting into the trench. The Left company had not yet returned. No further news. Afraid attack has failed.	
		10.25 pm	27th Inf. Bde was asked if the Brigade Commander wished for a Battalion of 52nd Inf. Bde (17th Division) to be moved forward to the GREEN LINE on account of the attacking companies having suffered heavy casualties. General MAXWELL replied that he did not need this. He asked that the artillery should not fire on trench immediately in front of his Brigade as men of 6th K.O.S.B. and 9th Scottish Rifles might be returning.	

A6945 Wt. W11422/M1160 350,000 12/16 D. D. & L. Forms/C./2118/14.

Instructions regarding War Diaries and Intelligence Summaries are contained in F. S. Regs., Part II. and the Staff Manual respectively. Title pages will be prepared in manuscript.

WAR DIARY
or
INTELLIGENCE SUMMARY.
(Erase heading not required.)

Army Form C. 2118.

Place	Date	Hour	Summary of Events and Information	Remarks and references to Appendices
RAILWAY CUTTING ST. LAURENT BLANGY	4th	1.30am	Verbal report received from 27th Infantry Brigade that all was now quiet and everyone of the attacking party who was within 100 yards of our trenches had been recovered. A good many 6th K.O.S.B. were coming in. 12th The Royal Scots in their attack on WIT TRENCH came under very heavy machine gun fire from WIT TRENCH just as they crossed the ridge before reaching the trench. The trench was strongly held and those of the Royal Scots who got in were ejected. A wounded Company Commander of 6th K.O.S. Borderers states that in their attack yesterday morning they crossed WIT TRENCH and went on to WOBBLE TRENCH from which they were met with a heavy rifle fire which accounted for a great many of his men. The above information was repeated to 17th Corps.	
		5.12 am	26th Infantry Brigade reported relief of 5th Camerons and 8th Black Watch by 10th A+S Highlanders and 7th Seaforths complete.	
		9.30am	Verbal instructions received from 17th Corps that part of 52nd Infantry Brigade, at present under orders of 9th Division, was to be employed on wiring and consolidating EFFIE trench in 9th Division's area	

A5834 Wt. W4973/M687 750,000 8/16 D. D. & L. Ltd. Forms/C.2118/13.

Instructions regarding War Diaries and Intelligence Summaries are contained in F. S. Regs., Part II. and the Staff Manual respectively. Title pages will be prepared in manuscript.

WAR DIARY
or
INTELLIGENCE SUMMARY.
(Erase heading not required.)

Army Form C. 2118.

Place	Date	Hour	Summary of Events and Information	Remarks and references to Appendices
		10.12	Instructions received that Divisions would proceed with consolidation of front system and improvement of communications.	
		2pm	200 men of 5th Infantry Brigade were employed on EFFIE TRENCH.	
			One Field Company and two companies 9th Seaforth Highlanders (Pioneers) were allotted to each Brigade for purposes of improvement of trenches during the night.	
		11.15pm	Orders issued for 4th S.A. Infantry to move from ARRAS to BLACK LINE tomorrow en route for trenches, to be at disposal of 26th Infantry Brigade.	AR
			A quiet day on the whole.	

Instructions regarding War Diaries and Intelligence Summaries are contained in F. S. Regs., Part II. and the Staff Manual respectively. Title pages will be prepared in manuscript.

WAR DIARY
or
INTELLIGENCE SUMMARY.
(Erase heading not required.)

Army Form C. 2118.

Place	Date	Hour	Summary of Events and Information	Remarks and references to Appendices
RAILWAY CUTTING	5th		Situation unchanged forward areas shelled intermittently.	
St LAURENT BLANGY			4 S A I move from ARRAS to BLACK LINE North of St LAURENT BLANGY and came under orders of 26th Infantry Brigade	
			South African Brigade was ordered to form three companies of 100 rifles from remaining battalions under one battalion staff this composite battalion to move to ARRAS en route for the trenches to be at disposal of 27th Infantry Brigade.	43
			Some thunder in afternoon.	
		9.15pm	26 Infantry Brigade order No 115 for relief of two battalions of 4th S A I on night May 6/7th	
			Scheme for future operations in outline received from 17th Corps.	

A5834 Wt. W4973/M687 750,000 8/16 D. D. & L. Ltd. Forms/C.2118/13.

Army Form C. 2118.

Instructions regarding War Diaries and Intelligence Summaries are contained in F. S. Regs., Part II. and the Staff Manual respectively. Title pages will be prepared in manuscript.

WAR DIARY
or
INTELLIGENCE SUMMARY.
(Erase heading not required.)

Place	Date	Hour	Summary of Events and Information	Remarks and references to Appendices
RAILWAY CUTTING ST LAURENT BLANGY	6th		Situation unchanged. Hostile artillery quieter.	
			A composite battalion consisting of three companies (fighting strength 100 bayonets) drawn from 1st, 2nd & 3rd the South African Regt was formed and moved up from MONCHY BRETON area to ARRAS and placed under orders of B.G.C 27th Infantry Brigade for assisting in holding the line.	
			26th Infantry Brigade carried out a battalion relief in Right subsector.	
	7th	4.30am	9th Division Artillery reported S.O.S on our left front. 27th Inf Brigade reported all quiet on their front though GAVRELLE was being heavily shelled.	
			Hostile artillery retaliated on our trenches more readily to-day than formerly and was on the whole more active.	
		9.30pm	Corps Order 20 40 for relief of 9th Division by 17th Division on nights 9/10 and 10/11 received	

A5834 Wt. W4973/M687 750,000 8/16 D. D. & L. Ltd. Forms/C.2118/13.

Instructions regarding War Diaries and Intelligence Summaries are contained in F. S. Regs., Part II. and the Staff Manual respectively. Title pages will be prepared in manuscript.

WAR DIARY
or
INTELLIGENCE SUMMARY.
(Erase heading not required.)

Army Form C. 2118.

Place	Date	Hour	Summary of Events and Information	Remarks and references to Appendices
RAILWAY CUTTING ST LAURENT BLANGY	May 8th	7am	9th Division order no 129 for relief of 17th Division on May 9/10 and 10/11 issued.	[illegible]
		9.30am	4th Division order no 33 for relief of part of 4th Division front by 17th Division on May 9/10th received.	
		12.30pm	17th Division order 136 for relief of 9th Division on May 9/10 and 10/11 received.	
		4pm	17th Corps (G1782) giving orders for moves of 9th Division to back areas on relief by 17th Division	
		7pm	Practice barrage fired on German trenches enemy retaliated on our front and support trenches for about 20 minutes.	
	May 9th	6am	9th Division order no 130 for moves of units to back areas issued.	[illegible]
			Weather fine and bright	
			Pioneers employed in digging new trenches in front of north end of CUBA and east from BRICKFIELD.	

A5834 Wt W4973/M687 750,000 8/16 D. D. & L. Ltd. Forms/C.2118/13.

Instructions regarding War Diaries and Intelligence Summaries are contained in F. S. Regs., Part II. and the Staff Manual respectively. Title pages will be prepared in manuscript.

WAR DIARY
or
INTELLIGENCE SUMMARY.
(Erase heading not required.)

Army Form C. 2118.

Place	Date	Hour	Summary of Events and Information	Remarks and references to Appendices
RAILWAY CUTTING ST LAURENT BLANGY	10th	3am	Relief of 27th Infantry Brigade by 52nd Infantry Brigade (17th Division) reported complete. On relief 27th Infantry Brigade billeted in ARRAS.	
			Corps Heavy artillery bombarded German trench on Divisional front.	
			A composite working party for work under A & Signals 17th Corps was assembled in BLACK LINE. This party consists of 350 - 26 Inf Bde, 250 - 27 Infantry Brigade 300 - SA Brigade.	
			Bright warm weather.	
		8.15pm	S O S signal was reported by 52nd Infantry Brigade as having been sent up from left of their right battalion.	
		8.44pm	S O S signal was reported by 26th Infantry Brigade as having been sent up on their front.	
			Artillery opened on ~~barrage~~ S O S lines.	
		9pm	All was reported quiet.	

A5834 Wt W4973/M687 750,000 8/16 D. D. & L. Ltd. Forms/C.2118/13.

Instructions regarding War Diaries and Intelligence Summaries are contained in F. S. Regs., Part II. and the Staff Manual respectively. Title pages will be prepared in manuscript.

WAR DIARY
or
INTELLIGENCE SUMMARY.
(Erase heading not required.)

Army Form C. 2118.

Place	Date	Hour	Summary of Events and Information	Remarks and references to Appendices
RAILWAY CUTTING ST LAURENT BLANGY	May 11th	10am	Divisional Headquarters closed at RAILWAY CUTTING on relief by 17th Division	
— CHELERS		11am	Divisional Headquarters opened at CHELERS.	
			A composite battalion consisting of 350 from 26th Infantry Brigade, 250 from 27th Infantry Brigade and 300 from S.A Brigade remained behind for work under A D Signals 17th Corps in 17th Division area.	
			Weather hot and dry.	
	12th	11am	Instructions received from 17th Corps for distribution of area which will necessitate movements of certain battalions again tomorrow.	
			Major General LUKIN proceeded to England on leave. The command of the Division devolved on Brigadier General TUDOR (RA).	
	13th	10am	Divisional HQrs closed at CHELERS and opened at ROELLECOURT.	

A5834 Wt. W4973/M687 750,000 8/16 D. D. & L. Ltd. Forms/C.2118/13.

Army Form C. 2118.

Instructions regarding War Diaries and Intelligence Summaries are contained in F. S. Regs., Part II. and the Staff Manual respectively. Title pages will be prepared in manuscript.

WAR DIARY
or
INTELLIGENCE SUMMARY.

(Erase heading not required.)

Place	Date	Hour	Summary of Events and Information	Remarks and references to Appendices
ROELLECOURT	14th		Composite working party which had been left for work in 17th Division's area rejoined the Division.	
			28th Machine Gun Company which had been left with two Sections of 26th M.G. Company to assist 17th Division in its operation on May 11th rejoined the Division.	
			9th Bn Seaforth Highlanders rejoined the Division and were billeted in ORLENCOURT.	
	15th		9th Bn Seaforth Highlanders moved from ORLENCOURT to BRIAS.	
	16th	12.30 pm	Orders received from 17th Corps for one Infantry Brigade to be earmarked to move to ARRAS at short notice, should the situation demand. (The enemy had attacked north of the SCARPE in the early morning.	
			The 26th Infantry Brigade was warned.	

Army Form C. 2118.

Instructions regarding War Diaries and Intelligence Summaries are contained in F. S. Regs., Part II. and the Staff Manual respectively. Title pages will be prepared in manuscript.

WAR DIARY
or
INTELLIGENCE SUMMARY.
(Erase heading not required.)

Place	Date	Hour	Summary of Events and Information	Remarks and references to Appendices
ROELLECOURT	17th		Weather fine and bright.	
			Training continued	
	18th		Training continued.	
	19th		G.O.C inspected 9th Bn Seaforth Highlanders.	
	20th		Training continued.	
	21st		Training continued.	
			There was a conference at H.Q. 17 Corps at 5 pm. G.O.C and G.S.O.1 attended.	
	22nd		27th Infantry Brigade moved from FOUFFLIN RICAMETZ area to MAGNICOURT en COMTE so as to be near MONCHY BRETON training area. Brigade H.Q. were established at VILLERS BRULIN.	
	23rd		Under orders received from 17 Corps 9th Division will be required to carry out an attack north of ROEUX early in June.	

A-831. Wt W.1973/M687 750,000 8/16 D. D. & L. Ltd. Forms/C.2118/13.

Army Form C. 2118.

Instructions regarding War Diaries and Intelligence Summaries are contained in F. S. Regs., Part II. and the Staff Manual respectively. Title pages will be prepared in manuscript.

WAR DIARY
or
INTELLIGENCE SUMMARY.
(Erase heading not required.)

Place	Date	Hour	Summary of Events and Information	Remarks and references to Appendices
ROELLE COURT	24th	8am	17th Corps Order No 44 for move of Division in relief of 51st Division on May 31st/1st June and June 1/2nd received.	
	25th	8pm	9th Division Order No 131 for relief of 51st Division issued.	
	26th	10.30	G.O.C. Third Army visited Brigade at Training on MONCHY BRETON Training area	
	27	11.15	G.O.C. 17th Corps presented ribbons of decorations awarded for gallantry during fighting in April to 26th Infantry Brigade	
	28th		Training continued	
	29th		26th Machine Gun Company moved to ARRAS in accordance with Order 131	
	30th		G.O.C. 17th Corps presented ribbons of decorations awarded for gallantry during fighting in April to 27th and South African Brigade on MONCHY BRETON area during the morning.	
			26th Infantry Brigade moved to ARRAS in accordance with Order 131	
		5pm	G.O.C. 9th Division attended a conference at Corps HQrs.	

A5834 Wt. W4973/M687 750,000 8/16 D. D. & L. Ltd. Forms/C.2118/13.

Army Form C. 2118.

Instructions regarding War Diaries and Intelligence Summaries are contained in F. S. Regs., Part II. and the Staff Manual respectively. Title pages will be prepared in manuscript.

WAR DIARY
or
INTELLIGENCE SUMMARY.

(Erase heading not required.)

Place	Date	Hour	Summary of Events and Information	Remarks and references to Appendices
ROELLECOURT	31st		27th Infantry Brigade. 9th Seaforth Highlanders, 197th M.G. Company and 90th Field Company R.E moved to ARRAS in accordance with order No 131.	
			26 Infantry Brigade relieved 153 Inf Brigade (51st Division) in trenches at ROEUX ("A" Subsector Right Division 17th Corps). relief complete at 1.25 am June 1st.	
			M. Henderson Major G S for G.O.C 9th Division	

A5834 Wt. W4973/M687 750,000 8/16 D. D. & L. Ltd. Forms/C.2118/13.

SECRET.

Copy No ______

9th DIVISION ORDER No. 127.

1.5.17.

1. 52nd Inf. Bde. (17th Division) is at the disposal of G.O.C. 9th Division as a reserve for forthcoming operations from midnight May 2nd/3rd.

2. On the morning of May 3rd. 52nd Inf. Bde. will move to following areas.

The Infantry will move by track N. of ST LAURENT BLANGY (vide attached tracing issued to 52nd Inf. Bde. only). Limbers will use the ST NICHOLAS - ST LAURENT BLANGY - ATHIES Road.

Brigade Headquarters	Railway Cutting H.8.c.0.3.
2 battalions Machine Gun Coy.	Trench system between l'ABBAYETTE and LE POINT du JOUR (H.9.a., H.9.c., H.8.d., H.14.a., H.14.b.)
2 battalions Trench Mortar By.	RAILWAY CUTTING (H.8.c. H.14.a.)

3. Units to arrive in allotted areas by 7 a.m.

4. ACKNOWLEDGE.

R Stewart

Lieutenant Colonel,
General Staff,
9th (Scottish) Division.

Issued at ~~8.30~~ 10 p.m.

Copies to:-
No. 1 to 26th Inf. Bde.
2 to 27th Inf. Bde.
3 to C.R.A.
4 to C.R.E.
5 to 9th Seaforths.
6 to 9th Signals.
7 to "Q".
8 to A.D.M.S.
9 to A.P.M.
10 to 197th Machine Gun Coy.
11 to 17th Division.
12 to 52nd Inf. Bde.
13) to 17th Corps.
14)
15 to 4th Division.
16 to 31st Division.

SECRET   9th Div. X 7/2529/3 dated 30-4-1917

PRELIMINARY INSTRUCTIONS NO. 1 FOR

OPERATIONS ON MAY 3RD.

Reference 1/10,000 Map(attached)

1. The XVllth Corps will resume the offensive on May 3rd, in conjunction with Vlth Corps on the right and Xlllth Corps on the left.

The attack will be preceded by two days bombardment.

2. The object of the operation of the XVllth Corps is to secure the line PLOUVAIN - 1.2.a.5.8.

Subsequent to this if the situation admits the Corps Reserve (17th Division) will be pushed through to secure a line between BIACHE - FRESNES and to harass the enemy in his retreat.

3. The operation will be carried out by the 4th Division on the right and the 9th Division on the left.

The actual line of the objective for these Divisions will be:-

RED LINE

River Bank in I.21.central - South West corner of PLOUVAIN - perimeter trench West of PLOUVAIN - PLOUVAIN STATION - WEED - WASTE - WHY trenches - WEAK trench to road at I.2.b.6.4 thence along road to the junction with WOBBLE trench.

Intermediate objectives will be:-

BLACK LINE

I.20 central to road at I.14.c.5.0 thence line of road across railway at I.14.a.4.4 - COD trench - road junction in I.2.c. - WOBBLE trench to I.2.a.3.9.

BLUE LINE

CARROT - CYPRUS - CANDY trenches - Mill and Copse at I.8.d.9.0 - Railway to PLOUVAIN STATION - WEED - WASTE - WHY - WEAK trenches to road at I.2.b.6.4 thence along road to the junction with WOBBLE trench.

On reaching the RED LINE patrols will be pushed out in order to gain ground towards the GREEN LINE on the map.

4. The dividing line between Divisions will be:-

(a) Between 4th and 9th Divisions

Junction of CASH and CUBA trenches to COPSE at I.8.d.9.0 (inclusive to 4th Division) - thence railway (inclusive to 9th Division)

(b) Between 9th Division and 31st Division (Xlllth Corps)

Point of junction on front line - junction of bank and road

...........at

at I.[illegible]a.5.8 (to 9th Division)

5. The Division will carry out the attack with two Brigades in line 26th on the right and 27th on the left.

Dividing line between Brigades will be as shown on attached map.

6. The exact line held by the Germans is uncertain, but he is known to be in the following places:-

ROEUX and the Wood West of it.
CHATEAU in I.13.d.
CHEMICAL WORKS in I.13.d.
Station and buildings North of the Railway in I.13.
A trench 200^x to 60^x East of our trenches between CAM and CASH trenches.
CUPID trench
COD trench
shell holes East of CUTHBERT trench.

The trenches on the HAUSA Wood spur, the PLOUVAIN defences, WINE trench and the BIACHE - FRESNES Line are probably held by reserved.

The enemy defences are organised in considerable depth and from prisoners' statements it appears that all small lengths of trench, shown on the map, will probably be found to be held by detachments in some cases with machine guns.

7. ROEUX, the CHEMICAL WORKS and the buildings North of the Railway will be subjected to continuous bombardment during the days preceding the attack. Similarly the trenches and woods immediately West and South West of PLOUVAIN will be systematically bombarded. The railway cutting from the ROEUX STATION Eastwards will be searched by night and by day for machine guns.

The wire on GREENLAND HILL, West of PLOUVAIN and on the BIACHE - FRESNES trench line will be cut during the preliminary bombardment.

8. The creeping barrage, will, generally speaking move forward at a rate of 100 yards every two minutes.

There will be pauses on the Black and Blue lines to admit of troops re-organising or being passed through for each further advance. The Red Line on being reached will be consolidated.

9. One Brigade 17th Division will be placed at the disposal of the 9th Division from midnight 2nd/3rd as a reserve to be used only in case of emergency. This Brigade will revert to the 17th Division when the latter is ordered forward.

10. It is the intention, should the general situation admit, to undertake a night advance after the battle of the 3rd with a view to disorganising the enemy, capturing his guns and gaining ground towards the DROCOURT - QUEANT Line.

On the front of this Corps this operation will be carried out by the 17th Division of which two Brigades will be concentrated in ARRAS and in Camp East of ST NICHOLAS by the evening of May 2nd; the third Brigade will be at "Y" huts. The Division will ~~xx~~ concentrate forward into the battle area on the 3rd May. One or portions of two Brigades will be prepared to pass through the front of the 9th Division on the RED LINE during the night May 3rd/4th; these troops will assault the PLOUVAIN - FRESNES line with the bayonet, reform and pass on th the GREEN LINE I.10.d., a., 4.c. & a. forming a temporary defensive flank along the railway as they advance. This advance will be carried out without rifle or artillery fire in order that all those who open fire may be recognised as enemies. Artillery fire during the advance will be restricted to counter battery work.

The........

The conditions which would make this operation possible are those which would result if the enemy is disorganised and wears out his strength by repeated counter attacks after we have gained the RED LINE or even before we reach it.

11. On the early morning of May 3rd gun limbers and wagons will be concentrated in the squares H.13 and 14 and will be ready to move forward in the evening and advance such batteries as are necessary to bring up for the proper artillery support of the GREEN LINE.
The frontage of the Corps would be reduced to 2700 yards by this move.

12. Major LUMSDEN, Acting Divisional Machine Gun Officer, will arrange to cover the advance by machine gun fire of the 28th and 197th Machine Gun companies.
The 26th and 27th Machine Gun companies will be at the disposal of G.O's C 26th and 27th Bdes. Some of the guns should be pushed well up with the leading troops to take advantage of opportunities which may occur as the advance progresses over the edge of GREENLAND HILL and PLOUVAIN and the approaches to BIACHE come under our fire by direct observation.

13. ACKNOWLEDGE.

Lieutenant-Colonel,
General Staff.
9th(Scottish) Division.

Adv. Hd. Qrs.
30th May 1917

Copies to:-
26th Bde
27th Bde
C R A
C R E
28th M.G. Coy
197th M.G. Coy
9th Seaforths
A.D.M.S.
Major LUMSDEN
"Q"

3

[illegible]

9th Division Operation Order
No. 123 128

Copy No.........

(Reference 1/10,000 Map
reproduced by J.Corps Topo Sector)

2nd May 1917

1. The XVllth Corps, with 4th Division on the Right and 9th Division on the left is to attack on May 3rd with a view to gaining ground towards the East. The 31st Division of the Xllth Corps will attack simultaneously on the left of the 9th Division.

2. The 9th Division will attack with 26th Infantry Brigade on the right and 27th Infantry Brigade on the left and capture the line WEED - WHY and WEAK trenches and the BIACHE - GAVRELLE road from its junction with WEAK trench to junction with Bank at I.2.a.5.8.
The 52nd Brigade of the 17th Division will be in Divisional Reserve.

3. The dividing line between Divisions and Brigades will be as laid down in "Preliminary Instructions No. 2" dated 1st May 1917.

4. The artillery protective barrage 200 yards East of the present front line will lift at Zero plus 4 minutes and move forward in accordance with instructions already issued.
A machine gun barrage will keep 400 yards in advance of the artillery barrage from Zero hour.

5. Zero hour will be at 3.45 a.m. on May 3rd.

6. Two contact planes will be detailed to call for flares at 6.15 am. Troops are to be reminded of the necessity for complying at once with this call.

7. On the objective being reached consolidation will be at once begun and this must be carried out energetically and without ceasing.
Patrols will also be pushed out to regain touch with the enemy and to capture any hostile batteries that may be within reach.

8. ACKNOWLEDGE.

Issued at 2 pm

Adv. Head Qrs.
2nd May 1917

P. Stewart
Lieutenant-Colonel,
General Staff.
9th (Scottish) Division.

Copies to:-

No. 1 26th Bde
2 27th Bde
3 52nd Bde
4. C.R.A.
5. C.R.E.
6. 28th M.G. Coy
7. 197th M.G. Coy
8. 9th Seaforths
9. A.D.M.S.
10. Major LUMSDEN
11. "Q"
12.) XVllth
13) Corps
15. do H.A.
16. 31st Division
17. 4th Division
18. 17th Division.
19. 9th Signals

War Diary (4)

S E C R E T.

9th Div. X 7/2529/7 dated 1/5/17

PRELIMINARY INSTRUCTIONS NO.2 FOR

OPERATIONS ON MAY 3RD.

Reference 1/10,000 Map (attached)

1. The XVllth Corps will resume the offensive on May 3rd in conjunction with the Vlth Corps on the right and Xlllth Corps on the left.
The attack will be preceded by two days bombardment.

2. The object of the operation of the XVllth Corps is to secure the line PLOUVAIN - Point I.2.a.5.8 junction of BANK with GAVRELLE - BIACHE Road.

3. The attack will be carried out by the 4th Division on the right and the 9th Division on the left. The 17th Division will be in Corps Reserve.

4. The final objective of the Divisions will be:-

RED LINE

River Bank in I.21 central - S.W. corner of PLOUVAIN - perimeter trench W. of PLOUVAIN - PLOUVAIN STATION - WEED - WHY - WEAK trenches - BIACHE - GAVRELLE road from junction with WEAK trench to junction with WOBBLE trench.

There will be two intermediate objectives in the 4th Division area viz.,

BLACK LINE

I.20 central to road at I.14.c.5.0 thence line of road across railway at I.14.a.4.4.

BLUE LINE

CARROT - CYPRUS - CANDY trenches - Mill at I.8.d.9.0.

5. The dividing lines between Divisions will be:-

(a) Between 4th Division and 9th Division

Junction of CASH and CUBA trenches to COPSE at I.13.d.9.0 (inclusive to 9th Division) - thence railway (inclusive to 9th Division).

(b) Between 9th Division and 51st Division (Xlllth Corps)

Point of junction on front line - junction of bank and Road I.2.a.5.8 (inclusive to 9th Division)

6. The Division will carry out the attack with two Brigades in line, 26th on the right and 27th on the left.
The 52nd Bde of the 17th Division will be at the disposal ofthe

the 9th Div......

9th Division from midnight May 2nd/3rd as a reserve to be used only in case of emergency.

7. The exact line held by the Germans in uncertain, but he is known to be in the following places.

ROEUX and the wood west of it.
CHATEAU in I.13.d.
CHEMICAL WORKS in I.13.d.
Station and buildings North of the Railway in I.13 .
A trench 200 x to 60 x East of our trenches between CAM and CASH trenches.
CUPID trench.
COD trench.
Shell holes East of CUTHBERT trench.

The trenches on the HAUSA Wood Spur, the PLOUVAIN defences, WINE trench and the BIACHE - FRESNES line are probably held by reserves.

The enemy defences are organised in considerable depth and from prisoner's statements it appears thatall small lengths of trench, shown on the map, will probably be found to be held by detachments in some cases with machine guns.

8. ROEUX, the CHEMICAL WORKS and the buildings North of the Railway will be subjected to continuous bombardment during the days preceding the attack. Similarly, the trenches and woods immediately West and South West of PLOUVAIN will be systematically bombarded. The railway cutting from the ROEUX STATION Eastwards will be searched by night and by day for machine guns.

The wire on GREENLAND HILL, West of PLOUVAIN and on the BIACHE - FRESNES trench line will be cut during the preliminary bombardment.

9. The creeping barrage will move forward at the rate of 100 yards every 2 minutes from Zero plus four minutes till Zero plus twenty four minutes after which it will advance at the rate of 100 yards every three minutes.

There will be pauses on the BLACK LINE and BLUE LINE on 4th Division front to admit of troops reorganising or being passed through for each further advance.

The RED LINE on being reached will be consolidated

10. On the early morning of May 3rd gun limbers and wagons will be concentrated in squares H.13 and 14 and will be ready to move forward in the evening and advance such batteries as are necessary to bring up for the proper artillery support of the GREEN Line.

The frontage of the Corps would be reduced to 2,700 yards by this move.

11. Major LUMSDEN MC, Acting Divisional Machine Gun Officer will arrange for covering fire by the guns of the 28th and 197th machine gun companies.

The 26th and 27th machine gun companies will be at the disposal of General Officers Commanding 26th and 27th Brigades. Some of the guns should be pushed well up with the leading troops to take advantage of opportunities which may occur as the advance progresses over the edge of GREENLAND HILL and PLOUVAIN and the approaches to BIACHE come under our fire by direct observation.

General Officer Commanding 26th Brigade will detail certain machine guns to fire from the COPSE in I.8.d. at the trenches West of PLOUVAIN and to command the exits from PLOUVAIN to prevent the enemy from emerging for a counter attack.

12.......

12. As the Infantry advances General Officers Commanding Brigades will arrange to establish strong points with machine guns to form defensive points in case of a strong counter attack being delivered by the enemy.

The guns of 28th Machine Gun Company will be at the disposal of the 27th Brigade and those of 197th Machine Gun Company at the disposal of General Officer Commanding 26th Brigade as soon as the work of covering fire is completed.

13. One Field Company R.E. and one company 9th Seaforths (Pioneers) will be at the disposal of each Brigadier to assist in consolidation.

The Third Field Company R.E. and the 9th Seaforths (less two companies) will be in reserve.

14. ACKNOWLEDGE by wire.

Adv. Head Qrs.
1st May 1917.

~~Lieut~~-Colonel,
General Staff.
9th(Scottish) Division.

Copies to:-

26th Bde
27th Bde
C.R.A.
C.R.E.
28th M.G. Coy
197th M.G. Coy
9th Seaforths
A.D.M.S.
Major LUMSDEN
"Q"
XVllth Corps
do H.A.
31st Division
4th Division
17th Division
52nd Brigade.

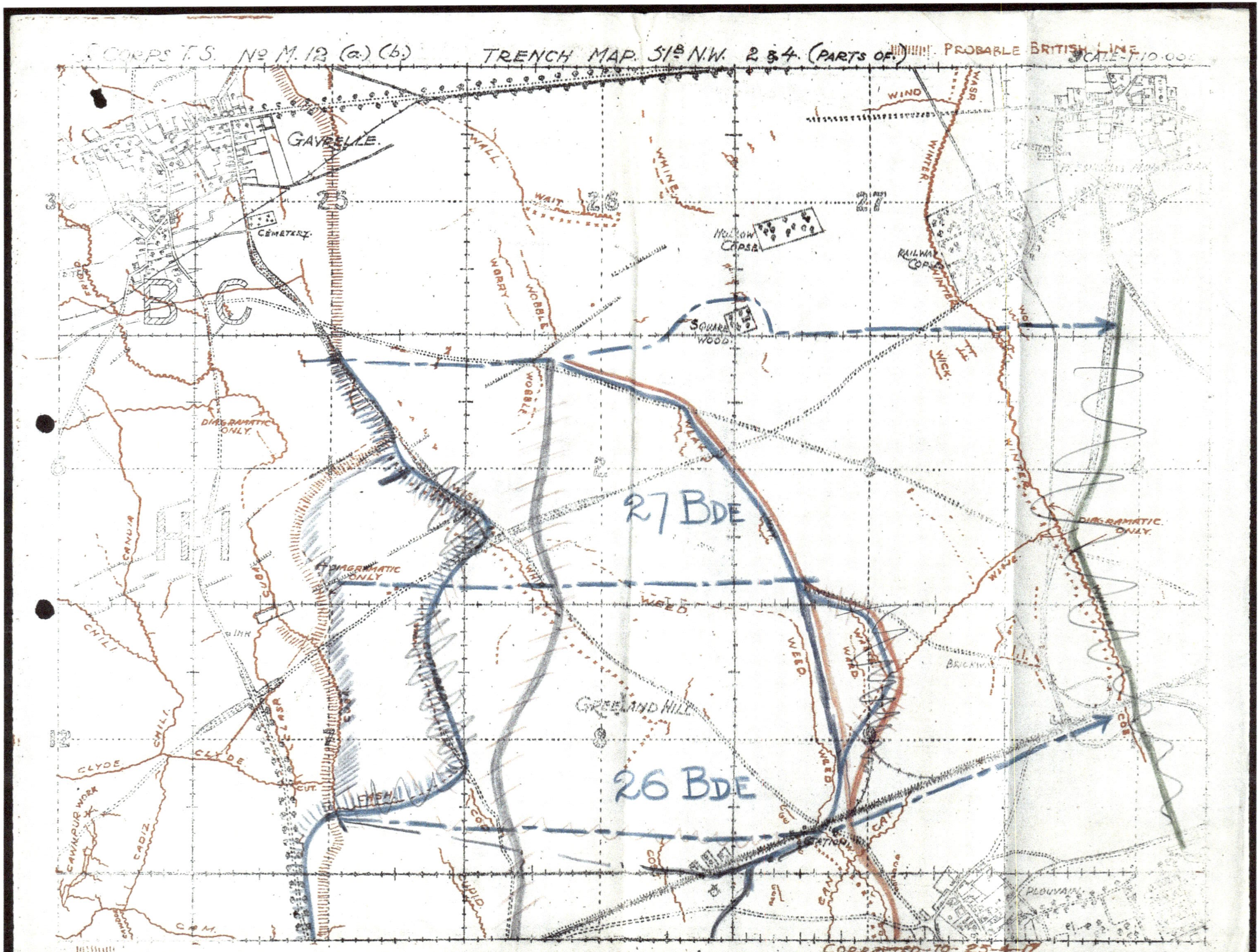

Corps T.S. No M.12 (a) (b)
TRENCH MAP. 51B N.W. 2 & 4. (PARTS OF.)
PROBABLE BRITISH LINE
SCALE 1:10.000
GAVRELLE.
CEMETERY.
HOLLOW COPSE
RAILWAY COPSE
SQUARE WOOD
GREENLAND HILL
PLOUVAIN
STATION
27 BDE
26 BDE
DIAGRAMMATIC ONLY
WALL
WAIT
WHINE
WINTER
WIND
WASP
WICK
WORRY
WOBBLE
WEED
WEAK
CHILI
CLYDE
CANDIA
CADIZ
CAWNPUR WORK
CUPID
CUBA
CORRECTED TO 25-4-17

War Diary.

9th Div. X. 7/2529/11

S E C R E T.

COVERING FIRE OF MACHINE GUNS

1. The Infantry advance on 3rd instant will be covered by the fire of the 28th and 197th Machine Gun Companies.

The 197th Machine Gun Company will cover the front of the 26th Brigade.

The 28th Machine Gun Company will cover the front of the 27th Brigade.

2. The guns will be placed in position in squares H.6.d. and H.12.b.

The ground to be covered and the lifts are shown on attached map.

3. On completion of the barrage table the 197th and 28th Machine Gun Company will act in accordance with instructions previously received from the 26th and 27th Infantry Brigades respectively.

Stewart

Lieut-Colonel
General Staff
9th(Scottish) Division

Adv. Head Qrs.
2nd May 1917

Copies to:-

26th Bde	"Q"
27th Bde	XVll Corps
C.R.A.	do H.A.
C.R.E.	51st D vision
28th M.G. Coy	4th do
197th M.G. Coy	17th do
9th Seaforths	52nd Brigade
A.D.M.S.	
Major LUMSDEN	

0 till 0+8

0+8 till 0+12

0+12 till 0+16

0+16 till 0+20

0+20 till 0+24

0+24 till 0+28

0+28 till 0+32

0+32 till 0+36

S E C R E T 9th Div. X 7/2529/3 dated 30-4-1917

PRELIMINARY INSTRUCTIONS NO. 1 FOR

OPERATIONS ON MAY 3RD.

Reference 1/10,000 Map(attached)

1. The XVllth Corps will resume the offensive on May 3rd, in conjunction with Vlth Corps on the right and Xlllth Corps on the left.

The attack will be preceded by two days bombardment.

2. The object of the operation of the XVllth Corps is to secure the line PLOUVAIN - 1.2.a.5.8.

Subsequent to this if the situation admits the Corps Reserve (17th Division) will be pushed through to secure a line between BIACHE - FRESNES and to harass the enemy in his retreat.

3. The operation will be carried out by the 4th Division on the right and the 9th Division on the left.

The actual line of the objective for these Divisions will be:-

RED LINE

River Bank in I.21.central - South West corner of PLOUVAIN - perimeter trench West of PLOUVAIN - PLOUVAIN STATION - WEED - WASTE - WHY trenches - WEAK trench to road at I.2.b.6.4 thence along road to the junction with WOBBLE trench.

Intermediate objectives will be:-

BLACK LINE

I.20 central to road at I.14.c.5.0 thence line of road across railway at I.14.a.4.4 - COD trench - road junction in I.2.c. - WOBBLE trench to I.2.a.8.9.

BLUE LINE

CARROT - CYPRUS - CANDY trenches - Mill and Copse at I.8.d.9.0 - Railway to PLOUVAIN STATION - WEED - WASTE - WHY - WEAK trenches to road at I.2.b.6.4 thence along road to the junction with WOBBLE trench.

On reaching the RED LINE patrols will be pushed out in order to gain ground towards the GREEN LINE on the map.

4. The dividing line between Divisions will be:-

(a) Between 4th and 9th Divisions

Junction of CASH and CUBA trenches to COPSE at I.8.d.9.0 (inclusive to 4th Division) - thence railway (inclusive to 9th Division)

(b) Between 9th Division and 31st Division (Xlllth Corps)

Point of junction on front line - junction of bank and road

...........at

at [illegible]2.a.5.8 (to 9th Division)

5. The Division will carry out the attack with two Brigades in line 26th on the right and 27th on the left.

Dividing line between Brigades will be as shown on attached map.

6. The exact line held by the Germans is uncertain, but he is known to be in the following places:-

ROEUX and the Wood West of it.
CHATEAU in I.13.d.
CHEMICAL WORKS in I.13.d.
Station and buildings North of the Railway in I.13.
A trench 200x to 60x East of our trenches between CAM and CASH trenches.
CUPID trench
COD trench
shell holes East of CUTHBERT trench.

The trenches on the HAUSA Wood spur, the PLOUVAIN defences, WINE trench and the BIACHE - FRESNES Line are probably held by reserved.

The enemy defences are organised in considerable depth and from prisoners' statements it appears that all small lengths of trench, shown on the map, will probably be found to be held by detachments in some cases with machine guns.

7. ROEUX, the CHEMICAL WORKS and the buildings North of the Railway will be subjected to continuous bombardment during the days preceding the attack. Similarly the trenches and woods immediately West and South West of PLOUVAIN will be systematically bombarded. The railway cutting from the ROEUX STATION Eastwards will be searched by night and by day for machine guns.

The wire on GREENLAND HILL, West of PLOUVAIN and on the BIACHE - FRESNES trench line will be cut during the preliminary bombardment.

8. The creeping barrage, will, generally speaking move forward at a rate of 100 yards every two minutes.

There will be pauses on the Black and Blue lines to admit of troops re-organising or being passed through for each further advance. The Red Line on being reached will be consolidated.

9. One Brigade 17th Division will be placed at the disposal of the 9th Division from midnight 2nd/3rd as a reserve to be used only in case of emergency. This Brigade will revert to the 17th Division when the latter is ordered forward.

10. It is the intention, should the general situation admit, to undertake a night advance after the battle of the 3rd with a view to disorganising the enemy, capturing his guns and gaining ground towards the DROCOURT - QUEANT Line.

On the front of this Corps this operation will be carried out by the 17th Division of which two Brigades will be concentrated in ARRAS and in Camp East of ST NICHOLAS by the evening of May 2nd; the third Brigade will be at "Y" huts. The Division will ~~xx~~ concentrate forward into the battle area on the 3rd May. One or portions of two Brigades will be prepared to pass through the front of the 9th Division on the RED LINE during the night May 3rd/4th; these troops will assault the PLOUVAIN - FRESNES Line with the bayonet, reform and pass on th the GREEN LINE I.10 d., a., 4.c. & [illegible] forming a temporary defensive flank along the railway as they advance. This advance will be carried out without rifle or artillery fire in order that all those who open fire may be recognised as enemies. Artillery fire during the advance will be restricted to counter battery work.

The........

The conditions which would make this operation possible are those which would result if the enemy is disorganised and ~~wears out~~ his strength by repeated counter attacks after we have gained the RED LINE or even before we reach it.

11. On the early morning of May 3rd gun limbers and wagons will be concentrated in the squares H.13 and 14 and will be ready to move forward in the evening and advance such batteries as are necessary to bring up for the proper artillery support of the GREEN LINE.
The frontage of the Corps would be reduced to 2700 yards by this move.

12. Major LUMSDEN, Acting Divisional Machine Gun Officer, will arrange to cover the advance by machine gun fire of the 28th and 197th Machine Gun companies.
The 26th and 27th Machine Gun companies will be at the disposal of G.O's C 26th and 27th Bdes. Some of the guns should be pushed well up with the leading troops to take advantage of opportunities which may occur as the advance progresses over the edge of GREENLAND HILL and PLOUVAIN and the approaches to BIACHE come under our fire by direct observation.

13. ACKNOWLEDGE.

Lieutenant-Colonel,
General Staff.
9th(Scottish) Division.

Adv. Hd. Qrs.
30th May 1917

Copies to:-
26th Bde
27th Bde
C R A
C R E
28th M.G. Coy
197th M.G. Coy
9th Seaforths
A.D.M.S.
Major LUMSDEN
"Q"

X. 7/2522/8
15.5.17.

To
9th. Division.
8th. Black Watch.
7th. Seaforth Hdrs.
5th. Cameron Hdrs.
10th. A. & S. Hldrs.
26th. M.G.Company.
26th. T.M.Battery.

G.O.C. to see on return
M.H.

Herewith account of the battle on 3rd. May 1917,
for your information.

R Lachlan Capt.
Captain,
Brigade Major,
26th. Infantry Brigade.

15/5/17.

26TH INFANTRY
15 MAY 1917
No. 2/643 b.
BRIGADE.

28th. Infantry Brigade.

Account of the battle on May 3rd. 1917.

1. The assembly was carried out in good order, and was completed by 3.am.
The brigade formed up for attack as ordered in brigade Order No.111.

2. The barrage opened at Zero, but appeared to be ragged, especially on the right flank, and some casualties were sustained in the assaulting battalions from our own artillery.

3. Owing to the darkness at Zero, direction was soon lost and there was no cohesion in the attack. The enemy appeared ready for our attack and opened heavy machine gun fire almost at once, from trenches and shell holes, which were closer to our front line than had been expected, and which had been missed by the barrage. Opposite the right flank of the attack, the enemy lights were sent up from his short lengths of trenches "echeloned" in depth, and this caused the 5th. Cameron Highlanders to mistake them for the enemy front line and to swing to their right, and cross the front of the 2nd. ESSEX Regiment. This caused the latter Regiment to shoot at the 5th. Cameron Highlanders who also sustained heavy casualties from enemy machine gun fire.

The 2 supporting companies, 10th. Arg. & Suth. Hdrs., kept straight on and apparently passed the left flank of the 5th. Cameron Highlanders, and they also came under heavy enfilade machine gun fire from the direction of the RAILWAY EMBANKMENT & the CHEMICAL WORKS.

The 6th. Black Watch on the left also lost cohesion, and as far as is known, only a few isolated groups of men ever reached the enemy front line. So great was the confusion owing to the intensity of the darkness, that the right battalions of the 27th. Brigade actually mistook our own front line for the German line, and advanced on it firing from the hip. This accounts for the fact that so many men of the 27th. Brigade eventually got into our trenches.

4. The German machine guns caused heavy casualties , and caused the attackers to return to our front line. Here a second attack was organised and a gallant attempt was made to capture the German front line, but it failed, and by this time, our barrage had almost, if not quite reached its final limit. The remnants of the assaulting battalions were driven back by heavy machine gun fire, to our own trenches, which were at once organised for defence against counter-attack.

5. When the enemy discovered that our attack had been repulsed, his artillery fire, which had been both intense and accurate, slackened down, and his snipers, lying scattered all over the ground in shell holes, became extremely active, and caused casualties.

6. Owing to the fact that so few officers were left from any of the assaulting ~~battalions~~ companies, it is impossible to collect any accurate accounts of what really took place, but in the opinion of those who are still with their battalions, the failure was caused by the darkness and our unprepared state for a night attack.

OBSERVATIONS ON THE ATTACK.

Assembly was easily carried out, and no interference from hostile artillery.

All ranks are agreed that the Hour of Zero was too early and that the darkness caused the attack to lose all direction and cohesion.

No attack on a large scale has been done by this Division at night, for a very long time, and it was not expected that such an operation was contemplated. Sufficient care and thought had not, therefore, been given to working out the necessary details to ensure the success of an attack in the dark. Had longer notice of the change of the Zero hour been given, it would still have been possible to lay out tapes and provide phosphorescent boards, taking careful compass bearings etc., the plan of attack would have been entirely altered, so as to ensure touch being kept from front to rear. I should have made successive advances on the 'Leap Frog' system instead of going straight through.

I was only informed at 2 p.m. that the Zero Hour had been changed - the alteration of 20 minutes having the effect of changing the whole character of the attack from a daylight to a night attack.

It is not necessary for troops to know the hour of Zero, but it is absolutely necessary that they should know some days beforehand if it is to be by day or by night.

All arrangements had been made for daylight observation and transmission of reports. From my Headquarters it was possible to see the whole field of operations, but owing to the dark, this was not used and it was most difficult to follow the progress of the attack.

THE ADVANCE.

The difficulty was accentuated in the dark by the fact that on the right flank the 4th Division front line was some 200 yards behind my Brigade and the line from these gradually ran back. The result was that as the men advanced, the enemy Very lights appeared on their right flank, and the whole attack of the 5th Cameron Highlanders swung round in that direction. The 10th A.& S.Highrs. supporting companies kept direction better, and went right through the gap left between the Cameron Hrs. and the Black Watch. They were, of course, a long way behind the barrage, but went right over CHARLIE and CUTHBERT trenches until they came under very heavy machine gun fire from all sides, and bombing counter-attacks from vicinity of GAVRELLE-PLOUVAIN road. Most of them appear to have got into shell holes, and are gradually making their way back, 68 having come inat night, but I fear the remainder are killed or prisoners.

The Black Watch attack was repulsed by machine gun and rifle fire, and bombs. They made a second attack and drove the enemy out of CHARLIE and CUTHBERT, killing a good many, but were unable to remain, owing to very heavy enfilade fire from machine guns in the embankment and CHEMICAL WORKS.

The whole attack was eventually withdrawn to the original front line, and the defence re-organised. This was rendered very difficult by 3 enemy aeroplanes who flew constantly up and down the line at a very low altitude, firing at our men. One was eventually brought down with machine gun fire, but the boldness of the enemy aeroplanes, which has noticeably increased lately, was quite unprecedented as far as the experience of this brigade goes.

ENEMY TACTICS.

The enemy did not appear to be in his trenches, but occupying shell holes every where with a very great number of machine guns, used both for frontal fire with his advanced troops, and also from the flanks.

He appeared to be quite ready for our attack as he opened at once with his artillery barrage, and machine gun and rifle fire. His artillery barrage was negligible as far as 'stopping' the advance goes.

His infantry used their rifles well and supplemented it with the bomb at close quarters.

The/

The machine guns however, are the real defence and are handled with great skill.

The 10th Arg. & Suth. Hdrs., who got near the embankment say they had guns on top of the embankment and others at the foot, and echeloned back in shell holes. It would seem, therefore, that he is using his machine gun as a very mobile weapon, though the rapidity with which certain grazing fire is brought to bear on certain zones, seems to show that he must have a certain number of guns in permanent positions firing on barrage lines.

OUR TACTICS.

It is difficult to write about these without appearing to criticise, but I think the following points may be worth consideration.

We have, with the very limited opportunities of training which can be allowed to troops engaged in trench and active warfare, been able to concentrate on one form of attack - the organised trench attack. This has been perfected, but neither Officers or men know any other. The fighting has, at present, got into the advanced stage when we cannot rely on complete artillery preparation or "Protection". The enemy's position is nebulous and constantly changing - he is constantly producing awkward little situations for us. His local Commanders appear to act with skill and determination, encroaching on us constantly with bombing attacks forming little pockets of snipers or machine guns in unexpected places, not waiting in definite lines of trenches, to be barraged by our artillery. Against this, we are using the same tactics as in the first phase. The barrage, I think, should now be shrapnel, but all ground in vicinity of enemy trenches, should be constantly searched by shrapnel at night, to get the enemy in his shell holes.

More smoke still is required to blind his machine guns, and gas, if possible.

Known bad pockets should be passed round, a feint or holding attack being made against such places. The actual position of the machine guns is not the bad pocket, but the place where the bullets from that gun sweep. We are apt to avoid the place where the machine guns are, and attempt to brush past in the zone where they kill.

As far as infantry are concerned, if the first organised attack is held up and they lose their barrage, there is a tendency to think that nothing more can be done. It certainly is no good launching a fresh attack or sacrificing more troops against machine guns in position, but I think the infantry of the old army, who were taught the old infantry advance by alternate rushes, supported by their own rifle and machine gun fire, who knew how to fight a battle of localities and tactical points, would gain much ground, even when the original attack has become disorganised, and would be constantly putting the enemy at a disadvantage. An extended wave gets into shell holes in pairs etc., without leadership, and it is lost. I think each extended line wants a pivot of troops in close formation, in close support.

We appear to be suffering from:-

(1). Want of leadership, which can in some way be corrected by less extended formation and more practice for Officers and N.C.O's handling and leading men.

(2). Want of initiative, which can in some way be remedied by fuller explanation of the general situation and the encouragement and direction of local enterprises during the lulls in main operations.

(3). Want of elasticity and scope in training and formations.

(4). Want of training of rank and file.

****

Army Form C. 2123.
(In books of 100).

"C" Form.
MESSAGES AND SIGNALS.

No. of Message........

Prefix........ Code........ Words........

£ s. d.

Charges to collect

Service Instructions.
Priority

Received.
From........
By........

Sent, or sent out.
At........m.
To........
By........

Office Stamp.

Handed in at........ Office........m. Received........m.

TO Hunt

*Sender's Number	Day of Month	In reply to Number	AAA
Bm 5	2		

moves complete

FROM

PLACE & TIME

* This line should be erased if not required.

(6334). Wt. W7496/M857. 500,000 Pads. 10/16. D. D. & L. (E489). Forms C/2123/3.

6

"C" Form

Army Form C. 2123.
(In books of 100.)

MESSAGES AND SIGNALS. No. of Message.....................

Prefix..............Code..............Words..........

£ s. d.

Charges to collect

Service Instructions.

Received
From Ahs
By Tkeo

Sent, or sent out
At......................m.
To..........................
By..........................

Office Stamp.

Handed in at..Office...................m. Received 4 6a m.

TO Riding

*Sender's Number | Day of Month 5 | In reply to Number | AAA

[illegible] Dfshs report enemy putting up a heavy barrage all along our front line

4 10 a.m.

FROM 32 Bde
PLACE & TIME 3 55 am

* This line should be erased if not required.

(B 8070) Wt. w. 7496—M857 250,000 Pads. 10/16 H & S (E436.) Forms/C.2123/3.

4

"C" Form
MESSAGES AND SIGNALS.

Army Form C. 2123.
(In books of 100.)

No. of Message........................

Prefix.........Code.........Words.........	Received	Sent, or sent out	Office Stamp.
£ s. d. Charges to collect	From............ By............	At..........m. To..........	
Service Instructions.		By..........	

Handed in at.............................Office..........m. Received..........m.

TO Riding

*Sender's Number	Day of Month	In reply to Number	AAA
	3		

700 spikes reports heavy rifle and machine gun fire on our zone

4.30 am

FROM 32 Bde
PLACE & TIME 4 20 am

* This line should be erased if not required.

(B 8070) Wt. w. 7496—M857 250,000 Pads. 10/16 H & S (E436.) Forms/C.2123/3.

8

"C" Form
MESSAGES AND SIGNALS.
Army Form C. 2123.
(In books of 100.)
No. of Message.....

Prefix.....Code.....Words.....	Received	Sent, or sent out	Office Stamp.
Charges to collect £ s. d.	From Spree	At.....m.	
Service Instructions.	By Akes	To.....	
		By.....	

Handed in at..... Office.....m. Received 4 24 m.

TO Riding

*Sender's Number	Day of Month	In reply to Number	AAA
	3		

No trench lights seen on our front for the last 10 minutes heavy machine gun fire from south of river aaa It appears the enemy have a strong barrage all along the front this commenced about 3 mins after zero

4.30 am

FROM
PLACE & TIME 100 32 Bde
4 15 am

* This line should be erased if not required.

(B 8070) Wt. w. 7496—M357 250,000 Pads. 10/16 H&S (E436.) Forms/C.2123/3.

"C" Form

Army Form C. 2123.
(In books of 100.)

MESSAGES AND SIGNALS. No. of Message

Prefix Code Words	Received	Sent, or sent out	Office Stamp.
£ s. d. Charges to collect	From AKC5 By Reo	At m.	
Service Instructions.		To	
		By	

Handed in at Office m. Received 4 34 a m.

TO Riding

*Sender's Number	Day of Month	In reply to Number	AAA
	3		

Hostile very lights appear to be going up further eastwards

4 35

FROM F.O.O. 1/Sher 32 Bde

PLACE & TIME 4 33 am

* This line should be erased if not required.

(B 8070) Wt. w. 7496—M857 250,000 Pads. 10/16 H & S (E436.) Forms/C.2123/3.

"C" Form.

MESSAGES AND SIGNALS.

Army Form C. 2123.
(In books of 100).

No. of Message..........

Prefix...... Code...... Words......	Received.	Sent, or sent out.	Office Stamp.
£ s. d. Charges to collect	From...... By cum	At......m. To...... By......	[stamp, illegible]
Service Instructions.			

Handed in at YCA Office 4.4? a.m. Received 5.0? a.m.

TO 9th Divn

*Sender's Number	Day of Month	In reply to Number	AAA
11001	3		

Hourly	report	no	2	4.30
am	aaa	Barrage	opened	3.45
am	aaa	Left	Bde	report
enemy	appeared	slow	in	replying
aaa	artillery	report	through	Liaison
with	right	bde	and	700
enemy	barrage	on	our	right
bde	commenced	13	seconds	after
ZERO	aaa	Report	from	arty
700	Just	received	states	enemy
coloured	lights	now	ceased	aaa
Addsd	13	Corps	reptd	2nd
and	9th	Divns		

HL 5.30 am [signature]

FROM 31 Divn
PLACE & TIME 4.30 am

* This line should be erased if not required.

(6334). Wt. W7496/M857. 500,000 Pads. 10/16. D. D. & L. (E 489). Forms C/2123/3.

11

"A" Form.
MESSAGES AND SIGNALS.

Army Form C.2121
(in pads of 100).
No. of Message ....

Prefix .... Code .... m. | Words | Charge
Office of Origin and Service Instructions.
Priority
M. Henderson

This message is on a/c of: .... Service.
(Signature of "Franking Officer.")

Sent
At .... m.
To ....
By ....

Recd. at .... m.
Date ....
From ....
By ....

TO 17th Corps
4th Division 31st Division

Sender's Number.	Day of Month.	In reply to Number.	AAA
* G 755	3		

Reports	at ~~state~~	4.55	state	light
not yet	good	enough	for	observation
aaa	Hostile	VERY	lights	which
were	originally	sent	up	in
front	~~are~~ are	now	being	sent
up	further	EAST	aaa Heavy	Hostile
barrage	which	fell	on	our
front	line	at	3.48	~~which~~
is	now	reported	to have	decreased

From 9th Division
Place
Time 5.15 am

The above may be forwarded as now corrected.
(Z) M. Henderson Major
Censor. Signature of Addressor or person authorised to telegraph in his name.
* This line should be erased if not required.

750,000. W 2186—M509. H. W. & V., Ld. 6/16.

12

"C" Form. Army Form C. 2123.
(In books of 100).

MESSAGES AND SIGNALS. No. of Message

Prefix SB Code EL Words 149	Received. From SO By mlor	Sent, or sent out. At ____m. To ____ By ____	Office Stamp.
£ s. d. Charges to collect			
Service Instructions. Priority			

Handed in at SO Office 5.35 a m. Received 6.13 a m.

TO Hunt

*Sender's Number	Day of Month	In reply to Number	AAA
Bm 56	3rd	—	

Situation	5.30	am	aaa	Telephone
line	DIS	forward	of	German
third	system	till	5.15	am
when	got	through	to	BRIQUETERIE
Station	in	CUBA	and	through
that	to	Station	an	WISH
aaa	CUBA	reports	enemy	barrage
in	front	of	CUBA	very
heavy	aaa	message	from	right
Battn	timed	5.10	am	reports
no	definite	news	but	think
Battn	is	getting	on	aaa
message	from	left	Battn	timed
4.40	am	reports	his	Battn
and	31st	Div	to	north
has	reached	WIT	but	that
he	was	not	in	touch

FROM

PLACE & TIME

* This line should be erased if not required.

(6334). Wt. W7496/M857. 500,000 Pads. 10/16. D. D. & L. (E 489). Forms C/2123/3.

FROM Cover

PLACE & TIME 5.50 am

* This line should be erased if not required.

(6334). Wt. W7496/M857. 500,000 Pads. 10/16. D. D. & L. (E 489). Forms C/2123/3.

AH

"C" Form. Army Form C. 2123.
(In books of 100).

MESSAGES AND SIGNALS. No. of Message

Prefix ...... Code ...... Words ......

£ s. d.

Charges to collect

Service Instructions.

Received. From ...... By ......

Sent, or sent out. At ...... m. To ...... By ......

Office Stamp.

Handed in at ...... Office ...... m. Received 6.13a m.

TO Hirst (2)

*Sender's Number BM 51 | Day of Month 3 | In reply to Number | AAA

with	right	Battn	on	that
trench	aaa	at	Zero	light
good	enough	to	see	40
yards	along	a	track	too
dark	to	see	arrival	of
enemys	barrage	but	sound	tells
of	its	arrival	at	Zero
plus	3	aaa	Smoke	and
dust	caused	by	our	barrage
and	carried	by	NE	wind
towards	our	front	prevented	any
view	and	still	prevents	it.
enemy	barrage	still	maintained	on
forward	areas	two	of	our
planes	seen	over	Bde	HQ
at	5.15	am		

6.17am

FROM Cover

PLACE & TIME 5.50am

*This line should be erased if not required.

(6334). Wt. W7496/M857. 500,000 Pads. 10/16. D. D. & L. (E 489). Forms C/2123/3.

13

"A" Form.

Army Form C. 2121.

MESSAGES AND SIGNALS.

No. of Message

Prefix ...... Code ...... m.	Words	Charge	This message is on a/c of:	Recd. at ...... m.
Office of Origin and Service Instructions.	Sent		...... Service.	Date
Priority	At ...... m.			From
	To			By
	By		(Signature of "Franking Officer.")	

TO				
	17th Corps	CRA		
	4th Div	26 Bde		
	31st Div	27 Bde		

Sender's Number.	Day of Month	In reply to Number	AAA
*G 705	5		

Reports	indicate	attack	of	right
Brigade	has	failed	with	considerable
loss	from	MG	fire	from
right	flank	aaa	Left	Bde
believed	to	have	made	a
little	progress	but	no	definite
information		yet	aaa	

From 9th Div

Place

Time 6.20 am

The above may be forwarded as now corrected.

(Z) G Pearson Capt

Censor.

Signature of Addressor or person authorised to telegraph in his name.

G.S.

* This line should be erased if not required.

(6691) Wt. W5148—M701. 50000. 8/16 Sir J. C. & S. E292.

14

"C" Form

Army Form C. 2123.
(In books of 100.)

MESSAGES AND SIGNALS. No. of Message..................

Prefix...........Code...........Words...........	Received	Sent, or sent out	Office Stamp.
£ s. d.	From [illegible]	At..................m.	
Charges to collect	By..................	To..................	
Service Instructions.		By..................	6 am

Handed in at.............................Office..............m. Received..............m.

TO Riding

*Sender's Number	Day of Month	In reply to Number	AAA
1/2/3			

Liaison officer reports CUTHBERT trench has now been evacuated by our infantry and asks for old SOS line

[initials]

6 am

FROM
PLACE & TIME Blazers (52 Bde)

* This line should be erased if not required.

(B 8070) Wt. w. 7496—M357 250,000 Pads. 10/18 H&S (E436.) Forms/C.2123/8.

15

"C" Form
MESSAGES AND SIGNALS.

Army Form C. 2123.
(In books of 100.)

No. of Message

Prefix . . . Code . . . Words . . .	Received	Sent, or sent out	Office Stamp.
£ s. d. Charges to collect	From 32 By FMS	At . . . m.	
Service Instructions.		To . . . By . . .	

Handed in at . . . Office . . . m. Received 6 45 A m.

TO Nicking

*Sender's Number	Day of Month	In reply to Number	AAA
	3/4		

FOO D/thed reports WOBBLES trench has been captured and advance continues 700 to 800 yards in front in direction of SQUARE WOOD.

6.50 am

FROM PLACE & TIME 32nd Bde 6 35 am

* This line should be erased if not required.

(B 8070) Wt. w. 7496—M857 250,000 Pads. 10/16 H&S (E436.) Forms/C.2123/3.

16

"C" Form.

Army Form C. 2123.
(In books of 100).

MESSAGES AND SIGNALS.

No. of Message........

Prefix........ Code........ Words........

£ s. d.

Charges to collect

Service Instructions. Priority

Received. From........ By Cam

Sent, or sent out. At........m. To........ By........

Office Stamp.

Handed in at YCA Operation Office 6·20 am. Received 6·56 am.

TO 9 Div

*Sender's Number	Day of Month	In reply to Number	AAA
J1004	3rd		

Aeroplane dropped message at Dhq 6·10 am as follows aaa Very lights seen at 5·10 and O1A50 C1C5·8 C13A34 B24b9·8 C25A76 aaa There is a very heavy enemy barrage aaa The Hun is putting up many very lights which appear to be white breaking into two red balls aaa Visibility very bad aaa Following from left Brigade aaa Reports from wounded officer point to the attack on OPPY not having been successful aaa Right and Centre bns suffered heavily in their assembly lines at /

FROM
PLACE & TIME

M Br[illegible]

* This line should be erased if not required.

(6334). Wt. W7496/M857. 500,000 Pads. 10/16. D. D. & L. (E 489). Forms C/2123/3.

"C" Form.

Army Form C. 2123.
(In books of 100).

MESSAGES AND SIGNALS.

No. of Message

Prefix Code Words	Received.	Sent, or sent out.	Office Stamp.
£ s. d. Charges to collect	From	At m.	ARMY ...V.17R
Service Instructions.	By	To	
		By	

Handed in at Office m. Received m.

TO 9 Divn 2

*Sender's Number	Day of Month	In reply to Number	AAA

1.35	am	and	2.55	am
which	seems	to	have	
disorganised	the	attack	aaa	no
information	from	left	Bn	aaa
Added	13	Corps	Repeated	2
and	9	Divns		

H.L.

FROM 31 Divn

PLACE & TIME 6-21 am

* This line should be erased if not required.

(6334). Wt. W7496/M857. 500,000 Pads. 10/16. D. D. & L. (E 489). Forms C/2123/3.

147

"C" Form

MESSAGES AND SIGNALS.

Army Form C. 2123.
(In books of 100.)

No. of Message..................

Prefix.............. Code.............. Words..............

£ s. d.

Charges to collect

Service Instructions.

Received From Blazer By Theo

Sent, or sent out At..............m. To.............. By..............

Office Stamp.

Handed in at.............................. Office..............m. Received 7.10 a.m.

TO Reding

*Sender's Number	Day of Month	In reply to Number	AAA
S 3/3	3		

Liadson officer reports WOBBLE trench has been captured aaa Patrols out 600 or 700 yards in front of SQUARE WOOD aaa slow progress in centre

4/20 am

FROM Blazer (52nd Bde)
PLACE & TIME 6.35 am

* This line should be erased if not required.

(B 8070) Wt. w. 7496–M357 250,000 Pads. 10/16 H & S (E436.) Forms/C.2123/3.

18

MESSAGES AND SIGNALS. No. of Message........

Prefix........ Code........ Words........	Received.	Sent, or sent out.	Office Stamp.
£ s. d.	From........	At........m.	
Charges to collect	By........	To........	
Service Instructions. Priority		By........	

Handed in at YCB Operator Office 7 3 ? m. Received 7 3 ? m.

TO 9 Div

*Sender's Number	Day of Month	In reply to Number	AAA
G 1906	3		

Hourly report 6.30 am aaa our right Bde appears to be back in original trench and have taken up defensive position aaa Our left Bde appear from flares seen to have post in OPPY wood aaa Situation of remainder of brigade not known aaa Left Bde have sent back prisoners captured in trench immediately west of OPPY wood all of 2nd Guards Reserve [illegible] aaa Aeroplane reports as follows timed 6.15 am aaa Lights seen at C7A45 C13A85 B12D66 B24B98 C19A55 C19A70 C20A86 aaa

FROM Addsd 13 Corps Reptd 2 Div + 9 Div

PLACE & TIME 31 Divn 7.2 am

* This line should be erased if not required.

(6334). Wt. W7496/M857. 500,000 Pads. 10/16. D. D. & L. (E 489). Forms C/2123/3.

PS 7-50 am DHL

19

"C" Form.

Army Form C. 2123.
(In books of 100).

MESSAGES AND SIGNALS.

No. of Message

Prefix Code Words

£ s. d.

Charges to collect

Received.
From
By MM

Sent, or sent out.
At m.
To
By

Office Stamp.

Service Instructions.
Priority Operation

Handed in at JA Office 7.56a m. Received 8.10a m.

TO 9 Divn

*Sender's Number	Day of Month	In reply to Number	AAA
G1012	3		

Enemy is counterattacking whole of right bde front in force and has taken Windmill aaa One of the two battn in Divn reserve has been sent up in support aaa SOS along whole Bde front on original line 8.10 am

FROM
PLACE & TIME
31 Divn
7.56 a m

* This line should be erased if not required.

(6334). Wt. W7496/M857. 500,000 Pads. 10/16. D. D. & L. (E 489). Forms C/2123/3.

70

"C" Form.

Army Form C. 2123.
(In books of 100).

MESSAGES AND SIGNALS. No. of Message

Prefix ... Code ... Words ... / £ s. d. / Charges to collect	Received. / From ... / By ...	Sent, or sent out. / At ... m. / To ... / By ...	Office Stamp.

Service Instructions. Priority

Handed in at RRc Office 8.20a m. Received 8.34a m.

TO Adv. 9th Divn.

*Sender's Number	Day of Month	In reply to Number	AAA
G B467	3/5		

General	attack	will	NOT	be
pressed	for	present	aaa	all
local	successes	of	4th	Div.
to	be	exploited	to	full
with	view	of	capturing	CEMETERY
CORONA	trench	CHEMICAL	WORKS	and
building	north	of	Railway	aaa
9th	Div.	will	continue	bombardments
of	points	which	held	up
their	attack	aaa	Heavies	to
bombard	ROEUX	CARROT	CYPRUS	
CANDY	trenches	and	Railway	East
of	CUPID	addsd	4th	and
9th	Divs	Repeated	GOCRA	

FROM 17 Corps

PLACE & TIME 8.10 Am

* This line should be erased if not required.

(6334). Wt. W7496/M857. 500,000 Pads. 10/16. D. D. & L. (E 489). Forms C/2123/3.

8.39 a.m.

21

"A" Form. Army Form C.2121 (in pads of 100).

MESSAGES AND SIGNALS.

No. of Message ....

Prefix .... Code .... m. | Words | Charge | *This message is on a/c of:* ....*Service.* | Recd. at ....m.

Office of Origin and Service Instructions.

Priority

Sent
At .... m.
To ....
By ....

(Signature of "Franking Officer.")

Date ....
From ....
By ....

TO 17th Corps

Sender's Number.	Day of Month.	In reply to Number.	AAA
*G 766	3		

Situation	appears	to	be	as
follows	aaa	Right	Brigade	attack
failed	and	original	front	line
is	now	held	aaa	Left
Brigade	aaa	Three	companies	of
each	of	the	two	leading
battalions	appear	to	have	crossed
WIT	trench	but	WIT	trench
is	now	occupied	by	Germans
aaa	Consequently	the	companies	which
passed	WIT	trench	are	for
the	present	cut	off	aaa
It	is	not	intended	to
attack	WIT	trench	till	higher
ground	to	South	can	be
secured	which	is	out	of
question	at	present	aaa	Meanwhile

From
Place
Time

The above may be forwarded as now corrected. (Z)

Censor. Signature of Addressor or person authorised to telegraph in his name.

* This line should be erased if not required.

750,000. W 2186 -M509. H. W. & V., Ld. 6/16.

"A" Form.

MESSAGES AND SIGNALS.

Army Form C.2121
(in pads of 100).
No. of Message ....

Prefix .... Code .... m. / Office of Origin and Service Instructions.	Words / Charge / Sent / At .... m. / To .... / By	This message is on a/c of: / .... Service. / (Signature of "Franking Officer.")	Recd. at .... m. / Date .... / From .... / By ....

TO 2

Sender's Number.	Day of Month.	In reply to Number.	AAA.
*			

original | fast | line | is | held

From 9 Division
Place
Time 9.10 a m

The above may be forwarded as now corrected.
(Z) M. Henderson Major
Censor.
Signature of Addressor or person authorised to telegraph in his name.

25

* This line should be erased if not required.

750,000. W 3186 -M569. H. W. & V., Ld. 6/16.

22

"C" Form.

MESSAGES AND SIGNALS.

Army Form C. 2123.
(In books of 100).

No. of Message

Prefix SM Code [illegible] Words 150 Charges to collect £ s. d. Service Instructions.	Received. From DO By Payne	Sent, or sent out. At m. To By 92 A	Office Stamp. TELEGRAPHS

Handed in at DO Office 9.20 m. Received 9.34 A m.

TO Hunt

*Sender's Number	Day of Month	In reply to Number	AAA
BM 9	3		

On	hearing	that	93rd	Bde
on	my	left	is	being
counter	attacked	I	ordered	up
one	coy	of	my	Reserve
Battn	to	CIDER	and	am
keeping	on	artillery	on	WIT
aaa	28th	Bty	has	
8	guns	now	barraging	the
ground	beyond	our	objective	in
the	direction	of	WAIT	TRENCH
and	SQUARE	WOOD	the	other
8	are	barraging	all	the
high	ground	east	of	CUTHBERT
so	as	to	protect	the
right	and	rear	of	my
troops	in	the	WOBBLE	direction
otherwise	no	change	cannot	do

FROM

PLACE & TIME 10.5 am

* This line should be erased if not required.

(6334). Wt. W7496/M857. 500,000 Pads. 10/16. D. D. & L. (E 489). Forms C/2123/3.

"C" Form.

MESSAGES AND SIGNALS.

Army Form C. 2123.
(In books of 100).

No. of Message

Prefix Code Words	Received.	Sent, or sent out.	Office Stamp.
£ s. d. Charges to collect	From By	At m. To By	
Service Instructions.			

Handed in at Office m. Received m.

TO (2)

*Sender's Number	Day of Month	In reply to Number	AAA
BM 9			

more on my front until high ground on my right is taken as it commands my area aaa 93rd Bde are in their front line and have no intention of reoccupying WT which will make it difficult for me to do so although it is important for us to get rid of the enemy interposing between my advanced people and my original front line

FROM
PLACE & TIME Cover. 9. 10 AM

10.5 am

* This line should be erased if not required.

(6334). Wt. W7496/M857. 500,000 Pads. 10/16. D. D. & L. (E 489). Forms C/2123/3.

23

"C" Form. Army Form C. 2123.
(In books of 100).

MESSAGES AND SIGNALS. No. of Message

Prefix SB Code Sg Words 40	Received. From SO By Payne	Sent, or sent out. At m. To By	Office Stamp.
Charges to collect £ s. d.			

Service Instructions. SO Priority

Handed in at SO Office 9.15 m. Received m.

TO Hunt

*Sender's Number	Day of Month	In reply to Number	AAA
BM 10	3		

Could an aeroplane be sent to reconnoitre the area of WOBBLE trench to ascertain if possible whether our men are there or not They will not light flares until they see an aeroplane

Corps asked 10.14 am
10 10 am

FROM PLACE & TIME Cover 9. 30 am

* This line should be erased if not required.

(6334). Wt. W7496/M857. 500,000 Pads. 10/16. D. D. & L. (E489). Forms C/2123/3.

24

"A" Form.

MESSAGES AND SIGNALS.

Army Form C.2121 (in pads of 100).

No. of Message

Prefix Code m. | Words | Charge | This message is on a/c of: Service. | Recd. at m.

Office of Origin and Service Instructions.

Priority

Sent At m. To By

(Signature of "Franking Officer.")

Date From By

TO XVII Corps

Sender's Number.	Day of Month.	In reply to Number.	AAA
*G 678	3		

Could	an	aeroplane	be	sent
to	reconnoitre	the	area	of
WOBBLE	trench	and	SQUARE	WOOD
to	ascertain	if	possible	whether
our	men	are	there	or
not	as	they	will	not
light	flares	until	they	see
an	aeroplane			

From 9th Division

Place

Time 10.15 am

The above may be forwarded as now corrected.

(Z) M. Henderson Major

Censor. Signature of Addressor or person authorised to telegraph in his name.

GS

* This line should be erased if not required.

750,000. W 2136 -M309. H. W. & V., Ld. 6/16.

25

"C" Form. Army Form C. 2123.

(In books of 100).

ME[SSAGES AND SIGNALS.] No. of Message

Prefix	Code	Words	Received.	Sent, or sent out.	Office Stamp.
£ s. d.			From	At m.	
Charges to collect			By	To	
Service Instructions. Priority				By	

Handed in at JCA 2 Office 9.55 m. Received 10.40 m.

TO 9 Divn

*Sender's Number	Day of Month	In reply to Number	AAA
G 1017	3		

Hourly	report	9.30	AM	aaa
We	hold	EASTERN	EDGE	of
GAVRELLE	to	RAILWAY	at	C19C62
along	railway	to	B24D28	aaa
mg	and	2	Coys	infantry
on	hill	80	aaa	LEFT
Bde.	in	forming	up	trenches
aaa	WINDMILL	has changed		hands
three	times	and	we are	at
present	making	a	new	attack
on	it	aaa	It	is now
known	that	LEFT	Bde.	was
hung	up	in	their	advance
through	OPPY	WOOD	by	very
thick	wire	thus	leaving	LEFT
OF	RIGHT	Bde.	Open	aaa
This	Bde	advancing	behind	barrage

FROM

PLACE & TIME 10.46 am

* This line should be erased if not required.

(6334). Wt. W7495/M857. 500,000 Pads. 10/16. D. D. & L. (E 489). Forms C/2123/3.

"C" Form.

Army Form C. 2123.
(In books of 100).

MESSAGES AND SIGNALS. No. of Message

Prefix Code Words | Received. From By | Sent, or sent out. At m. To By | Office Stamp.

£ s. d.

Charges to collect

Service Instructions.

Handed in at Office m. Received 10.40 m.

TO 11

*Sender's Number | Day of Month | In reply to Number | AAA

was ~~[illegible]~~ very heavily counter attacked from OPPY WOOD and village after barrage had passed and their LEFT FLANK ROLLED up aaa we are making a strong front at B12C63 to join with 2nd Divn aaa

Addsd 13 Corps Repeated 2nd and 9th Divns

FROM 31 Divn

PLACE & TIME 9.50 am

* This line should be erased if not required.

(6334). Wt. W7496/M857. 500,000 Pads. 10/16. D. D. & L. (E 489). Forms C/2123/3.

26

"C" Form.

MESSAGES AND SIGNALS.

Army Form C. 2123.
(In books of 100).

No. of Message

Prefix Code Words

£ s. d.

Charges to collect

Service Instructions. Priority

Received. From By

Sent, or sent out. At m. To By

Office Stamp.

Handed in at R.A.C. Office 10.44 a m. Received 10.49 a m.

TO 9 Divn.

Sender's Number	Day of Month	In reply to Number	AAA
JB 472	3		

In Confirmation telephone message Send machine to call for flares and reconnoitre area WOBBLE trench and SQUARE wood to ascertain if possible our men there or not aaa Addressed 13 Sqdn RFC Repeated 9 Divn

10.54 am

FROM 17 Corps

PLACE & TIME 10.40 am

* This line should be erased if not required.

(6334). Wt. W7496/M857. 500,000 Pads. 10/16. D. D. & L. (E489). Forms C/2123/3.

24

"A" Form. Army Form C. 2121.

MESSAGES AND SIGNALS.

No. of Message

Prefix ... Code ... m.	Words / Charge	This message is on a/c of:	Recd. at ... m.
Office of Origin and Service Instructions. PRIORITY	Sent At ... m. To ... By ...	... Service.	Date
		(Signature of "Franking Officer.")	From
			By

TO { 27 Bde

Sender's Number.	Day of Month	In reply to Number	AAA
* G 704			

An aeroplane has been told to call for flares and reconnoitre SQUARE WOOD and WO[illegible] trench ~~aaa~~ to ascertain if our troops are in this area aaa

From 9th Div
Place
Time 11 am

The above may be forwarded as now corrected. (Z) [illegible] Capt

Censor. Signature of Addressor or person authorised to telegraph in his name.

* This line should be erased if not required.

(6691) Wt. W5148—M701. 50000. 8/16 Sir J. C. & S. E292.

28

MESSAGES AND SIGNALS. No. of Message..........

Prefix.......... Code.......... Words..........

£ s. d.

Charges to collect

Service Instructions.

Received From.......... By..........

Sent, or sent out At..........m. To.......... By..........

Office Stamp.

Handed in at RFC Office 12.38p m. Received 12.45p m.

TO 9 Divn

*Sender's Number	Day of Month	In reply to Number	AAA
G B 474	3/5	—	

Contact Patrol Aeroplane will fly along Corps front and call for FLARES at two PM today paying special attention to CHEMICAL WORKS aaa Addressed 4th and 9th Divisions Repeated 13 Squadron RFC

Brigades informed

HL

12-40

FROM 17th Corps

PLACE & TIME 12·30 PM

* This line should be erased if not required.

Wt. 432—M437 500,000 Pads. H W V 5/16 Forms C.2123.

"A" Form.

MESSAGES AND SIGNALS.

Army Form C.2121
(in pads of 100).
No. of Message ....

Prefix .... Code .... m. Office of Origin and Service Instructions.	Words	Charge	This message is on a/c of: .... Service.	Recd. at .... m.
	Sent At .... m. To .... By		(Signature of "Franking Officer.")	Date .... From .... By ....

TO 2

Sender's Number.	Day of Month.	In reply to Number.	AAA
*			

South	aaa	Acknowledge	aaa	addressed
27th	Inf	Bde	and	C.R.A
with	9th	Division	repeated	26th
Inf	Bde	17th	Corps	31st
Division	4th	Division	52nd	Inf
Bde				

From 9th Div

Place

Time 12-50 pm

The above may be forwarded as now corrected.

(Z) M Henderson Capt

.... Censor.

Signature of Addressor or person authorised to telegraph in his name.

* This line should be erased if not required.

45

750,000. W 2186 –M509. H. W. & V., Ld. 6/16.

29

"A" Form.

Army Form C.2121
(in pads of 100).
No. of Message..........

MESSAGES AND SIGNALS.

Prefix ....Code............m.	Words	Charge	This message is on a/c of:	Recd. at..............m.
Office of Origin and Service Instructions.	Sent		..........................Service.	Date..................
Priority	At..............m.			From..................
	To..................			
	By X		(Signature of "Franking Officer.")	By..................

TO { 26th Inf Bde — C.R.E. — 4 Division
C.R.A. with 9 Division — 17th Corps — 52nd Inf Bde
27th Inf Bde — 31st Division }

Sender's Number.	Day of Month.	In reply to Number.	AAA
*G 771	3		

27th	Inf	Brigade	will	assault
WIT	trench	between	cross roads	I.2.c
and	northern	boundary	of	9th
Division	at	I.1.b.7.8	at	an
hour	to	be	notified	later
aaa	WHIP	and	WIT	trenches
and	WOBBLE	trench	NORTH	of
I.2.a.5.8	will	be	intensely	bombarded
from	ZERO	hour	aaa	at
ZERO	plus	2	minutes	the
artillery	fire	will	lift	off
the	~~part~~ portion	of	the	trench
to	be	assaulted	aaa	a
smoke	barrage	will	be	placed
South	of	the	crossroads	in
I.2.c	to	conceal	the	advance
from	the	high	ground	on

From 9th Div

Place

Time 12.50 pm

The above may be forwarded as now corrected. (Z)

Censor. Signature of Addressor or person authorised to telegraph in his name.

* This line should be erased if not required.

750,000. W 2136-M569. H. W. & V., Ld. 6/16.

30

"C" Form (Duplicate).
MESSAGES AND SIGNALS.

Army Form C. 2123.
(In books of 50's in duplicate.)
No. of Message..................

Service Instructions.

Charges to Pay. £ s. d.

Office Stamp. 3.V.17 R TELEGRAPHS

Handed in at YCA Office 12.44 p.m. Received 1.13 p.m.

TO 9 Divn

Sender's Number	Day of Month	In reply to Number	AAA
G1023	3		

We	are	now	in	touch
with	9th	Divn	SE	of GAVRELLE
aaa	Added	13	corps	Repted
9	Div			

1.25 pm

FROM 31 Divn
PLACE & TIME 12.40 pm

Wt. 432—M437 500,000 Pads. H W V 5/16 Forms C.2123.

31

Army Form C. 2121
(in pads of 100).

"A" Form
MESSAGES AND SIGNALS.

No. of Message..................

Prefix..............Code..................m. | Words. | Charge.

Office of Origin and Service Instructions.

PRIORITY

Sent
At..................m.
To....................
By....................

This message is on a/c of:
..............................Service
....
(Signature of "Franking Officer.")

Recd. at............m.
Date....................
From....................
By....................

TO 27 I Bde

Sender's Number.	Day of Month.	In reply to Number.	AAA
*G 774	3		

31st Div report that they are now in touch with you aaa

From 9th Div
Place
Time 1.29pm

The above may be forwarded as now corrected.
(Z)
.... Censor.
[illegible] Capt
Signature of Addressor or person authorised to telegraph in his name.

*This line should be erased if not required.

(18565.) Wt. W12952/M1294. 187,500 Pads. 1/17 McC. & Co., Ltd. (E. 813.)

32

"C" Form.

Army Form C. 2123.
(In books of 100).

MESSAGES AND SIGNALS.

No. of Message

Prefix SM Code Ak Words 40
£ s. d.
Charges to collect
Service Instructions.

Received.
From So Texey
By Payne

Sent, or sent out.
At m.
To
By

Office Stamp.

Handed in at So Office 12.55 p m. Received 1.40 p m.

TO Hunt

*Sender's Number	Day of Month	In reply to Number	AAA
BM 13	3		

Message from OC BREAK timed
11.40 am says that he
is in touch with OC
[illegible] Bow on left The
OC [illegible] Bow reports he
holds the line from C25a5.7
to C25c8.2 Added Hunt Repeated
Hull

Phone informed 2.10

FROM
PLACE & TIME Cover 1.15 pm

* This line should be erased if not required.

(6334). Wt. W7496/M857. 500,000 Pads. 10/16. D. D. & L. (E 489). Forms C/2123/3.

359

MESSAGES AND SIGNALS. No. of Message

Service Instructions.	Charges to Pay. £ s. d.	Office Stamp.
am		

Handed in at YCA Office 2.15 p.m. Received 2.55 p.m.

TO 9 Div

Sender's Number	Day of Month	In reply to Number	AAA
R 1728	3.5.17		

Enemy is seen in C19B preparing for another attack on GAVRELLE windmill artillery is engaging him

Repeated to 27 Infy Bde

3 6

FROM 31 Div

PLACE & TIME 2.6 pm.

Wt. 482—M437 500,000 Pads. H W V 5/16 Forms C.2123.

24

"A" Form.

MESSAGES AND SIGNALS.

Army Form C.2121 (in pads of 100).

No. of Message ....

Prefix .... Code .... m. | Words | Charge

Office of Origin and Service Instructions.

Sent — At .... m. To .... By ....

This message is on a/c of: .... Service.

(Signature of "Franking Officer.")

Recd. at .... m. Date .... From .... By ....

TO 27 Inf Bde

Sender's Number	Day of Month	In reply to Number	
* G 776	3		AAA

31st	Division	wires	~~begun~~ timed	2.6
pm	begins	enemy	is	seen
in	C.19.b	preparing	for	another
attack	on	GAVRELLE	windmill	artillery
is	engaging	him		

From 9th Div

Place

Time 3.6 pm

The above may be forwarded as now corrected. (Z) M Henderson Major GS

Censor. Signature of Addressor or person authorised to telegraph in his name.

* This line should be erased if not required.

750,000. W 2186 –M569. H. W. & V., Ld. 6/16.

35

MESSAGES AND SIGNALS. No. of Message

Prefix...... Code...... Words...... £ s. d. Charges to collect	Received From Z By 2	Sent, or sent out At......m. To...... By......	Office Stamp.
Service Instructions.			

Handed in at...... Office......m. Received 3 12 m.

TO Pudding

*Sender's Number	Day of Month	In reply to Number	AAA
EX2	3		

FOO reports 2 57 pm . White Lights are being sent up from I 7 a 33

3 28

FROM
PLACE & TIME Blazer

* This line should be erased if not required.

(B 8070) Wt. w. 7496—M857 250,000 Pads. 10/16 H&S (E436.) Forms/C.2123/3.

36

"C" Form (Original).
MESSAGES AND SIGNALS.

Army Form C. 2123.
(In books of 50's in duplicate.)

No. of Message..................

Prefix.......Code.......Words....... / £ s. d. / Charges to collect	Received / From............ / By............	Sent, or sent out / At..........m. / To.......... / By..........	Office Stamp.

Service Instructions.

Handed in at YFA Office 2.45 p m. Received 3.16 p m.

TO 9 Divn

*Sender's Number	Day of Month	In reply to Number	AAA
G 1032	3		

4th	Counter	attack	on	mill
by	us	succeeded	but	with
heavy	loss	aaa	mill	now
held	by	us.	but	fighting
still	going	on	otherwise	situation
unchanged	aaa	we	are	in
touch	with	Divn	on	right
aaa	Enemy	heavy	arty	very
active	against	our	left	Bde
aaa	Addsd	13	Corps	Reptd
2	and	9	Divn	

3.30

FROM 31st Divn
PLACE & TIME 2.40 pm

* This line should be erased if not required.

Wt. 432—M437 500,000 Pads. H W V 5.16 Forms C. 2123.

74

"A" Form.
MESSAGES AND SIGNALS.

Army Form C.2121
(in pads of 100).
No. of Message..........

Prefix .... Code .... m. Office of Origin and Service Instructions.	Words	Charge	This message is on a/c of: .... Service. (Signature of "Franking Officer.")	Recd. at .... m. Date .... From .... By ....
Priority	Sent At .... m. To .... By			

TO { 27th Inf Bde — C.R.E — 4th Division
C.R.A. with 9th Division — 17th Corps — 52nd Inf Bde
26th Inf Bde — 31st Division

Sender's Number.	Day of Month.	In reply to Number.	AAA
* G 777	3		

with	reference	my	G 771	aaa
ZERO	will	be	8	p.m.
aaa	acknowledge	aaa	addressed	27th
Inf	Bde	and	C.R.A.	with
9th	Division	repeated	26th	Inf
Bde	C.R.E	17th	Corps	31st
Division	4th	Division	52nd	Inf
Bde				

From 9th Div
Place
Time 4 pm
The above may be forwarded as now corrected.
Censor.
(Z) M. Henderson Major
Signature of Addressor or person authorised to telegraph in his name.
* This line should be erased if not required.

750,000. W 2186 –M569. H. W. & V., Ld. 6/16.

28

"A" Form.

MESSAGES AND SIGNALS. 98

Army Form C.2121 (in pads of 100).

No. of Message

Prefix .... Code .... m. Office of Origin and Service Instructions.	Words	Charge	This message is on a/c of: .... Service. (Signature of "Franking Officer.")	Recd. at .... m. Date .... From .... By ....
	Sent At.........m. To......... By.........			

ARMY TELEGRAPHS -3 V.17

TO { 4th Corps 9th [illegible] Divn

Sender's Number.	Day of Month.	In reply to Number.	AAA
* 361	3		

Situation so far as can be ascertained is as follows aaa We are holding original front line with exception of posts at I 13 central in some of enclosures and buildings near CHATEAU and possibly in Chemical Works aaa Enemy have been advancing into CORONA Trench and it would appear we now have no troops on BLACK LINE aaa Situation in CLOVER Trench not clear aaa 1 Coy R.I. Bde and 1 Coy 9th Div have been sent to clear up situation aaa Enemy has made several strong counter attacks aaa Hampshire Regt. have been placed at disposal of 12th Bde and are moving [illegible] aaa This leaves 1 battn as Div Reserve

From 4th Div

Place

Time 4-55 pm

The above may be forwarded as now corrected. (Z)

Censor. Signature of Addressor or person authorised to telegraph in his name.

* This line should be erased if not required.

750,000. W 2186–M509. H. W. & V., Ld. 6/16.

39

"A" Form
MESSAGES AND SIGNALS.

Army Form C. 2121
(in pads of 100).

No. of Message..................

Prefix..............Code..................m. | Words. | Charge.
Office of Origin and Service Instructions.

Priority

Sent
At..............m.
To..............
By..............

This message is on a/c of:
..............................Service.
....
(Signature of "Franking Officer.")

Recd. at............m.
Date....................
From....................
By.......................

TO 26th Bde CRE
27th Bde 9th Seaforths

Sender's Number.	Day of Month.	In reply to Number.	AAA
* G 781	3/5/17		

One Field Company RE and two Pioneer Companies will be at the disposal of each Bde tonight for work on clearing front line and communication trenches aaa OC 9th Seaforths will arrange to place one additional Company at the disposal of each Bde for the purpose aaa ~~Communication~~ Connection between WISH line and the Buckfield in CUBA should be made by the

From
Place
Time

The above may be forwarded as now corrected. (Z)
Censor.
Signature of Addressor or person authorised to telegraph in his name.

*This line should be erased if not required.

(18865.) Wt. W12952/M1294. 187,500 Pads. 1/17. McC. & Co., Ltd. (E. 313.)

"A" Form
MESSAGES AND SIGNALS.

Army Form C. 2121
(in pads of 100).

No. of Message..................

Prefix.............Code.................m.	Words.	Charge.	This message is on a/c of:	Recd. at............m.
Office of Origin and Service Instructions.	Sent		..............................Service.	Date....................
	At..................m.			From..................
	To....................			
	By.....................		(Signature of "Franking Officer.")	By......................

TO

Sender's Number. *	Day of Month.	In reply to Number.	AAA

construction of intermediate strong points which can subsequently be connected by a continuous trench aaa acknowledge

From 9th Div
Place
Time 8 35 pm

The above may be forwarded as now corrected. (Z)

Censor. Signature of Addressor or person authorised to telegraph in his name.

*This line should be erased if not required.

(18965.) Wt. W12952/M1294. 187,500 Pads. 1/17 McC. & Co., Ltd. (E. 813.)

40

"C" Form. Army Form C. 2123.

(In books of 100).

MESSAGES AND SIGNALS. No. of Message

Prefix ... Code ... Words ...	Received.	Sent, or sent out.	Office Stamp.
£ s. d. Charges to collect	From	At ... m.	TELEGRAPHS 3.V.17
Service Instructions.	By A.N.V.	To	
		By	

Handed in at RRC Priority [?] Office 1.20 p m. Received 1.2? p m.

TO adv 9th Div

*Sender's Number	Day of Month	* In reply to Number	AAA
AB 283	3/5		

Divisions will consolidate and improve the positions held aaa Touch will be kept with the enemy by means of patrols aaa Addsd adv 4th And 9th Divns Repted 17th Div GOCRA and 13 Sqdn RFC

1.35 pm [illegible]

FROM PLACE & TIME 17 Corps 1-15 pm

* This line should be erased if not required.

(6334). Wt. W7496/M857. 500,000 Pads. 10/16. D. D. & L. (E 469). Forms C/2123/3.

41

"A" Form.
MESSAGES AND SIGNALS.

Army Form C.2121
(in pads of 100).
No. of Message ....

Prefix ....Code ....m.	Words	Charge	*This message is on a/c of:*	Recd. at ....m.
Office of Origin and Service Instructions.	Sent		............................*Service.*	Date ....
	At.... ....m.			From ....
	To			
	By		(Signature of "Franking Officer.")	By ....

TO: 26 Inf Bde, 27 Inf Bde, CRA, CRE

Sender's Number.	Day of Month.	In reply to Number.	AAA
* G 783	3		

17	Corps	were	being	Divisions
will	consolidate	and	improve	the
positions	held	and	touch	will
be	kept	with	the	enemy
by	means	of	patrols	only
[illegible]	to	information	and	necessary
action	addressed	26	27	Inf
Bdes	and	CRE	repeated	CRA
for	information			

From 9 Div
Place
Time 7 45 pm

The above may be forwarded as now corrected. (Z) M. Henderson Major

Censor. Signature of Addressor or person authorised to telegraph in his name.

Lt C

* This line should be erased if not required.

750,000. W 2186 –M509. H. W. & V., Ld. 6/16.

Copy.

42

4th S.A.I.
26th Inf. Bde.
S.A. Bde.
&
9th Div. Train

G. 813. 4th.

From receipt of this order 4th. S.A.I. will cease to work under C.E. of Corps aaa. This Battalion will move tomorrow May 5th afternoon to trench area in vicinity of ATHIES exact area will be notified later aaa Battalion will be prepared to take over trenches under orders of B.G.C. 26th Inf. Bde. on night of May 6th/7th aaa. Acknowledge aaa addressed 4th. S.A.I. repeated 26th Inf. Bde. S. African Bde. & 9th Div. Train.

9th. Division

11 30 pm.

Copy

43

Priority.

S. A. Bde.
Q.

G. 822. 5/5/14.

One Company from each of the 1st, 2nd and 3rd S.A. Regts. will move to ARRAS today aaa Arrangements for busses are being made by Q aaa Strength of each Company will be 100 duty N.C.O's. and other ranks aaa Acknowledge aaa Addressed S.A. Bde. repeated Q.

9th Division.

11-20

44

Copy No______

9th Division Order No. 129.

8.5.17.

1. 9th Division (less Artillery) will be relieved in the line by 17th Division (less Artillery). Reliefs in front line to be completed by 4.30 a.m. on May 11th.

2. Reliefs will be carried out as follows:-

Night 9th/10th. 27th Inf. Bde. will be relieved by 52nd Inf. Bde.

Night 10th/11th. 26th Inf. Bde. will be relieved by 50th Inf. Bde. from I.7.d.15.35 to a point about 200 yards South of the BRICKFIELD, the remainder of the 26th Inf. Brigade front being taken over by 52nd Inf. Bde.

Details of reliefs to be arranged between Brigade Commanders concerned.

3. The Artillery now covering the front of the 9th Division will from the hour of the G.O.C. 17th Division assuming command cover the whole front of the 17th Division (Junction of CAM Trench and ROEUX - GAVRELLE Road to I.1.b.1.7).

4. The relief of the Machine Gun Companies in each Brigade Area will be carried out 24 hours before the Infantry reliefs.

5. Relief of Field Companies R.E. and Pioneers will be carried out under arrangements to be made between the C.R.Es. concerned.

6. Relief of Field Ambulances will be arranged by the A.Ds.M.S. concerned.

7. All coloured lights and rockets and ground flares at present held by Units of the 9th Division will be handed over on relief.

8. The 9th Bn. Seaforth Highlanders will from 6 a.m. May 11th come under orders of C.E. XVII Corps.

9. On relief, 28th Machine Gun Coy. and 2 sections of 26th Machine Gun Coy. and one battalion S.African Bde. made up to strength capable of producing 800 working men will remain attached to 17th Division. This Battalion will be employed under A.D.Signals.

10. The 9th Division (less troops mentioned in paras 8 and 9) will on relief move to a rest area under orders which will be issued later.

11. G.O.C. 9th Division will hand over command of the front at 10 a.m. on May 11th at which hour Divisional Headquarters will close in RAILWAY CUTTING (H.~~14~~8.a.1.9).

12. ACKNOWLEDGE.

[signature]
Lieutenant Colonel,
General Staff,
9th (Scottish) Division.

Issued at 7 a.m.

Distribution.....

Copies to:-

No. 1 to 26th Inf. Bde.
2 to 27th Inf. Bde.
3 to 1st S.African Bde.
4 to C.R.A.
5 to C.R.E.
6 to 9th Seaforths.
7 to 9th Div. Train.
8 to 9th Signals.
9 to "Q".
10 to A.D.M.S.
11 to A.D.V.S.
12 to A.P.M.
13 to 197th Machine Gun Coy.
14) to 17th Corps.
15)
16 to 31st Division.
17 to 17th Division.
18 to 4th Division.
19 to 52nd Inf. Bde.
20 to 28th Machine Gun Coy.
21 to War Diary.
22 to File.

45

SECRET

AMENDMENT NO. 1 TO 9TH DIVISION O.O. 130.

9th May 1917

With reference to March Table issued with O.O. 130.

(a) Items 5 and 6.

The destination of the 27th Infantry Brigade will be the area:-

BAILLEUL AUX CORNAILLES
MARQUAY
FOUFFLIN RICAMETZ
TERNAS

(b) Items 6,14 and 16.

The 63rd, 64th and 90th Field Coys. R.E. will proceed to GOUY EN TERNOIS.

(c) Items 13,14,15,16

For May 11th read May 12th.

Acknowledge

M. Henderson Major
for Lieut-Colonel,
General Staff.
9th (Scottish) Division.

Issued at 2 p.m.

Copies to:-

recepients of O.O. 130

S E C R E T

9TH (SCOTTISH) DIVISION
OPERATION ORDER 20

Copy No.......

Sheet 51.c. 1/40,000
Sheet 36.b. do
Trench Map
Sheet 51.b. 1/10,000

1. Moves of Units 9th Division will be carried out in accordance with attached March Table on May 9th, 10th and 11th.

2. The party of 250 men from 27th Infantry Brigade for work under 17th Division will move to BLACK LINE on May 9th and will be accommodated with composite Battalion from 1st., 2nd, 3rd and 4th S.A. Regiments.

The party of 350 men from 26th Infantry Brigade will move to BLACK LINE on May 10th.

3. 28th Machine Gun Company with two sections of 26th Machine Gun Company will remain in present billets and come under orders of G.O.C. 17th Division from 10 am. May 11th.

4. 9th Divisional H.Q. will close at RAILWAY CUTTING H.14.a. at 10 am on May 11th and open at CHELERS at 11 am.

A Staff Officer 9th Division will be at CHELERS from 10 am to receive messages.

5. ACKNOWLEDGE.

Lieut-Colonel,
General Staff.
9th(Scottish)Division.

Issued at 6 am.

Issued to:-

1. 26th Bde
2. 27th Bde
3. S.A. Bde
4. C.R.A.
5. C.R.E.
6. 9th Seaforths
7. 9th Signals
8. 9th Train
9. "Q"
10. A.D.M.S.
11. D.A.D.O.S.
12. A.P.M.
13. 197th M.G. Coy
14.)
15.) XVll Corps
16. 17th Div.
17. 4th Div
18. 28th M.G. Coy
19. 51st Div.
20. 3rd Div

MARCH TABLE to accompany 9th Division Order No. 130.

Item	Unit	Date	[illegible]	From	To	Remarks.
1.	27th Inf. Bde.	Night 9/10th.	March.	Trenches	ARRAS	On relief by 52nd I.Bde.
2.	Composite Bn. 1st, 2nd, 3rd, S.A.I.	-	-	-	Black Line	" " " " "
3.	90th Fld.Coy.	"	"	"	ARRAS	On relief.
4.	197th M.G.Coy.	"	"	"	Transport Lines ST NICHOLAS.	"
5.	27th I.Bde.and 90th Fld.Coy. (Personnel)	May 10th.	Tactical train.	ARRAS	CHELERS MONT-en-TERNOIS MONCHEAUX GOUY-en-TERNOIS	Train arrangements will be notified by 9th Div."Q".
6.	27th Inf.Bde. & 90th Fld.Coy. (Transport)	May 10th.	March	ST NICHOLAS.		No restrictions as to time or route. Intervals of 200x to be kept between each Battalion transport & 90th Field Coy.
7.	197th M.G.Coy.	"	Tactical train.	ARRAS	HERLIN-le-VERT.	
8.	64th Fld.Co.RE.	"	March.	Trenches	Y Huts.	On relief.
9.	9th Seaforths.	"	"	"	Destination to be notified later.	
10.	26th Inf.Bde.	Night 10/11th.	Bus	Trenches.	Y Huts.	Arrangements for busses will be notified by 9th Div."Q".
11.	4th S.A.I.	"	"	"	Y Huts.	do
12.	63rd Fld.Co.RE.	"	"	"	Y Huts.	do

[illegible]em.	Unit	Date	Route	From	To	Remarks.
[illegible]3.	26th Inf.Bde.	May 11th.	March.	Y. Huts.	PENIN, AVERDOINGT MAIZIERES TINCQUES.	To move under orders of GOC. 26th Bde. No restrictions as to time or route. Intervals of 200x to be kept between Coys.& Secs. of transport & 400 yards between battalions.
[illegible].	63rd Fld.Coy.	"	"	"		
[illegible]5.	4th S.A.I.	"	"	"	MONCHY [illegible]. BRETON	
[illegible]6.	* 64th Fld.Coy.RE.	"	"	"	"	
[illegible].	Div. H.Qrs.	"	"	Line.	CHELERS.	

* S.African Bde. to arrange accommodation.

Copy

46

26th Bde
27th Bde
S.A. Bde.
C.R.A.
C.R.E.

G.993 16/5

Orders have been received for one Inf. Bde. to be earmarked to send up as reinforcement to ARRAS in case situation demands aaa 26th. Bde. is detailed for this duty aaa

Addressed 26th Bde. repeated 27th and S.A. Bdes. C.R.A. and C.R.E.

9th Division.

1-10pm.

44

SECRET.

Copy No. 28

9TH DIVISION ORDER NO. 131.

25th May, 1917.

Ref. 1/100,000 LENS.
1/20,000 Trench Maps
51.b.N.W.
51.c.N.E.

1. The 9th Division (less Artillery) will relieve the 51st Division (less Artillery) in the Right Sector XVIIth Corps on May 31st/1st June and 1st/2nd June.

Relief to be completed by 4 a.m. June 2nd.

2. Moves will be carried out in accordance with attached Movement Table.

Orders regarding bussing and train arrangements will be issued later.

3. The 26th Infantry Brigade will relieve the 154th Infantry Brigade in the right Subsector on the night May 31st/June 1st., the 27th Infantry Brigade will relieve the 153rd Infantry Brigade in the left Subsector on the night 1st/2nd June. The S. African Brigade will be in Divisional Reserve.

Headquarters of Brigades are situated as follows :-

154th Brigade	Railway Cutting H.14.a.1.9.
153rd Brigade	H.16.d.1.7.
152nd Brigade	1 Rue d'Ancre, ARRAS.

4. Details of relief will be arranged direct between Brigadiers concerned.

Command will pass on completion of the Infantry reliefs, which will be reported by wire to Divisional Headquarters.

5. (a) The Boundary between the 9th and 34th Divisions will be :-

Junction of CROOK and CHAPLIN Trenches (inclusive to 9th Division) - Communication trench from CALABAR to CUTE Trench at I.13.a.80.95. (exclusive to 9th Division) Junction of CAMEL and CADIZ Trenches at H.18.b.45.70 (inclusive to 9th Division) thence CAMEL Trench to 9th Division as far as road junction H.17.a.80.95 - thence SUNKEN ROAD to junction with GAVRELLE Switch at H.10.d.75.55. thence to railway bridge H.8.c.0.0. and due West along grid line to old British front line at G.11.d.9.0.

(b) The Boundary between 26th and 27th Brigades will on first taking over the line be the same as that between the 154th and 153rd Brigades. After completion of the relief on the 2nd June the boundary will be :-

Junction of CRUSH Trench with the railway (inclusive to 27th Brigade) - Junction of CRETE and COLON Trenches (inclusive to 27th Brigade) - Junction of CUSP and CORFU Trenches I.13.a.7.1. (inclusive to 26th Brigade) - Junction of

........CORONA.......

CORONA Trench and CORONA SUPPORT I.13.d.9.2. (inclusive to 26th Brigade) - and thence a line to the bend of the SUNKEN ROAD at I.14.c.5.4.

Any readjustment of troops necessary will be made under arrangements between G.O's.C. 26th and 27th Brigades.

6. Reliefs of Field Coys. R.E. and Field Ambulances will be arranged direct between C.R.E's. and A.D's.M.S. concerned.

7. The relief of th 8th Royal Scots (Pioneers) be the 9th Seaforths (Pioneers) will be carried out on 31st May details being arranged between Officers commanding the two Battalions.

The 9th Seaforths will relieve the Lewis Gun ~~Detachments of~~ the 8th Royal Scots employed on Anti-Aircraft work at

H.14.b.3.4.	one gun.
H.15.b.6.7.	one gun.
H.15.b.7.3.	two guns.
H.16.b.7.6.	one gun.

Headquarters, 8th Royal Scots are at G.18.c.5.5.

8. (a) The Artillery at present covering the front of the 51st Division will cover the front of the 9th Division.

(b) The C.R.A., 9th Division, will assume command at 10 a.m. on 2nd June.

9. G.O.C., 9th Division, will assume command at 10 a.m. 2nd June at which Divisional Headquarters will close at ROELLECOURT and open at G.16.b.7.7. (near CANDLE FACTORY).

10. Movements of 9th Division from ARRAS will be by road south of River SCARPE to BLANGY, thence across River SCARPE to Cross Roads G.18.c.5.4. - ATHIES.

The road via St NICHOLAS to St LAURENT BLANGY has been allotted to the 17th and 34th Divisions.

11. G.O.C., S.African Brigade, will detail 4 Officers and 160 men for work with 184th Tunnelling Co. R.E. This party will move to ARRAS on 31st May and will report to Headquarters 184th Tunnelling Coy. at G.21.b.25.55. at noon on 1st June.

12. ACKNOWLEDGE.

K Stewart.
Lieutenant Colonel,
General Staff,
9th(Scottish) Division.

Issued at .... 8 pm

Copies to

No. 1	26th Bde.	No. 16.	A.P.M.
2	27th Bde.	17.	"Q"
3.	S.A.Bde.	18.	D.A.D.O.S.
4 to 9.	C.R.A.	19.	197th M.G.Coy.
10.	C.R.E.	20.	Divl. M.G.Officer.
11.	9th Seaforths	21 & 22.	17th Corps
12.	9th Div. Train.	23.	17th Corps H.A.
13.	9th Signals.	24.	29th Division.
14.	A.D.M.S.	25.	34th Division.
15.	A.D.V.S.	26.	51st Division.
		27.	File.

MOVEMENT TABLE TO ACCOMPANY 9th DIVISION ORDER
No. 131 dated 25/5/17.

Item	Date	Unit.	From	To	Bus, Train or Road.	Remarks.
1.	May 29th	26th M.G.Coy.	MARQUAY	ARRAS	Personnel by bus Transport by road.	
2.	May 30th	26th M.G.Coy.	ARRAS	Line		To relieve 154th M.G.Co.
3.	May 30th	26th Inf. Bde. 63rd Fld. Coy. R.E.	ROELLECOURT Area	ARRAS	ditto	On arrival in ARRAS come under orders of 51st Div. tactically.
4.	May 30th	27th M.G.Coy.	HOUVELIN & MAGNICOURT	ARRAS	ditto	
5.	May 31st	27th M.G.Coy.	ARRAS	Line		To relieve 152nd M.G.Coy.
6.	May 31st	9th Seaforths (Pioneers)	BRYAS	Camp G.18.c.	Personnel by bus to ARRAS. Transport by road.	To relieve 8th Royal Scots.
7.	May 31st (morning)	2 Battalions 26th Inf. Bde.	ARRAS	STIRLING Camp H.13.d.		To relieve 2 Battns. 154th Bde.
8.	May 31st (afternoon)	2 Battalions 26th Inf. Bde.	ARRAS	STIRLING Camp.		
9.	May 31st (evening)	2 Battalions 26th Inf. Bde.	STIRLING Camp	Line		To relieve 154th Bde.

Item.	Date.	Unit	From	To	Bus, Train or Road	Remarks.
10.	May 31st	27th Inf. Bde. 90th Fld. Co. R.E.	MAGNICOURT VILLERS BRULIN Area	ARRAS	PERSONNEL by bus Transport by Road	On arrival at ARRAS come under orders of 51st Div. tactically
11.	May 31st	197th M.G. Co	CHELERS	ARRAS	ditto	
12.	June 1st (morning)	2 Battalions 27th Inf. Bde.	ARRAS	FIFE Camp H.13.a.2.5. Balmoral Camp G.18.a.0.4.		To relieve 2 Battalions 153rd Brigade.
13.	June 1st (afternoon)	2 Battalions 27th Brigade	ARRAS	FIFE and BALMORAL Camps		
14.	June 1st (evening)	2 Battalions 27th Brigade	FIFE and BALMORAL Camps	Line		To relieve 153rd Brigade during night 1st/2nd June.
15.	June 1st	S.A. Inf. Bde 64th Fld. Coy. R.E. and 28th M.G. Coy	MONCHY BRETON area	ARRAS	Personnel by Train Transport by Road	Entrain at LIGNY ST FLOCHEL detrain at ARRAS.

CASUALTIES FROM 28/4/17 to 11/5/17. 28-4-17 to 15-5-17

UNIT	OFFICERS			OTHER RANKS			TOTALS		REINFORCEMENTS	
	K.	W.	M.	K.	W.	M.	OFFICERS	OTHER RANKS	OFFICERS	O.R.
8th Black Watch	3	6	3	10	135	55	12	200	9	205
7th Seaforths	-	3	-	14	99	10	3	123	7	109
5th Camerons	2	14	2	23	192	64	18	279	1	35
10th A. & S. Hrs.	1	3	2	17	99	62	6	178	4	25
26th M.G. Company	-	-	-	-	5	-	-	5	-	15
11th Royal Scots	1	6	-	12	104	17	7	133	17	54
12th -do-	1	1	2	18	85	40	4	145	16	107
6th K.O.S.B.	-	4	11	51	142	200	15	393	8	158
9th Scottish Rifles	2	7	2	13	188	66	11	267	6	219
27th M.G. Coy.	1	2	1	-	21	8	4	29	3	32
28th M.G. Coy.	-	4	-	1	17	-	4	18	1	28
197th M.G. Coy.	1	-	-	4	16	-	1	20	-	15
9th Seaforths	1	2	-	2	17	-	3	19	1	16
TOTALS	13	52	23	165	1120	522	88	1807	73	1018

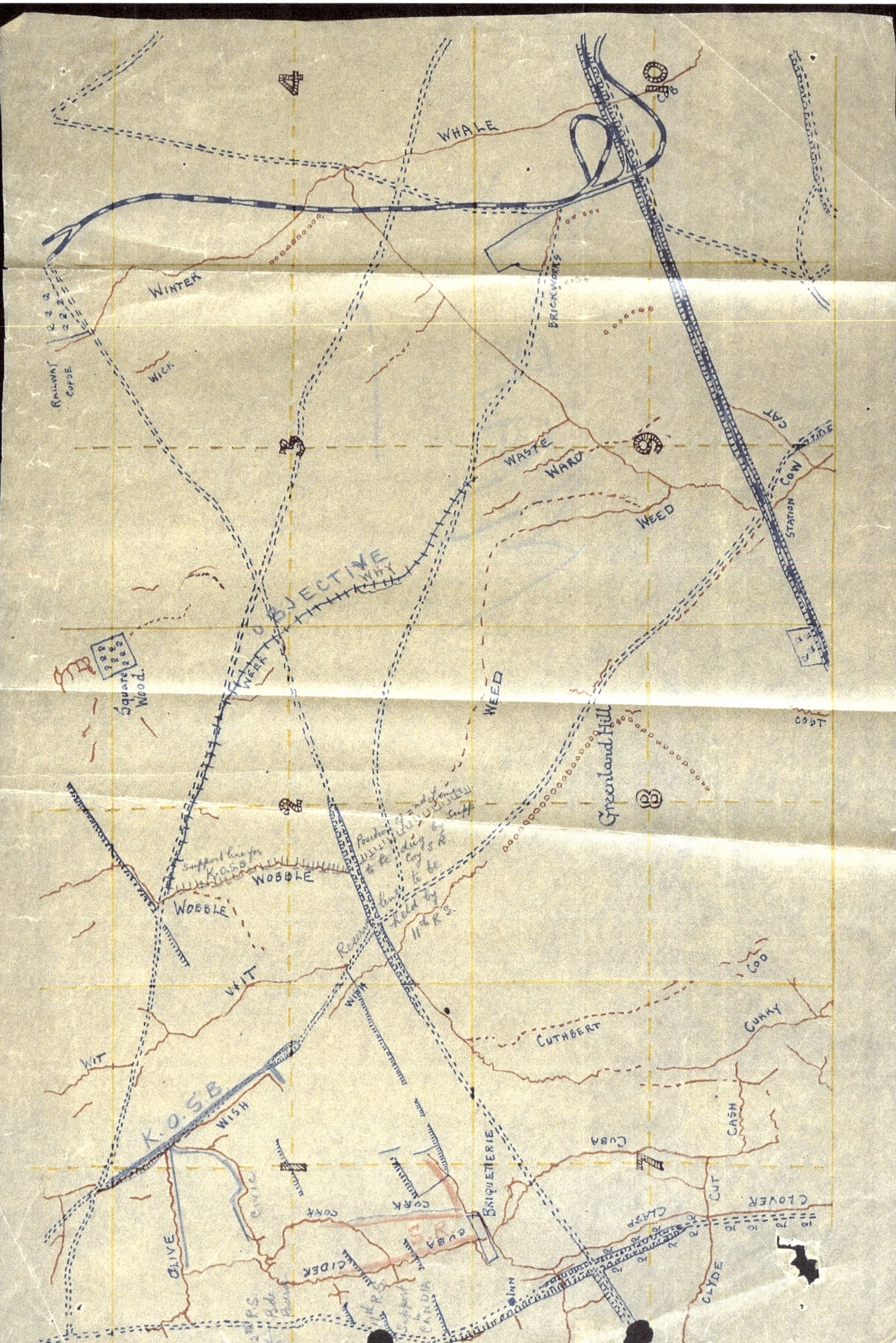
WHALE
WINTER
WICK
RAILWAY COPSE
BRICKWORKS
CAT
WASTE
WARD
WEED
COW
STATION
OBJECTIVE
WHY
WEEK
Square Wood.
WEED
Greenland Hill
COOT
Support line for K.O.S.B.
WOBBLE
WOBBLE
WIT
WIT
WISH
K.O.S.B.
WISH
CUTHBERT
CURRY
COD
CUBA
CASH
CUT
CLOVER
CLYDE
CASA
BRIQUETTERIE
CORK
CORK
CIVIC
OLIVE
CIDER
CUBA
INN
CANDIA

NARRATIVE OF EVENTS

P A R T 1.

E V E N T S P R I O R T O M A Y 3 R D.

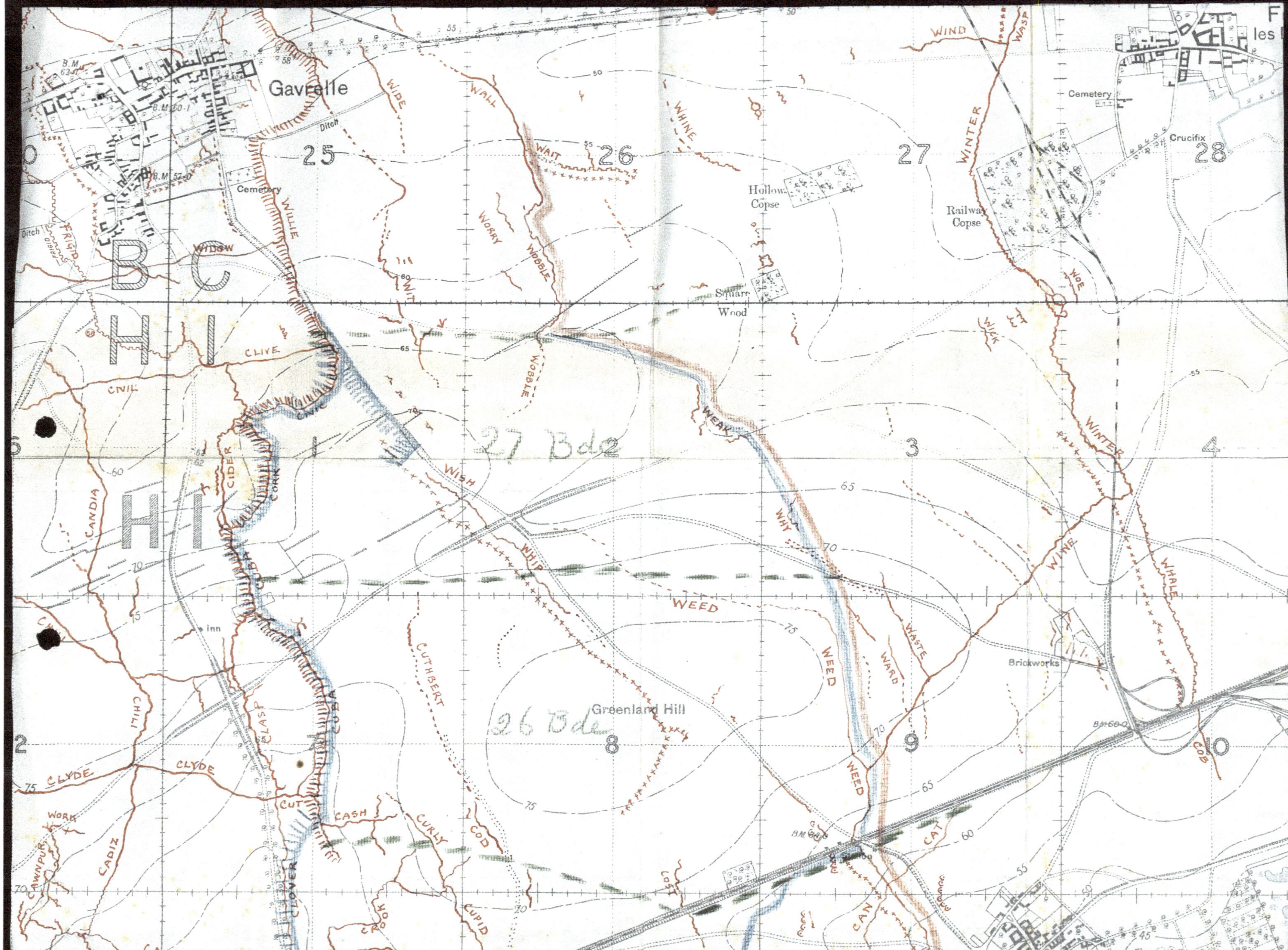

Gavrelle
Cemetery
Ditch
Hollow Copse
Railway Copse
Square Wood
Cemetery
Crucifix
Brickworks
Greenland Hill
Inn
27 Bde
26 Bde
WIND
WASP
WINTER
WOE
WICK
WHALE
COB
WINE
WASTE
WARD
WEED
WHY
WEAK
WHINE
WAIT
WOBBLE
WORRY
WALL
WIDE
WIT
WILLIE
WIDOW
FRIGID
WISH
WHIP
CUTHBERT
CLIVE
CIDER
CORK
CUBA
CLASP
CANDIA
CHILI
CLYDE
CUT
CASH
CURLY
COD
CUPID
CROOK
CLOVER
CADIZ
WORK
CAWNPUR
CAT
CAN
LOST
les
B
C
H
I
25
26
27
28
3
4
8
9
10
2

MAP 1

-	Workmen's dwellings.
marchandises	Goods yard.
-	Convent.
-	Slag heap.
-	Cross.
-	Inner dock.
e, Dét[illegible]	Destroyed.
"	Weir.
-	Dyke, causeway.
, Distie	Distillery.
e douane	Custom-house.
de douane	Custom warehouse.
ère, Dynamre	Dynamite magazine.
rie -	Dynamite factory.
-	Sluice, Lock.
Eclse	Sluice.
-	School.
-	Stable.
-	Church.
-	Enamel works.
ère, Embre	Landing-place.
, Estamt	Inn.
-	Pond.
Fabe	Factory.
roduits chimiques	Chemical works.
ience	Pottery.
-	Farm.
Filre	Spinning mill.
Fondie	Foundry.
Fontne	Spring, fountain.
-	Forest.
radoub	Dry dock.
-	Smithy.
-	Mine, Pit.
-	Moat, Ditch.
-	Kiln.
ux	Lime-kiln.

Four à coke	Coke oven.
Ganterie	Glove Factory.
Gare	Station.
Garenne	Warren.
Garnison	Garrison.
Gazomètre	Gasometer.
Glacerie, Fabe de glaces	Mirror Factory.
Glacière	Ice factory.
Grue	Crane.
Gué	Ford.
Guérite	Sentry-box, Turret.
" à signaux	Signal-box (Ry.)
Halte	Halt.
Hangar	Shed, Hangar.
Hôpital	Hospital.
Hôtel-de-Ville	Town hall.
Houillère	Colliery.
Huilerie	Oil factory.
Imprimerie, Imprie	Printing works.
Jetée	Pier.
Laminerie	Rolling mills.
Ligne / Laisse de haute marée	High water mark.
" de basse marée	Low " "
Maison Forestière, Mon. Fre.	Forester's house.
Malterie	Malt-house.
Marbrerie	Marble works.
Marais	Marsh.
Marais salant	Saltern, Salt marsh.
Marché	Market.
Mare	Pool.
Meule	Rick.
Minière	Mine.
Monastère	Monastery.
Moulin, Min	Mill.
" à vapeur	Steam mill.
Mur	Wall.
" crénelé	Loop-holed wall.

Nacelle	Ferry.
Orme	Elm.
Orphelinat	Orphanage.
Oseraies	Osier-beds.
Ouvrage	Fort.
Ouvrages hydrauliques	Water works.
Papeterie	Paper-mill.
Parc	Park, yard.
" aérostatique	Aviation ground.
" à charbon	Coal yard.
" à pétrole	Petrol store.
Passage à niveau P.N.	Level-crossing.
Passerelle, Passlle	Foot-bridge.
Pepinière	Nursery-garden.
Peuplier	Poplar tree.
Phare	Light-house.
Pilier, Pilr	Post.
Plaine d'exercice	Drill ground.
Pompe	Pump.
Ponceau	Culvert.
Pont	Bridge.
" levis	Drawbridge.
Poste / Station de garde-côte	Coast-guard station.
Poteau Pau	Post.
Poterie	Pottery.
Poudrière, Poudre / Magasin à poudre	Powder magazine.
Prise d'eau	Water supply.
Puits	Pit-head, Shaft, Well.
" artésien	Artesian well.
" d'aérage / " ventilateur	Ventilating shaft.
" de sondage	Boring.
Quai	Quay, Platform.
" aux bestiaux	Cattle platform.
" aux / des marchandises	Goods platform.
Raccordement	Junction.
Raffinerie	Refinery.
" de sucre	Sugar refinery
Râperie	Beet-root factory.

Remblai	Emba[nkment]
Remise des / aux Machines	Engin[e shed]
Réservoir, Résr	Reser[voir]
Route cavalière	Bridle[-path]
Rubanerie	Ribbo[n factory]
Ruine / Ruines / En ruine / Ruiné - e	Ruin.
Sablière	Sand-[pit]
Sablonnière, Sablonre	"
Sapin	Fir tre[e]
Saule	Willo[w]
Saunerie	Salt-w[orks]
Scierie, Scie	Saw-m[ill]
Sondage	Boring
Source	Spring
Sucrerie, Sucie	Sugar
Tannerie	Tanne[ry]
Tir à la cible	Rifle r[ange]
Tissage	Weavi[ng]
Tôlerie	Rolling
Tombeau	Tomb.
Tour	Tower.
Tourbière	Peat-bo[g]
Tourelle	Small t[ower]
Tuilerie	Tile wo[rks]
Usine à gaz	Gas wo[rks]
" électrique / " d'électricité	Electri[c]
" métallurgique	Metal w[orks]
" à agglomérés	Brique[tte]
Verrerie, Verrie	Glass w[orks]
Viaduc	Viaduc[t]
Vivier	Fish P[ond]
Voie de chargement / " " déchargement / " " d'évitement / " " formation / " " manœuvre	Siding
Zinguerie	Zinc wo[rks]

PART 1.

EVENTS PRIOR TO MAY 3RD.

1. The 9th Division (less Artillery, R.E. and Pioneers) was relieved from the battle front by 51st Division on April 14th/15th.

2. On completion of relief the Divisional H.Q. were established at HERMAVILLE, but later moved to CHELERS, the Brigades being distributed :-

26th Infantry Brigade	BAILLEUL-AUX-CORNAILLES
27th Infantry Brigade	PENIN
S.A. Infantry Brigade	MONCHY BRETON

3. On April 28th orders were received for 9th Division to relieve 37th Division in the Left Sector of the Corps front on nights 28th/29th and 29th/30th April.

4. Owing to lack of reinforcements it had been decided to leave the 1st South African Brigade in the MONCHY BRETON Area.

5. G.O.C. 9th Division assumed command of Left Sector at 10 a.m. on April 30th.

6. A Brigade (52nd) of 17th Division was placed at disposal of G.O.C. 9th Division on evening of May 2nd.

P A R T 11.

P L A N A N D D I S P O S I T I O N F O R

M A Y 3 R D.

PART 11.

PLAN AND DISPOSITION FOR OPERATION ON MAY 3RD.

1. The Division was to take part in an offensive in co-operation with 4th Division (17th Corps) on right and 31st Division (X111 Corps) on Left on May 3rd.

The first and fifth Armies were also attacking.

A message was received at Divisional H.Q. on evening of May 2nd that tomorrow's battle would be the biggest the British Army had ever taken part in.

2. The Division was attacking with 26th Infantry Brigade on the Right and 27th Infantry Brigade on the Left, the 52nd Brigade 17th Division being placed at the disposal of G.O.C. as a reserve.

The Divisional objective being the capture of the line WEED - WHY and WEAK trenches and the BIACHE - GAVRELLE road from its junction with WEAK trench to junction with BANK at I.2.a.5.8.

3. The Artillery barrage was to open at ZERO (3.45 a.m.) 200 yards east of our front trench for 4 minutes, and from there move forward. A Machine Gun barrage was to move 400 yards in advance of the Artillery barrage.

4. On the objective being reached consolidation was to be at once begun. Patrols were also to be pushed out to regain touch with the enemy and capture any hostile batteries that might be within reach.

5. The 26th Infantry Brigade was disposed for attack:-

5th Cameron Hrs	Right Assaulting Battalion
8th Black Watch	Left Assaulting Battalion
10th A.& S. Hrs.	Support
7th Seaforth Hrs.	Brigade Reserve.

6..........

6. The 27th Infantry Brigade was disposed as follows :-

9th Scottish Rifles	Right Assaulting Battalion
6th K.O.S.B.	Left Assaulting Battalion
11th Royal Scots	Support Battalion
12th Royal Scots	Brigade Reserve

7. The 52nd Infantry Brigade (17th Division)

9th Northumberland Fusiliers 10th Lancashire Fusiliers	) BROWN) LINE
9th West Riding Regiment 12th Manchester Regiment	) BLUE LINE) RAILWAY CUTTING

P A R T 111.

E V E N T S O N M A Y 3 R D.

PART 111.

EVENTS ON MAY 3RD.

1. ZERO hour was at 3.45 a.m. at which hour our artillery barrage opened and the attacking wave of Infantry advanced.

2. At this early hour it was quite dark and the attacking troops lost direction almost immediately. The enemy who appeared to be ready for our attack opened heavy machine gun fire almost at once from trenches and shell holes, which were closer to our front line than had been expected and which had consequently missed the barrage.

3. 5th Cameron Hrs., who were on the Right of the 26th Infantry Brigade's attack drawn off by hostile lights being sent up from short lengths of trenches echeloned on depth swung to their Right and crossed the front of the 2nd Essex Regiment (4th Division) who in the darkness mistook them for enemy and fired on them.

4. The 8th Black Watch on the Left of the ~~27~~ 26th Infantry Brigade also lost cohesion and as far as could be ascertained only a few isolated groups of men ever reached the enemy's front trench.

The two supporting companies of 10th A.& S. Hrs. kept straight on and apparently passed the left flank of the 5th Cameron Hrs. and they also came under heavy enfilade machine gun fire from the direction of the RAILWAY EMBANKMENT and CHEMICAL WORKS.

5. The 9th Scottish Rifles on the right of 27th Infantry Brigade failed to pick up the lamp to guide their left and in spite of compass bearings the two assaulting companies swung to their right and some of the men on the

right..........

swung to such an extent as to mistake the front line of 26th Brigade for the German line and advanced on it firing from the hip. The remainder of these companies struck CUTHBERT earlier than was intended. Only one wounded officer of these companies returned and reported that this trench was quite undamaged by artillery fire and was occupied by the enemy at about one man per yard. The Left Company probably crossed WHIP trench, but nothing is known of it, or the Right Company, both of which appear to have pressed on. The supporting companies as they advanced came under hostile machine gun fire and dug themselves in 200 yards or so beyond CORK trench.

6. The 11th Royal Scots, supporting battalion, seeing nothing in the dark, pushed up as ordered, the two companies for the occupation of WISH and WHIP trenches, but these became involved with the rear of the Scottish Rifles who were held up by machine gun fire. Part of these companies dug themselves in with the Scottish Rifles, the remainder were withdrawn to CUBA. The rear two companies also halted in CUBA.

7. On the Left the situation at once became involved. Shortly after the attack began O.C. 6th K.O.S.B., supporting company telephoned back from WIT trench that as the assaulting companies had left that trench and gone on to WOBBLE, he himself was following them to occupy WOBBLE according to his orders.

8. From this it would appear clear that three companies of 6th K.O.S.B. crossed WIT trench and carried on towards their objective.

9. Later the O.C. 9th Scottish Rifles and Major HAMILTON (90th Field Coy. R.E.) not knowing that the rear part of the Scottish Rifles had been held

up moved across to the right of K.O.S.B. in WISH and on arrival there saw one party of about 50 Germans enter WIT near its South end and one further North, both these parties were taken to be prisoners sent back by Scottish Rifles and K.O.S.B's. An officer and 2 men were actually sent to bring the right party in; all three were hit. On receiving this report it was realised that WIT trench was re-occupied, or at any rate occupied, and that the enemy now interposed between the three companies of K.O.S.B's and the remainder of the Brigade.

10. At 4.15 am F.O.O. reported that there had been no hostile lights for last ten minutes, but there was heavy machine gun fire from South Bank of River SCARPE, the hostile barrage had commenced about three minutes after ZERO.

11. At 5.50 a.m. General KENNEDY reported verbally that he was unable to give definite information yet, but from reports of wounded it appeared that our assaulting troops were all back in our front line; the casualties being caused by machine gun fire from the Right.

12. At 6.12 am General KENNEDY reported that there was an officer of the 5th Cameron Hrs with about 40 men consolid-ating in CUTHBERT trench, but he appeared to be isolated. This party was later withdrawn.

13. At 6.17 am a report was received from 27th Infantry Brigade stating that hostile barrage was heavy in front of CUBA. Right Battalion (Scottish Rifles) at 5.10 am reported they had no definite news but thought battalion was making progress. Left Battalion (K.O.S.B) at 4.40 am reported battalion and Right of 31st Division had reached WIT trench, but was not in touch with Right.

14. At 6.30 am the 52nd Brigade (17th Division) which had been placed at disposal of G.O.C. 9th Division and had spent night in ST. NICHOLAS, moved two battalions to **BROWN** LINE and two battalions to BLUE LINE.

15. Consequent on these reports from 26th and 27th Infantry Brigades, H.Q. XV11 Corps and Divisions on flanks were informed that reports indicated attack of our Right Brigade had failed with loss. Left Brigade believed to have made a little progress, but no definite information.

16. At 6.50 am General KENNEDY (26th Inf. Bde) reported that the cause of the trouble was machine guns in the Embankment, he thought between CUPID and COST. In the meanwhile he had ordered the Artillery to bring back the barrage to CUTHBERT but not South of CASH or North of grid line between I.7 and I.1.

17. Contact aeroplanes reported at 7 am that there were no flares shown in advance of our original front line.

18. At 7 am 31st Division, on our left, reported very heavy hostile barrage. The attack on OPPY had apparently failed. Right and Left Battalions had suffered heavily during assembly which appeared to have disorganised the attack.

19. At 7.20 am F.O.O. 32nd Bde. R.F.A. reported that WOBBLE trench had been captured and that patrols were out 600 or 700 yards in front of SQUARE WOOD. Slow progress in centre.

20. Enquiry was then made of 27th Inf. Bde regarding above report of F.O.O. The Brigade Major replied that he had no information to confirm this. The Germans were

reported......

reported to be still in WIT trench (which is West of WOBBLE) firing on our troops in our original front line.

21. At 7.45 am information was received from XVll Corps that 4th Division had been ordered not to renew their attack. Artillery fire was being brought back. The Heavy Artillery to fire on CANDY, CYPRUS, and CARROT trenches and on ROEUX where more than 400 yards from our line.

22. At 7.45 am General MAXWELL (27th Inf. Bde) reported that three companies of Left Battalion (6th K.O.S.B) were beyond WIT trench somewhere, one company and three M.G's still in our front trench. WIT trench appeared to be occupied by Germans along its whole length on our front and also to the North of us. The Brigade of 31st Division on his Left did not know position of its troops in front. The situation on the Right was that 9th Scottish Rifles had got about three companies in the "BLUE" beyond WISH trench and perhaps beyond WIT trench. There was at one time nobody in lower portion of WISH trench. Behind in CORK trench there was a conglomeration of men who were the remainder of the Scottish Rifles trickled back and some of the two companies 11th Royal Scots, who were to have occupied WISH and WIT trenches, behind the Scottish Rifles, ~~more~~ NONE of these two companies got forward. In CUBA trench there were six platoons 11th Royal Scots and one machine gun in action and one knocked out. There were two platoons of 11th Royal Scots in shell holes in front of 8th Black Watch's left, all the Black Watch were back in CUBA. Three companies of his reserve battalion (12th Royal Scots) were still in FAMPOUX line (GREEN line)

General MAXWELL had ordered artillery to keep intermittent bombardment on WIT trench. The right of 27th Brigade was entirely swept by enemy holding ground in front of 26th Brigade. General MAXWELL did not propose to make any effort to get into WIT trench for the time being, as it would be hopeless till southern part is cleared and until 31st Division take their part.

23. At 7.50 am 31st Division reported that they were unable to make any progress and that their Right Brigade was back on defensive in original front line. About twenty minutes later 31st Division reported that enemy was counter attacking along whole front of their Right Brigade in force and had taken the WINDMILL at GAVRELLE, two battalions from Divisional Reserve had been sent up in support.

24. At 8.39 am orders were received from XV11 Corps that general attack was not to be pressed for the present. All local successes of 4th Division were to be exploited to the full with a view to capturing CEMETERY, CORONA trench CHEMICAL WORKS and buildings North of Railway. 9th Division was to continue bombardment of points which had held up their attack. Heavy Artillery was to bombard ROEUX, CARROT, CYPRUS and CANDY trenches and Railway East of CUPID. The above order was repeated to 26th and 27th Infantry Brigades and C.R.A.

25. At 9.10 am the H.Q. XV11 Corps were informed that attack of Right Brigade had failed and that original line was now held. Three companies of each leading Battalions of the Left Brigade appeared to have crossed WIT trench, but WIT trench was now occupied by Germans.

Consequently these companies which passed WIT

trench......

trench were for the present cut off. It was not intended to attack WIT trench till higher ground to south can be secured, meanwhile original front line was held.

26. At 9.50 am a report was received from XV11 Corps H.A. that our men had been seen in SQUARE WOOD. 27th Infantry Brigade and 31st Division were informed.

27. At request of 27th Infantry Brigade arrangements were made with 17th Corps for an aeroplane to reconnoitre area round WOBBLE trench and SQUARE WOOD and call for flares to ascertain if possible if any of our men were there or not. The aeroplane flew over the area at 11.40 am and called for flares, but none were shown. Apparently there were no troops British or German in WOBBLE trench, but visibility was bad, owing to smoke. The aeroplane had been fired on by hostile machine guns from West end of WEED trench.

28. General KENNEDY (26th Infantry Brigade) reported at 11.15 am that the approximate strength of his Brigade was :-

8th Black Watch	205
7th Seaforth Hrs.	intact
5th Camerons	143
10th A.& S. Hrs.	300

29. At 12.50 pm orders were issued for 27th Infantry Brigade to assault WIT trench between cross roads (WISH cross roads I.2.c.) and northern boundary of 9th Division

at........

I.1.b.7.8 at an hour to be notified later. WHIP and WIT trenches and WOBBLE trench N. of I.2.a.5.8 were to be intensely bombarded from ZERO hour. At Zero plus 2 minutes the artillery fire was to lift off the portion of the trench to be assaulted. A smoke barrage was to be placed South of the WISH cross roads to conceal the advance from the high ground to south.

Units were notified later that the hour of assault would be 8 p.m.

30. At 1.25 p.m. touch was re-established with 31st Division S.E. of GAVRELLE in our original line.

31. 4th Division reported at 5.55 p.m. that they were holding original front line with exception of posts near ROEUX Station (I.13.central) in some enclosures and buildings near CHATEAU and possibly in CHEMICAL WORKS. Enemy had been advancing into CORONA trench. Situation in CLOVER trench was not clear. The enemy had made several strong counter attacks. One Company, Rifle Brigade(4th Division) and one company (9th Division) had been sent to clear up situation.

32. At 6.50 pm orders were issued for one Field Company R.E. and two companies 9th Seaforth Hrs. (Pioneers) to be at the disposal of each Brigade on night May 3rd/4th. for work in clearing the front line and communication trenches. Connection between WISH trench and BRICKFIELD in CUBA to be made by the construction of intermediate strong points which can be subsequently connected by a continuous trench

33......

33. At 7.35 pm orders were received from XV11 Corps for Divisions to consolidate and improve positions held. Touch was to be kept with the enemy by means of patrols.

These instructions were repeated to all concerned.

34. At 8 p.m. two companies 12th Royal Scots attacked WIT trench. The trench was strongly held and the Royal Scots in their attack came under very heavy machine gun fire from WIT trench just as they crossed the RIDGE before reaching the trench. Those of the Royal Scots who got in were ejected.

35. The attack enabled a good many K.O.S.B's to return to our lines.

A P P E N D I C E S.

I N D E X   T O   A P P E N D I C E S.

APPENDIX 1.

ACCOUNT OF THE BATTLE ON MAY 3RD ,1917.

26th INFANTRY BRIGADE.

1. The assembly was carried out in good order, and was completed by 3 a.m.

The brigade formed up for attack as ordered in Brigade Order No. 111.

2. The barrage opened at ZERO, but appeared to be ragged, especially on the right flank, and some casualties were sustained in the assaulting battalions from our own artillery.

3. Owing to the darkness at Zero, direction was soon lost and there was no cohesion in the attack. The enemy appeared ready for our attack and opened heavy machine gun fire almost at once, from trenches and shell holes, which were closer to our front line than had been expected, and which had been missed by the barrage. Opposite the right flank of the attack, the enemy lights were sent up from his short lengths of trenches "echeloned" in depth, and this caused the 5th Cameron Highlanders to mistake them for the enemy front line and to swing to their right, and cross the front of the 2nd ESSEX Regiment. This caused the latter Regiment to shoot at the 5th Cameron Highlanders who also sustained heavy casualties from enemy Machine Gun fire.

The 2 Supporting Companies, 10th Argyll and Sutherland Highlanders kept straight on and apparently passed the left flank of the 5th Cameron Highlanders,

Highlanders ....

Highlanders, and they also came under Heavy enfilade Machine Gun fire from the direction of the RAILWAY EMBANKMENT and the CHEMICAL WORKS.

The 8th Black Watch on the left also lost cohesion, and as far as is known, only a few isolated groups of men ever reached the enemy front line. So great was the confusion owing to the intensity of the darkness, that the right Battalions of the 27th. Brigade actually mistook our own front line for the German line, and advanced on it firing from the hip. This accounts for the fact that so many men of the 27th Brigade eventually got into our trenches.

4. The German Machine Guns caused heavy casualties, and caused the attackers to return to our front line. Here a second attack was organised and a gallant attempt was made to capture the German front line, but it failed, and by this time, our barrage had almost, if not quite reached its final limit. The remnants of the assaulting Battalions were driven back by heavy Machine Gun fire, to our own trenches, which were at once organised for defence against counter-attack.

5. When the enemy discovered tha our attack had been repulsed, his Artillery fire, which had been both intense and accurate, slackened down, and his snipers, lying scattered all over the ground in shell holes, became extremely active, and caused casualties.

6/.............

6. Owing to the fact that so few Officers were left from any of the assaulting Companies, it is impossible to collect any accurate accounts of what really took place, but in the opinion of those who are still with their Battalions, the failure was caused by the darkness and our unprepared state for a night attack.

==*=*=*=*=*=*=*=*=*=*=*

OBSERVATIONS ON THE ATTACK.

Assembly was easily carried out, and no interference from Hostile Artillery.

All ranks are agreed that the hour of ZERO was too early and that the darkness caused the attack to lose all direction and cohesion.

No attack on a large scale has been done by this Division at night, for a very long time, and it was not expected that such an operation was contemplated. Sufficient care and thought had not, therefore, been given to working out the necessary details to ensure the success of an attack in the dark. Had longer notice of the change of the ZERO hour been given, it would still have been possible to lay out tapes and provide phosphorescent boards, taking careful compass bearings etc., the plan of attack would have been entirely altered, so as to ensure touch being kept from front to rear. I should have made successive advances on the "Leap Frog" system instead of going straight through.

I was only informed at 2 pm. that the ZERO hour had been changed - the alteration of 20 minutes having the effect of changing the whole character of the attack from a daylight to a night attack.

It................

It is not necessary for troops to know the hour of ZERO, but it is absolutely necessary that they should know some days beforehand if it is to be by day or by night.

All arrangements had been made for daylight observation and transmission of reports. From my Headquarters it was possible to see the whole field of operations, but owing to the dark, this was not used and it was most difficult to follow the progress of the attack.

THE ADVANCE.

The difficulty was accentuated in the dark by the fact that on the right flank the 4th Division front line was some 200 yards behind my Brigade and the line from there gradually ran back. The result was that as the men advanced, the enemy Very Lights appeared on their right flank, and the whole attack of the 5th Cameron Highlanders swung round in that direction. The 10th Argyll and Sutherland Highlanders supporting companies kept direction better, and went right through the gap left between the Cameron Highlanders and the Black Watch. They were, ofcourse, a long way behind the barrage, but went right over CHARLIE

and ....

CUTHBERT trenches until they came under very heavy Machine Gun fire from all sides, and bombing counter-attacks from vicinity of GAVRELLE - PLOUVAIN road. Most of them appear to have got into shell holes, and are gradually making their way back, 68 having come in at night, but I fear the remainder are killed or prisoners.

The Black Watch attack was repulsed by machine gun and rifle fire, and bombs. They made a second attack and drove the enemy out of CHARLIE and CUTHBERT, killing a good many, but were unable to remain, owing to very heavy enfilade fire from Machine Guns in the EMBANKMENT and CHEMICAL WORKS.

The whole attack was eventually withdrawn to the original front line, and the defebce re-organised. This was rendered very difficult by 3 enemy aeroplanes who flew constantly up and down the line at a very low altitude, firing at our men. One was eventually brought down with Machine Gun fire, but the boldness of the enemy aeroplanes, which has noticeably increased lately, was quite unprecedented as far as the experience of this Brigade goes.

ENEMY TACTICS.

The enemy did not appear to be in his trenches, but occupying shell holes everywhere with a

very..................

very great number of machine guns, used both for frontal fire with his advanced troops, and also from the flanks.

He appeared to be quite ready for our attack as he opened at once with his Artillery barrage, and machine gun and rifle fire. His artillery barrage was negligible as far as "stopping" the advance goes.

His Infantry used their rifles well and supplemented it with the bomb at close quarters.

The machine guns however, are the real defence and are handled with great skill.

The 10th Argyll and Sutherland Highlanders who got near the embankment say they had guns on top of the embankment and others at the foot, and echeloned back in shell holes. It would seem, therefore, that he is using his machine gun as a very mobile weapon, though the rapidity with which certain grazing fire is brought to bear on certain zones, seems to show that he must have a certain number of guns in permanent positions firing on barrage lines.

OUR TACTICS.

It is difficult to write about these without

appearing................

appearing to criticise ,but I think the following points may be worth consideration.

We have, with the very limited opportunities of training which can be allowed to troops engaged in trench and active warfare, been able to concentrate on one form of attack - the organised trench attack. This has been perfected, but neither Officers or men know any other. The fighting has, at present, got into the advanced stage when we cannot rely on complete artillery preparation or "Protection". The enemy's position is nebulous and constantly changing - he is constantly producing awkward little situations for us, his local Commanders appear to act with skill and determination, encroaching on us constantly with bombing attacks forming little pockets of snipers or Machine Guns in unexpected places, not waiting in definite lines of trenches, to be barraged by our Artillery. Against this, we are using the same tactics as in the first phase. The barrage, I think, should now be shrapnel,but all ground in vicinity of enemy trenches, should be constantly searched at night, to get the enemy in his shell holes.

More smoke still is required to blind his Machine Guns, and gas, if possible.

Known bad pockets should be passed round, a feint or holding attack being made against such places. The actual position of the Machine Guns is not the bad pocket, but the place where the

bullets...............

bullets from that gun sweep. We are apt to avoid the place where the Machine Guns are, and attempt to brush past in the Zone where they kill.

As far as Infantry are concerned, if the first organised attack is held up and they lose their barrage, there is a tendency to think that nothing more can be done. It certainly is no good launching a fresh attack or sacrificing more troops against Machine Guns in position, but I think the Infantry of the old army, who were taught the old Infantry advance by alternate rushes, supported by their own rifle and machine gun fire, who knew how to fight a battle of localities and tactical points, would gain much ground, even when the original attack has become disorganised, and would be constantly putting the enemy at a disadvantage. An extended wave gets into shell holes in pairs etc., without leadership, and it is lost. I think each extended line wants a pivot of troops in close formation, in close support.

We appear to be suffering from:-

(1) Want of leadership, which can in some way be corrected by less extended formation and more practice for Officers and N.C.O'S handling and leading men.

(2) Want of initiative, which can in some way be remedied by fuller explanation of the general situation, and the encouragement and direction of local

enterprises.................

enterprises during the lulls in main operations.

(3) Want of elasticity and scope in training and formations.

(4) Want of training of rank and file.

APPENDIX 2.

27th INFANTRY BRIGADE.

REPORT ON THE ATTACK ON 3RD MAY, 1917.

1. Objective of Brigade, as shewn on plan. As it would not be possible to discover and pick up the small features i.e. road track, WEAK and WHY Trenches, assaulting Battalions were directed to halt behind the protective barrage and as soon as there was light enough to see the above, to occupy the line made by them and dig in.

2. Distribution of Brigade at ZERO.

9th Scottish Rifles, right assaulting Battalion formed up in CORK and CUBA. (echeloned behind the right of Left assaulting Battalion which occupied a more advanced trench), right on BRIQUETERIE in touch with 20th Brigade.

6th K.O.S.B., left assaulting Battalion, formed up in WISH Trench, CLIVE and CIVIC, with left in touch with 93rd Brigade of 31st Division.

Support Battalion.	11th Royal Scots in CANDIA.
Brigade Reserve.	12th Royal Scots in German third system trenches.
27th M.G. Company.	1 section with each Assaulting Battalion. Half Section with Support Battalion. 1 section to remain in North portion of WISH. Half section to remain in South portion of WISH, and in WHIP when reached and passed by the attack of the Right Battalion.
Stokes Battery.	To remain in third system till required, the ammunition being dumped in WISH.
28th Machine Gun Coy.	Was employed under the Division for barrage fire during the attack, but was subsequently attached to this Brigade.

3.

3. <u>Orders for Brigade Action at ZERO. (3-45 a.m.)</u>

<u>Right Battalion.</u>(Scottish Rifles) with two Companies in front line, each in two waves, and two in close support in columns of platoon, to leave their front trenches at Zero and, moving with their left on a lamp placed as a guide to it on the extremity of the K.O.S.B. right, to get level with the latter Battalion and push on with it when the barrage straightened out and crept eastwards. Support Company to dig a second line left on road as a support to front line.

<u>Left Battalion.</u>(K.O.S.B.) with two companies in front line and one in support was to leave the fourth company in reserve in front trench. Right of Battalion on a due East bearing, left on road track in touch with 93rd Brigade of 31st. Division. Assaulting Companies to leave WISH Trench at ZERO to get under the barrage. Support Company to occupy WOBBLE as a second lime to the new one to be occupied.

<u>Support Battalion.</u>(11th Royal Scots) two companies to occupy WISH and WHIP Trenches. Two Companies to stand fast in CUBA prepared to fill a gap if one occurred between Brigade right and 26th. Brigade left.

<u>Reserve Battalion.</u>(12th Royal Scots) to remain

in....................

in German third system as Brigade Reserve.

4. Narrative.

At Zero, 3-45 a.m. it was just possible to see some 40 to 50 Yards along a white path or track: otherwise it was dark and direction except with compass impossible. The advance of this Brigade was at an oblique angle to the front held.

At ZERO, the right Battalion got clear of its trenches the lamp to guide the left was not picked up and in spite of compass bearings the two assaulting companies swung up their left shoulders, so that instead of going due East they moved S.S.E. the right thereby striking CUTHBERT trench earlier than intended. Only one wounded Officer of these Companies returned and reports that this trench was quite undamaged by Artillery Fire and was occupied by the enemy at about 1 man per yard. Some killing was done in this trench, the Officer himself (a very good one) shooting three Germans. The left Company probably crossed WHIP, but nothing is known of it or the right company, both of which appear to have pressed on. The supporting Companies as they advanced came under Machine Gun fire and dug themselves in 200 Yards or so beyond CORK Trench, right on the bank.

The right Company of the 26th Brigade lost direction to the left at ZERO and was mixed up with the rear companies of the Scottish Rifles.

The...............

The Supporting Battalion 11th Royal Scots seeing nothing in the dark pushed up, as ordered, the two Companies for the occupation of WISH and WHIP trenches, but these became involved with the rear of the Scottish Rifles held up by Machine Gun fire. Some dug in with the Scottish Rifles, the remainder were withdrawn to CUBA.

The rear two Companies also halted in CUBA.

On the left the situation was, and still is, involved.

Shortly after the attack began, O.C., 6th K.O.S.B. Supporting Company telephoned back from WIT Trench that as the Assaulting Companies had left that trench and gone on to WOBBLE, he himself was following them to occupy WOBBLE according to his orders.

It seemed absolutely clear from this that three K.O.S.B. Companies had crossed WIT, and carried on towards the objective. O.C.,K.O.S.B. reported, somewhat later, that Scottish Rifles on right and 26th Brigade on Scottish Rifles right were held up, and he therefore was sending a platoon to block South end of WIT to protect his right.

Later again, O.C. Scottish Rifles and Major HAMILTON R.E. not knowing that the rear part of the Scottish Rifles had been held up moved across to K.O.S.B. right (in WISH) and on arrival there saw one party of about 50 Germans enter WIT near its South end and one further North: they took both these parties to be prisoners sent back by Scottish Rifles and K.O.S.B.

and.............

and actually sent an Officer and two men to bring the right party in. All three were hit by some other enemy. On receiving this report verbally from Major HAMILTON I realized that WIT was re-occupied, or at any rate occupied and that the enemy now interposed between us and three companies of K.O.S.B.

Enquiry from the Brigade on my left elicited the fact that it had not reached WIT at all and had no hope of doing so. I accordingly asked for Artillery fire on that part of WIT opposite my front in the hope of clearing the Germans out, and this fire was kept on, first for a considerable period, and then intermittently during the morning.

No news came back from the K.O.S.B. and the only possible information of them was that received from the artillery that some of our men were seen in SQUARE WOOD.

This situation did not change all day.

Unwilling to leave troops, which had got on, unsupported and cut off, I decided to attack WIT Trench with the object of holding it during the night to allow K.O.S.B. to return under cover of darkness to our lines instead of into German hands.

At 8 p.m. therefore while there was still good light, one and a half companies from the Reserve Battalion (12th Royal Scots) were ordered to make the attack, covered on each flank by artillery fire and Machine Gun barrage to obscure the view of enemy Machine Guns. These flank barrages to continue till

darkness...........

darkness set in. An Officer patrol was, after the capture of WIT, to go out and find K.O.S.B's.

At 8 p.m. Artillery opened for one minute on WIT, and the 6 platoons attacked.

For long (nearly an hour) it was thought that they had succeeded, but as no report came back, but only a few wounded men it was realised that it had failed. M.G. fire from the right appears to have swept the 200 yards of "No Man's Land" with such effect that of about 150 who started no less than 120 were casualties of whom 80 are missing.

As a result of the attack however, a considerable number of K.O.S.B's came in, mostly from the right half of the attack front. Included amongst these was Captain TILTMAN Commanding the Right Assaulting Company K.O.S.B. He reported that until he returned to our lines and learnt we were attacking WIT, he thought he was in front of WOBBLE. Not only did he cross a trench, a poor one, in the morning which he took to be WIT, but he re-crossed it again and halted in it on coming back when our 8 p.m. attack began. The only explanation is that he took the small sections of trench about 80 yards beyond our front line for WIT.

But this, though apparently the truth as regards the Right Assaulting Company, could not apply to the Left Company and the Support Company, in front of which there is no such subsidiary line between their starting trench and WIT itself. The only conclusion to be drawn therefore is that WIT trench opposite our Left was either unoccupied or over-run by the K.O.S.B's. left assaulting Company and Support Company and must have been re-occupied after they passed beyond. The message from the Support Company Commander already referred to makes it perfectly clear that a trench was crossed, and as there is no semblence of one, even by the latest air photographs, except WIT, it must have been WIT that this

K.O.S.B. crossed. How far they advanced beyond will now never be known, as the whole of them have disappeared. But whatever the truth, I should under similar circumstances act no differently again, and I believe the G.O.C. would not have me act differently. Troops which press on deserve to be supported in every way, and those which have the confidence that they will be so supported, and that they will be assisted if they get into trouble will go further than those who have not this confidence.

The alternative of clearing WIT with the reserve battalion much earlier in the day presented itself to me, but had to be rejected, for with Brigades held up in their original front lines both on right and left, it would have resulted in nothing but the inevitable loss of any such troops sent on the mission. To wait for the approach of darkness was, I think, the only chance.

I regret that the casualties suffered by the Brigade are heavy. Of an approximate number of 2,200 bayonets when the Brigade went into action, 38 officers and 912 other ranks ~~and~~ are killed, wounded and missing.

If however the attack was unsuccesful and casualties heavy, I shbmit that an enemy which cannot take advantage of a successful defence by counter attack is one that is either ignorant of war or has little stomach for it. The Germans are not ignorant of war; counter attack, to their credit, was almost their religion. A satisfactory conclusion can there be drawn from their absolute failure to strike back on May 3rd.

An interesting incident occurred at 1 am on night of 2nd/3rd May. While the support battalion was forming up in CANDIA trench an enemy aeroplane, flying low, fired tracer bullets along it and then signalled with a light.

This was immediately followed by coloured lights sent up from the enemy's front line, and a few minutes later a heavy artillery barrage fell on CANDIA and CUBA positions for about 20 minutes. Just previous to Zero the enemy again bombarded these two trenches.

I shall submit, later, names of officers, N.C.Os and men whose services I desire to bring to the notice of the G.O.C.

CASUALTIES FROM 28/4/17 TO 11/5/17.

28/4/17 to 15/5/17.

UNIT.	OFFICERS.			OTHER RANKS.			TOTALS.		REINFORCEMENTS.	
	K.	W.	M.	K.	W.	M.	OFFS.	O.R.	OFFICERS.	O.R.
8th Black Watch	3	6	3	23	142	43	12	208	9	205
7th Seaforths	-	3	-	14	78	~~4~~6	3	98	7	109
5th Cameron Hrs.	2	14	2	20	188	81	18	289	1	35
10th A. & S. Hrs.	1	3	2	19	99	28	6	144	4	25
26th M. G. Coy.	-	-	-	-	5	1	-	6	-	15
11th Royal Scots	1	6	-	15	105	12	7	132	17	54
12th Royal Scots	1	1	2	24	89	23	4	136	16	107
6th K. O. S. B.	-	4	11	21	171	200	15	392	8	158
9th Scottish Rifles	2	7	2	17	205	59	11	281	6	219
27th M. G. Coy.	1	2	1	1	18	8	4	27	3	32
28th M. G. Coy.	-	4	-	1	17	-	4	18	1	28
197th M. G. Coy.	1	-	-	4	16	-	1	20	-	15
9th Seaforth Hrs.	1	2	-	2	17	-	3	19	1	16
TOTALS	13	52	23	161	1150	459	88	1770	73	1018

W. 15517—M. 141. 250,000. 1/16. L.S.&Co. Forms/W 3091/2.

Army Form W. 3091.

Cover for Documents.

Nature of Enclosures.

General Staff 9th (Scottish) Division

War Diary

for

May 3rd 1917

with Appendices

Notes, or Letters written.

Army Form C. 2118.

Instructions regarding War Diaries and Intelligence Summaries are contained in F. S. Regs., Part II, and the Staff Manual respectively. Title pages will be prepared in manuscript.

WAR DIARY
or
INTELLIGENCE SUMMARY.
(Erase heading not required.)

Place	Date	Hour	Summary of Events and Information	Remarks and references to Appendices
RAILWAY CUTTING ST.LAURENT BLANGY	3rd May 1917	3.45am	ZERO hour, our artillery put down barrage and assaulting Infantry advanced.	
		4.3am	A message timed 3.30 am was received from 27th Infantry Brigade reporting that movement into assembly area was complete.	1
		4.10am	32nd Bde. R.F.A. reported that enemy was putting down heavy barrage all along our front line. The same Brigade reported heavy rifle and machine gun fire on our front about half an hour later.	2/3
		4.15am	F.O.O. reported that there had been no hostile lights for last ten minutes. Heavy M.G. fire from South of RIVER. Enemy barrage commenced about 3 minutes after ZERO.	4
		4.55 am	Report from 32nd Bde. R.F.A. (timed 4.35) stated that hostile lights were going up further East.	5
		4.55 am	General KENNEDY (26th Inf. Bde) reported that his Brigade observer reported that enemy's Very Lights were being sent up from much further EAST. Hostile barrage had slackened considerably. A certain amount of M.G. fire from RIGHT. It was still too dark for observation.	
		5.3 am	31st Division (on our LEFT) reported our barrage opened at 3.45 am. Enemy appeared slow in replying. Enemy barrage on Right Brigade commenced 10 minutes after ZERO. Coloured lights now ceased.	6
		5.15 am	Following report (G.755) was sent to 17th Corps and repeated to 4th and 31st Divisions. Reports that at 4.55 am state that light was not good for observation. Hostile Very Lights being sent up further EAST. Barrage now decreased.	7
		5.20 am	A report was received from 4th Division (on our Right) that their Right Brigade was getting on well. Left Company Somerset Light Infantry had got into ROEUX. Right Company was held up.	
		5.50 am	General KENNEDY (26th Inf. Bde) reported that he was unable to give definite information yet, but from reports of wounded it appeared that our assaulting troops were all back in our front line, the casualties being caused by M.G. fire from Right.	

A6945 Wt. W11422/M1160 350,000 12/16 D. D. & L. Forms/C./2118/14.

Army Form C. 2118.

Instructions regarding War Diaries and Intelligence Summaries are contained in F. S. Regs., Part II, and the Staff Manual respectively. Title pages will be prepared in manuscript.

WAR DIARY
or
INTELLIGENCE SUMMARY.
(Erase heading not required.)

Place	Date	Hour	Summary of Events and Information	Remarks and references to Appendices
RAILWAY CUTTING ST LAURENT BLANGY	3rd May	6.12.	General KENNEDY (26th Inf. Bde) reported an officer of 5th Camerons in CUTHBERT trench, consolidating, has about 40 men with him but appeared to be isolated.	
		6.17am	27th Inf. Bde reported telephone communications forward of old German 3rd system broken. Enemy's barrage reported heavy in front of CUBA. Right Battalion at 5.10 am had reported no definite news but think Battalion is getting on. Left Battalion at 4.40 am reported Battalion and right of 31st Division had reached WIT trench, but was not in touch on Right.	8
		6.20am	XVII Corps and Divisions on flanks informed that reports indicate attack of Right Brigade has failed with loss. Left Brigade believed to have made a little progress, but no definite information.	9
		6.50am	52nd Bde. R.F.A. reported that CUTHBERT trench was now evacuated by our Infantry.	10
		6.50am	52nd Bde. R.F.A. reported that WOBBLE trench had been captured, and advance continued 700 to 800 yards in direction of SQUARE WOOD.	11
		6.50 am	General KENNEDY (26th Inf. Bde) reported that cause of the trouble was machine guns in EMBANKMENT, he thought between CUPID and COST. He had told the artillery to bring back barrage to CUTHBERT, but not South of CASH or North of grid line between I.7 and I.1.	
		7.0 am	Map dropped by contact aeroplane showed no flares in advance of our original front line.	
		7.0am	31st Division reported very heavy hostile barrage. Germans putting up many lights, white breaking into two red balls. Attack on OPPY apparently failed. Right and Left Battalions suffered heavily during assembly, which seems to be disorganised the attack. 52	12
		7.20am	52nd Bde. R.F.A. reported that WOBBLE trench had been captured. Patrols out 600 or 700 yards in front of SQUARE WOOD. Slow progress in centre. On enquiry being made Brigade Major 27th Inf. Bde. stated message from F.O.O. regarding capture of WOBBLE trench had been repeated to him. He had no information to confirm this. Germans were reported to be still in WIT trench (West of WOBBLE) firing on our troops in our original front line.	13

A6945 Wt. W11422/M1160 350,000 12/16 D. D. & L. Forms/C./2118/14.

Instructions regarding War Diaries and Intelligence Summaries are contained in F. S. Regs., Par. II. and the Staff Manual respectively. Title pages will be prepared in manuscript.

WAR DIARY
or
INTELLIGENCE SUMMARY.
(Erase heading not required.)

Army Form C. 2118.

Place	Date	Hour	Summary of Events and Information	Remarks and references to Appendices
RAILWAY CUTTING ST LAURENT BLANGY	3rd May	7.45am	B.G., G.S. XVII Corps informed G.S.O.1 that he had told 4th Division not to renew their attack, Artillery fire was being brought back. The Heavy Artillery to fire on CANDY, CYPRUS, and CARROT trenches and on ROLUX where more than 400 yards from our line.	
		7.45am	General MAXWELL (27th Inf. Bde) reported that three companies of Left Battalion (6th K.O.S.B) are beyond WIT trench somewhere. WIT trench appears to be occupied by the Germans. It is occupied all along its length, and also occupied to North of us. Brigade on his Left does not know where its people are. One company and three machine guns still in old front line. The situation on the right was that 9th Scottish Rifles had got three companies at least, half of this, or three companies in the "BLUE" beyond WISH and perhaps WIT. There was at one time nobody in lower portion of WISH. Behind in CORK trench a conglomeration of men who are the remainder of the Scottish Rifles trickled back, and some of the two companies of the 11th Royal Scots, who were to have taken WISH and WIT trenches, behind the Scottish Rifles. None of these two companies got forward. In CUBA there are 6 platoons 11th Royal Scots and one machine gun in action and one knocked out. Two platoons of the 11th Royal Scots in shell holes in front of 8th Black Watch's Left, all the Black Watch are in CUBA. Three companies of Reserve Battalion (12th Royal Scots) still in the GREEN LINE. Have asked F.O.O. to keep intermittent bombardment on WIT. Our right is entirely swept by enemy, who are holding 26th Inf. Bde's Area. That he did not propose to make any effort to get into WIT for the time being because Lt-Col. SMYTHE (O.C. Left Battn.) reports it would be hopeless to do this until southern part is cleared and from his own point of view until Brigade on Left takes their part of WIT trench.	
		7.50am	31st Division reported that they had been able to make no progress, and that Right Brigade was back on defensive in original front trench.	14
		8.10 am	31st Division reported enemy was counter-attacking whole front of their Right Brigade in force and had taken the MILL at GAVRELLE, Two Battalions from Divisional Reserve had been sent up in support.	15

Army Form C. 2118.

Instructions regarding War Diaries and Intelligence Summaries are contained in F. S. Regs., Par. II, and the Staff Manual respectively. Title pages will be prepared in manuscript.

WAR DIARY
or
INTELLIGENCE SUMMARY.
(Erase heading not required.)

Place	Date	Hour	Summary of Events and Information	Remarks and references to Appendices
RAILWAY CUTTING ST. LAURENT BLANGY	3rd. May	8.39am	Orders received from XVII Corps that general attack was not to be pressed for present. All local successes of 4th Division to be exploited to full, with a view of capturing CEMETERY, CORONA trench, CHEMICAL WORKS, and buildings North of RAILWAY. 9th Division to continue bombardment of points which held up their attack. Heavy Artillery was to bombard ROEUX, CARROT, CYPRUS, and CANDY trenches and RAILWAY East of CUPID. The above order was repeated to 26th and 27th Inf. Bdes and C.R.A.	16
		9.10am	The following report was sent to the XVII Corps:- Right Brigade attack has failed and original front line is now held. Left Brigade, three Companies of each of the two leading battalions appear to have crossed WIT trench, but WIT trench is now occupied by Germans, Consequently the companies which passed WIT trench are for the present out off. It is not intended to attack WIT trench till higher ground to south can be secured, which is out of the question at present. Meanwhile original front line is held.	17
		9.50am	Report received from Corps H.A. through Liaison Officer that our men are in SQUARE WOOD. G.S.O.1 informed 27th Inf. Bde and 31st Division and inquired about 31st Division's barrage going on to SQUARE WOOD. 31st Division were also informed as to situation as far as we knew it.	
		10.5am	27th Inf. Bde. reported that on hearing that 93rd Inf. Bde, on their left, was being counter attacked, General MAXWELL had ordered up one company of Reserve battalion to CIDER trench and was keeping artillery on to WIT trench. 28th M.G. Coy has 8 guns now barraging the ground beyond our objective in the direction of WAIT trench and SQUARE WOOD, the other 8 are barraging all the high ground East of CUTHBERT so as to protect the Right and rear of 27th Inf. Bde troops in the direction of WOBBLE, otherwise no change. 27th Inf. Bde unable to do more on its front until high ground on right is taken as it commands their area. 93rd Inf. Bde. are in their front line and have no intention of reoccupying WIT, which will make it difficult for 27th Inf. Bde to do so although it is important for them to get rid of the enemy interposing between their advance men and original front line.	18

Instructions regarding War Diaries and Intelligence Summaries are contained in F. S. Regs., Part II. and the Staff Manual respectively. Title pages will be prepared in manuscript.

Army Form C. 2118.

WAR DIARY
or
INTELLIGENCE SUMMARY.
(Erase heading not required.)

Place	Date	Hour	Summary of Events and Information	Remarks and references to Appendices
RAILWAY CUTTING ST.LAURENT BLANGY	3rd May	10.5am	27th Inf. Bde were informed that Major HAMILTON (90th Field Coy.R.E.) had reported that the Germans were on Hill 80 N.W. of GAVRELLE. General MAXWELL replied that the Germans were towards HILL 80.	
		10.10am	27th Inf. Bde asked if an aeroplane could be sent to reconnoitre area of WOBBLE trench to ascertain if possible whether our men are there or not.	19
		10.10am	G.O.C. reported situation verbally to G.O.C. 17th Corps. Our infantry seen in SQUARE WOOD, WIT trench occupied by Germans who came in to it from the North. WIT trench cannot be retaken unless ground is retaken on right, and also unless the Right Brigade of 31st Division could attack on our Left. 31st Division were unable to do this, were only just managing to hold their original line. Smoke was required on right of 27th Inf. Bde.	
		10.50am	XVII Corps were asked if an aeroplane could be sent to reconnoitre the area of WOBBLE trench and SQUARE WOOD to ascertain if possible whether our men are there or not.	20
		10.25am	27th Inf. Bde were asked if they were in touch with 31st Division on their Left, the Brigade replied that their Left troops could see troops on Right of 31st Division in original trench. This information was repeated to H.Q. XVII Corps.	
		10.46am	31st Division reported that they were holding Eastern edge of GAVRELLE to RAILWAY. The WINDMILL had changed hands three times. They were then organising a new attack on it. Apparently their Left Brigade was checked in their advance in OPPY WOOD which enabled the enemy to counter attack exposed left flank of Right Brigade and roll it up.	21
		10.54am	Information received from 17th Corps that an aeroplane was being sent to call for "flares" and reconnoitre area WOBBLE trench and SQUARE WOOD to ascertain if possible if our men were there or not. 27th Inf. Brigade were informed.	22 23

A6945 Wt. W11422/M1160 350,000 12/16 D. D. & L. Forms/C./2118/14.

Instructions regarding War Diaries and Intelligence Summaries are contained in F. S. Regs., Part II. and the Staff Manual respectively. Title pages will be prepared in manuscript.

WAR DIARY
or
INTELLIGENCE SUMMARY.
(*Erase heading not required.*)

Army Form C. 2118.

Place	Date	Hour	Summary of Events and Information	Remarks and references to Appendices
RAILWAY CUTTING ST LAURENT BLANGY	30th May	11.15am	General KENNEDY (26th Inf. Bde) reported that the approximate strength of his Brigade was now as follows:-	
			8th Black Watch 205 7th Seaforth Hrs. intact 5th Cameron Hrs. 145 10th A. & S. Hrs. 300	
		11.45am	26th Inf. Bde were informed that 4th Division had some men dug in on road West of CHEMICAL WORKS. They were going to push along CORONA trench and try and take the CEMETERY.	
		12.30pm	Instructions were sent to 27th Inf. Bde to establish connection with 31st Division, and to report when touch had been gained.	
		12.40pm	XVII Corps reported that contact patrol aeroplanes would fly along Corps front and call for flares at 2 pm, paying special attention to CHEMICAL WORKS.	
		12.45pm	XVII Corps reported that contact aeroplane called for flares at 11.40 and 11.50 am but none were shown. Apparently there were no troops British or German in WOBBLE trench, but visibility bad owing to smoke. Aeroplane was fired on by hostile machine guns from West end of WEED trench.	
		12.50pm	26th Inf. Bde reported that units in the front trenches state that CHILI trench was being heavily shelled by 4.2 and 5.9 howitzers from N.E., counter battery action required. The necessary arrangements were made made accordingly with Heavy Artillery.	

A6945 Wt. W11422/M1160 350,000 12/16 D. D. & L. Forms/C./2118/14.

Army Form C. 2118.

WAR DIARY
or
INTELLIGENCE SUMMARY.
(Erase heading not required.)

Instructions regarding War Diaries and Intelligence Summaries are contained in F. S. Regs., Par. II. and the Staff Manual respectively. Title pages will be prepared in manuscript.

Place	Date	Hour	Summary of Events and Information	Remarks and references to Appendices
RAILWAY CUTTING ST. LAURENT BLANGY	3rd May	12.50	9th Division message G.771 was issued, this ordered 27th Infantry Brigade to assault WIT trench between cross roads I.2.c. and northern boundary of 9th Division at I.1.b.7.8 at an hour to be notified later. WHIP and WIT trenches and WOBBLE trench N. of I.2.a.5.8 will be intensely bombarded from ZERO hour. At ZERO plus 2 minutes the artillery fire will lift off the portion of the trench to be assaulted. A smoke barrage will be placed South of the cross roads in I.2.c. and conceal the advance from the high ground on south.	25
		1.25	31st Division reported that their right was now in touch with our left (27th Inf. Bde) S.E. of GAVRELLE.	26
		1.27	The above information was reported to 27th Inf. Bde.	27
		2.0	27th Inf. Bde reported that 6th K.O.S.B. were now in touch with 15th West Yorkshire Regt (31st Division)	28
		3.6	31st Division reported that enemy had been seen in valley N.E. of GAVRELLE (C.19.b.) preparing for another attack on GAVRELLE WINDMILL. Artillery was engaging him. The above information was repeated to 27th Inf. Bde.	29 30
		3.6	Instructions from XV11 Corps Artillery for support of attack by 27th Inf. Bde were received.	
		3.28.	F.O.O. 52nd Brigade reported at 2.57 pm white lights were being sent up from CUBA trench I.7.a.3.3. It was ascertained later that these lights were sent up by our troops as our artillery was shooting short.	31
		3.30	31st Division reported that they had recaptured WINDMILL at GAVRELLE.	32
		4 pm	All concerned were notified that ZERO hour for attack by 27th Inf. Bde would be 8 p.m.	33

Instructions regarding War Diaries and Intelligence Summaries are contained in F. S. Regs., Par. II, and the Staff Manual respectively. Title pages will be prepared in manuscript.

WAR DIARY
or
INTELLIGENCE SUMMARY.
(Erase heading not required.)

Army Form C. 2118.

Place	Date	Hour	Summary of Events and Information	Remarks and references to Appendices
RAILWAY CUTTING ST. LAURENT BLANGY	3rd May	5.55	4th Division reported that they were holding original front line with exception of posts at I.13.central in some enclosures and buildings near CHATEAU and possibly in CHEMICAL WORKS. Enemy have been advancing into CORONA trench. Situation in CLOVER trench not clear. Enemy had made several strong counter attacks. One company Rifle Brigade and one company 9th Division have been sent to clear up situation.	34
		6.50	Orders were issued for one Field Company R.E. and two companies Pioneers to be at disposal of each Brigade tonight for work in clearing front line and communication trenches. O.C. 9th Seaforths to arrange to place one additional company at disposal of each Brigade for the purpose. Connection between WISH trench and the BRICKFIELD in CUBA to be made by the construction of intermediate strong points which can be subsequently connected by a continuous trench.	35
		7.35	Orders received from XVII Corps for Divisions to consolidate and improve the positions held. Touch to be kept with the enemy by means of patrols. The above order was repeated to C.R.A., C.R.E. 26th and 27th Infantry Brigades.	36 37
		8.0pm	27th Bde attacked WIT trench with 12th Royal Scots (two companies)	
		9.15	General MAXWELL reported verbally that both companies got into the trench. The right company was knocked out by hostile machine gun fire after getting into the trench. The Left company had not yet returned. No further news. Afraid attack has failed.	
		10.25 pm	27th Inf. Bde was asked if the Brigade Commander wished for a Battalion of 52nd Inf. Bde (17th Division) to be moved forward to the GREEN LINE on account of the attacking companies having suffered heavy casualties. General MAXWELL replied that he did not need this. He asked that the artillery should not fire on trench immediately in front of his Brigade as men of 6th K.O.S.B. and 9th Scottish Rifles might be returning.	

A6945 Wt. W11422/M1160 350,000 12/16 D. D. & L. Forms/C./2118/14.

"C" Form.

Army Form C. 2123.
(In books of 100).

MESSAGES AND SIGNALS.

No. of Message

Prefix B Code GK Words 9	Received. From Bo By Miller	Sent, or sent out. At m. To By	Office Stamp.
Charges to collect £ s. d.			
Service Instructions. Priority			

Handed in at Bo Office 3.50 m. Received 3.58 m.

TO Hunt

Sender's Number	Day of Month	In reply to Number	AAA
Bm 5	3		

Moves complete

FROM Bowers
PLACE & TIME 3.30 am

* This line should be erased if not required.

(6384). Wt. W7495/M857. 500,000 Pads. 10/16. D. D. & L. (E 489). Forms C/2123/3.

"A" Form
Army Form C. 2121
(in pads of 100).

MESSAGES AND SIGNALS.

No. of Message.................

Prefix.............Code.................m.	Words. / Charge.	This message is on a/c of:	Recd. at............m.
Office of Origin and Service Instructions.	Sent	..............................Service.	Date ....
	At..................m.		From ....
	To......................		
	By......................	(Signature of "Franking Officer.")	By.......................

TO [illegible]

Sender's Number.	Day of Month.	In reply to Number.	AAA
*			

F.O. D/32 reports enemy putting up a heavy barrage all along our front line

Recd 4.10 am

From 32nd Bde

Place

Time 5.55 am

The above may be forwarded as now corrected. (Z)

.... *Censor.*

Signature of Addressor or person authorised to telegraph in his name.

* This line should be erased if not required.

(18965.) Wt. W12952/M1294. 187,500 Pads. 1/17 McC. & Co., Ltd. (E. 818.)

3

Army Form C. 2121
(in pads of 100).

"A" Form
MESSAGES AND SIGNALS.

No. of Message..................

Prefix..............Code..................m.

Office of Origin and Service Instructions.

Words.	Charge.

Sent
At..................m.
To......................
By......................

This message is on a/c of:
..............................*Service.*
....
(Signature of "Franking Officer.")

Recd. at...........m.
Date......................
From......................
By........................

TO C.O. [illegible]

Sender's Number.	Day of Month.	In reply to Number.	AAA
*			

[illegible] D/32 [illegible]
heavy [illegible] and machine
[illegible]
[illegible]

[illegible]

From [illegible]
Place
Time [illegible]

The above may be forwarded as now corrected. (Z)
.... Censor.
Signature of Addressor or person authorised to telegraph in his name.

*This line should be erased if not required.

(18965.) Wt. W12952/M1294. 187,500 Pads. 1/17 McC. & Co., Ltd. (E. 818.)

"A" Form

Army Form C. 2121
(in pads of 100).

MESSAGES AND SIGNALS.

No. of Message................

Prefix..............Code..................m. | Words. | Charge. | *This message is on a/c of:* | Recd. at............m.

Office of Origin and Service Instructions.

Sent
At..................m.
To......................
By......................

..............................*Service.*

(Signature of "Franking Officer.")

Date......................
From......................
By........................

TO CRA

Sender's Number.	Day of Month.	In reply to Number.	AAA
*	3		

No trench lights seen on our front for the last 15 minutes. Heavy machine gun fire from South of [illegible]. It appears that enemy have a strong barrage all along the front. This commenced about 5 minutes after zero.

Recd 4.30 am

From FOO 32nd Bde
Place
Time 4.15 am

The above may be forwarded as now corrected. (Z)

Censor. Signature of Addressor or person authorised to telegraph in his name.

* This line should be erased if not required.

(18965.) Wt. W12952/M1294. 187,500 Pads. 1/17 McC. & Co., Ltd. (E. 818.)

(5)

"A" Form

Army Form C. 2121
(in pads of 100).

MESSAGES AND SIGNALS.

No. of Message..................

Prefix.............Code.................m.	Words. / Charge.	*This message is on a/c of:*	Recd. at...........m.
Office of Origin and Service Instructions.	Sent	..........................*Service.*	Date ....
	At..................m.		From ....
	To		By......................
	By.......................	(Signature of "Franking Officer.")	

TO { CRA

Sender's Number.	Day of Month.	In reply to Number.	AAA
*	3		

Hostile Very Lights appear to be going up [illegible] towards

Recd. 4.55 am

From	F.O.O. D/Head
Place	
Time	4.50 am

The above may be forwarded as now corrected. (Z)

Censor. Signature of Addressor or person authorised to telegraph in his name.

*This line should be erased if not required.

(18965.) Wt. W12952/M1294. 187,500 Pads. 1/17 M^cC. & Co., Ltd. (E. 818.)

Army Form C. 2123.
(In books of 100).

"C" Form.

MESSAGES AND SIGNALS. No. of Message ......

Prefix ...... Code ...... Words ...... £ s. d. Charges to collect	Received. From ...... By	Sent, or sent out. At ...... m. To ...... By	Office Stamp.

Service Instructions.

Handed in at YCA Office 4.30 a m. Received 5 a m.

TO 9th Divn

*Sender's Number	Day of Month	In reply to Number	AAA
G 100	3		

Third report No 2 4.30 am aaa Barrage opened 3.45 am aaa Left Bde reports enemy appeared slow on [illegible] [illegible] artillery [illegible] through Lihons with eighty [illegible] aaa The enemy barrage [illegible] aaa right Bde commenced 13 seconds after ZERO aaa Report from Arty 3.0 just [illegible] states only [illegible] [illegible] [illegible] [illegible] [illegible] 13 Corps reptd 2nd and 9th Divns

S T a

FROM PLACE & TIME: 31 Divn 4.30 am

* This line should be erased if not required.

(6334). Wt. W7496/M857. 500,000 Pads. 10/16. D. D. & L. (E489). Forms C/2123/3.

7

"A" Form
MESSAGES AND SIGNALS.

Army Form C. 2121
(in pads of 100).

No. of Message.................

Prefix............Code..................m.	Words. / Charge.	*This message is on a/c of:*	Recd. at............m.
Office of Origin and Service Instructions.	Sent	...............................*Service.*	Date.....................
	At....................m.		From..................
	To......................		
	By......................	(Signature of "Franking Officer.")	By........................

TO { 17th Corps
4th Division
31st Division

Sender's Number.	Day of Month.	In reply to Number.	AAA
* G 405	3		

Report at 4.05. [illegible] light
not yet been enough for
observation aaa Very
lights which were originally
sent up in front line now
being sent up further East
aaa Hostile barrage
which fell on our front
line at 3.38 is now reported
to have ceased.

From	4th Division
Place	
Time	5-15 am

The above may be forwarded as now corrected. (Z)

Censor. Signature of Addressor or person authorised to telegraph in his name.

* This line should be erased if not required.

(18965.) Wt. W12952/M1294. 187,500 Pads. 1/17 McC. & Co., Ltd. (E. 818.)

"A" Form

Army Form C. 2121 (in pads of 100).

MESSAGES AND SIGNALS.

No. of Message.................

Prefix.............Code.................m. Office of Origin and Service Instructions.	Words. Charge. Sent At.................m. To.................... By....................	This message is on a/c of: ....Service. (Signature of "Franking Officer.")	Recd. at............m. Date.............. From.............. By..............

TO 7th Division

Sender's Number.	Day of Month.	In reply to Number.	AAA
* BM 56	3rd		

Situation 5.30 am aaa Alphonse [illegible] DIS [illegible] [illegible] [illegible] [illegible] third Rylstone hill 6.15 am [illegible] [illegible] through to BRIQUETERIE Station on CUBA and through Mar [illegible] Station on HISH aaa CUBA reports enemy barrage in front of CUBA very heavy aaa Message from right batt timed 5.10 am reports no [illegible] news but think [illegible] [illegible] on aaa Message from left batt timed 4.40 am reports his [illegible] and 31st Div [illegible] had reached [illegible] that he was not in touch

From

Place

Time

The above may be forwarded as now corrected. (Z)

Censor. Signature of Addressor or person authorised to telegraph in his name.

* This line should be erased if not required.

(18965.) Wt. W12952/M1294. 187,500 Pads. 1/17 McC. & Co., Ltd. (E. 818.)

"C" Form.

MESSAGES AND SIGNALS.

Army Form C. 2123.
(In books of 100).

No. of Message..................

Prefix........ Code........ Words........	Received.	Sent, or sent out.	Office Stamp.
£ s. d. Charges to collect	From........ By........	At........m. To........ By........	[illegible]
Service Instructions.			

Handed in at.................... Office........m. Received 6.14 am m.

TO [illegible] (5)

*Sender's Number	Day of Month	In reply to Number	AAA
[illegible]	[illegible]		

with	right	Battn	on	that
front	was	at	zero	light
was	enough	to	see	40
yards	along	a	track	top
[illegible]	to	see	arrival	of
enemy	barrage	but	around	[illegible]
of	it	arrival	at	Zero
plus	3	aaa	Smoke	and
dust	caused	by	our	barrage
and	carried	by	NE	wind
towards	our	front	prevents	any
view	and	still	prevents	it
enemy	barrage	still	maintained	on
forward	area	two	of	our
planes	seen	over	Bde	HQ
at	5.15	am	6.14 am	

FROM [illegible]

PLACE & TIME 5.50 am

* This line should be erased if not required.

(6334). Wt. W7496/M857. 500,000 Pads. 10/16. D. D. & L. (E 489). Forms C/2123/3.

9

"A" Form

MESSAGES AND SIGNALS.

Army Form C. 2121 (in pads of 100).

No. of Message..................

Prefix............Code..............m.	Words. / Charge.	This message is on a/c of:	Recd. at............m.
Office of Origin and Service Instructions.	Sent	..............................Service.	Date....................
Priority	At................m.		From....................
	To......................		
	By......................	(Signature of "Franking Officer.")	By......................

TO { [illegible] Corps — [illegible]
{ [illegible] Divn — [illegible]
{ [illegible] Divn — [illegible]

Sender's Number.	Day of Month.	In reply to Number.	AAA
* G 458	5		

Reports indicate attack [illegible] right brigade [illegible] [illegible] [illegible] from M.G. fire from [illegible] [illegible] [illegible] [illegible] [illegible] [illegible] [illegible] [illegible] [illegible] [illegible] [illegible] [illegible]

From [illegible] Division
Place
Time 6-20am

The above may be forwarded as now corrected. (Z)

Censor. Signature of Addressor or person authorised to telegraph in his name.

* This line should be erased if not required.

(18965.) Wt. W12952/M1294. 187,500 Pads. 1/17 McC. & Co., Ltd. (E. 818.)

10

Army Form C. 2121
(in pads of 100).

"A" Form
MESSAGES AND SIGNALS.

No. of Message..................

Prefix..............Code..................m. / Office of Origin and Service Instructions.	Words. / Charge. / Sent / At....................m. / To.................... / By....................	This message is on a/c of: ....Service. / (Signature of "Franking Officer.")	Recd. at............m. / Date.................. / From.................. / By....................

TO { [illegible]

Sender's Number.	Day of Month.	In reply to Number.	AAA
* [illegible]	3		

Liaison officer reports
CUTHBERT Trench has now
been evacuated by our
Infy and also by
[illegible] [illegible] fire

From [illegible]
Place
Time

The above may be forwarded as now corrected. (Z)

.... *Censor.* .... Signature of Addressor or person authorised to telegraph in his name.

* This line should be erased if not required.

(18965.) Wt. W12952/M1294. 187,500 Pads. 1/17 McC. & Co., Ltd. (E. 818.)

"A" Form

Army Form C. 2121
(in pads of 100).

MESSAGES AND SIGNALS.

No. of Message..................

Prefix..............Code.................m.	Words.	Charge.	This message is on a/c of:	Recd. at............m.
Office of Origin and Service Instructions.	Sent		..............................Service.	Date..................
....	At...................m.			From..................
....	To......................		....	
....	By......................		(Signature of "Franking Officer.")	By......................

TO

Sender's Number.	Day of Month.	In reply to Number.	AAA
*			

From

Place

Time

The above may be forwarded as now corrected. (Z)

....Censor.

....Signature of Addressor or person authorised to telegraph in his name.

* This line should be erased if not required.

(18965.) Wt. W12952/M1294. 187,500 Pads. 1/17 McC. & Co., Ltd. (E. 818.)

12

Prefix .... Code .... Words .... £ s. d. Charges to collect	Received. From .... By	Sent, or sent out. At .... m. To .... By	Office Stamp.
Service Instructions. Priority			

Handed in at Y.C.A. Operations Office 6.20 a.m. Received 6.36 a.m.

TO 9 Divn

*Sender's Number	Day of Month	In reply to Number.	AAA
G1004	3rd		

aeroplane	dropped	message	at	Dhq.
6.10	a.m	as	follows	aaa
Very	lights	seen	at	5.10
and	C1A50	C1C55	C13A34	B24b7/8
C25A76	aaa	There	is	a
very	heavy	enemy	barrage	aaa
The	Hun	is	putting	up
many	very	lights	which	appear
to	be	white	breaking	into
two	red	balls	aaa	Visibility
very	bad	aaa	Following	from
left	Brigade	aaa	Reports	from
a	wounded	officer	point	to
the	attack	on	OPPY	not
having	been	successful	aaa	Right
and	Centre	Bns	suffered	heavily
in	their	assembly	lines	at

FROM
PLACE & TIME

* This line should be erased if not required.
(6334). Wt. W7496/M857. 500,000 Pads. 10/16. D. D. & L. (E 489). Forms C/2123/3.

FROM 31 Divn
PLACE & TIME 6-21 a.m

* This line should be erased if not required.
(6334). Wt. W7496/M857. 500,000 Pads. 10/16. D. D. & L. (E 489). Forms C/2123/3.

13

"A" Form
MESSAGES AND SIGNALS.

Army Form C. 2121
(in pads of 100).

No. of Message..................

Prefix.........Code..............m.	Words.	Charge.	This message is on a/c of:	Recd. at..........m.
Office of Origin and Service Instructions.	Sent		..................Service.	Date................
	At..............m.			From................
	To..................			
	By..................		(Signature of "Franking Officer.")	By..................

TO CRA

Sender's Number.	Day of Month.	In reply to Number.	
* [illegible]	3		AAA

Liaison Officer reports HOBBIE Trench has been captured and Patrols out 600 or 700 yards in front of SQUARE WOOD and slow progress in Centre

[illegible]

From [illegible]
Place
Time 6.35 a.m.

The above may be forwarded as now corrected. (Z)

Censor. Signature of Addressor or person authorised to telegraph in his name.

* This line should be erased if not required.

(18965.) Wt. W12952/M1294. 187,500 Pads. 1/17 McC. & Co., Ltd. (E. 818.)

Army Form C. 2121
(in pads of 100).

"A" Form
MESSAGES AND SIGNALS.

No. of Message..................

Prefix.............Code.................m. Office of Origin and Service Instructions.	Words.	Charge.	This message is on a/c of: ....Service. (Signature of "Franking Officer.")	Recd. at...........m. Date............... From............... By...............
	Sent At..................m. To.................. By..................			

TO { 9th Div [?]

Sender's Number.	Day of Month.	In reply to Number.	AAA
* G 1906 [?]	3		

Handby [?] report 5.30 am aaa Our right Bde appears to be back in original trenches and have taken up defensive position aaa Our left Bde appears from reports [?] to have posts in Oppy Wood aaa Situation of remainder of Brigade not known aaa Left Bde have sent back for engineers [?] to work on trench immediately West of Oppy Wood [illegible] 2nd Guards Reserve Division aaa Aeroplane reports as follows: lines [?] 6.15 am aaa lights seen at C 7 a 4.5 [illegible] B 24 b 7.8 C 19 a 9.5 [illegible] C 25 a 8.0 aaa [illegible]

From	2nd [?] 9th Div [?]	
Place	3rd Div [?]	
Time		7.20 [?]

The above may be forwarded as now corrected.

Censor. | (Z) Signature of Addressor or person authorised to telegraph in his name.

*This line should be erased if not required.

(18965.) Wt. W12952/M1294. 187,500 Pads. 1/17 McC. & Co., Ltd. (E. 818.)

"C" Form. Army Form C. 2123.
(In books of 100).

MESSAGES AND SIGNALS. No. of Message

Prefix Code Words

£ s. d.

Charges to collect

Service Instructions. Priority Operations

Received. From By

Sent, or sent out. At m. To By

Office Stamp.

Handed in at YA Office 2.51 m. Received 8.10 m.

TO 34 Divn

*Sender's Number	Day of Month	In reply to Number	AAA
S.1012	3		

Enemy is counter attacking whole of right Bde front in force and has taken windmill aaa One of the two battns in Divn reserve has been sent up in support aaa But along whole Bde front on original line 8.10am

FROM 31 Divn

PLACE & TIME 7.56 am

* This line should be erased if not required.

(6334). Wt. W7496/M857. 500,000 Pads. 10/16. D. D. & L. (E 489). Forms C/2123/3.

H. A. G.

16

"C" Form. Army Form C. 2123.
(In books of 100).

MESSAGES AND SIGNALS. No. of Message.........

Prefix...... Code...... Words......	Received.	Sent, or sent out.	Office Stamp.
£ s. d.	From......	At...... m.	
Charges to collect	By......	To......	
Service Instructions. Priority		By......	

Handed in at ...... Office 8.20 m. Received 8.34 a m.

TO Adv. 9th Div

*Sender's Number	Day of Month	In reply to Number	AAA
G.13467	9/5		

Formal	attack	will	NOT	be
pressed	for	present	aaa	all
local	successes	of	4th	Div.
to	be	exploited	to	full
with	view	of	capturing	CEMETERY
CORONA	trench	CHEMICAL	WORKS	and
buildings	north	of	Railway	aaa
9th	Div.	will	continue	bombardment
of	points	which	held	up
their	attack	aaa	Heavies	to
bombard	ROEUX	CARROT.	CYPRUS	
CANDY	trenches	and	Railway	East
of	CUPID	addsd	4th	and
9th	Divs	Repeated	GOCRA	

H

FROM 17 Corps

PLACE & TIME 8.10 am

* This line should be erased if not required.

(6334). Wt. W7496/M857. 500,000 Pads. 10/16. D. D. & L. (E 489). Forms C/2123/3.

8.39 a.m.

14

"A" Form
MESSAGES AND SIGNALS.

Army Form C. 2121
(in pads of 100).

No. of Message.................

Prefix..............Code..................m. Office of Origin and Service Instructions.	Words. / Charge. Sent At....................m. To.................... By....................	*This message is on a/c of:* ....*Service.* (Signature of "Franking Officer.")	Recd. at..........m. Date.................... From.................... By....................

TO { 19th Corps

Sender's Number.	Day of Month.	In reply to Number.	AAA
* G466			

Situation appears to be as follows aaa Right Bde. attack failed and original front line is now held aaa Left Brigade aaa 2 companies of each of the two leading battalions appear to have reached WIT trench line WIT trench is now occupied by Germans [?] consequently the companies which passed WIT trench are for the present cut off [?] It is not intended to attack WIT trench till higher formation [?] [illegible] can be secured which is not a question at present and meanwhile original

From
Place
Time

The above may be forwarded as now corrected. **(Z)**
Censor. Signature of Addressor or person authorised to telegraph in his name.
*This line should be erased if not required.

(18965.) Wt. W12952/M1294. 187,500 Pads. 1/17 McC. & Co., Ltd. (E. 818.)

Time
The above may be forwarded as now corrected. **(Z)**
Censor. Signature of Addressor or person authorised to telegraph in his name.
*This line should be erased if not required.
(18965.) Wt. W12952/M1294. 187,500 Pads. 1/17 McC. & Co., Ltd. (E. 818.)

18

"C" Form.

MESSAGES AND SIGNALS.

Army Form C. 2123.
(In books of 100).

No. of Message..................

Prefix.......... Code.......... Words..........	Received.	Sent, or sent out.	Office Stamp.
£ s. d.	From..................	At..................m.	
Charges to collect	By..................	To..................	
Service Instructions.		By..................	

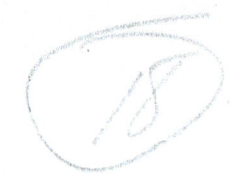

Handed in at...Office..................m. Received..................m.

TO [illegible]

*Sender's Number	Day of Month	In reply to Number	AAA
BM 1	2		

Am hearing that [illegible] in my [illegible] [illegible] [illegible] up [illegible] [illegible] [illegible] the direction of [illegible] smoke with the [illegible] barraging at the high ground [illegible] to protect the flank, and [illegible] of [illegible] in the WOBBLE direction [illegible]

FROM

PLACE & TIME 10. 5. am

* This line should be erased if not required.

(6334). Wt. W7496/M857. 500,000 Pads. 10/16. D. D. & L. (E 489). Forms C/2123/3.

MESSAGES AND SIGNALS.

No. of Message..................

Prefix........ Code........ Words........ £ s. d. Charges to collect	Received. From.............. By..............	Sent, or sent out. At..............m. To.............. By..............	Office Stamp.
Service Instructions.			

Handed in at...Office..............m. Received..............m.

TO (2)

*Sender's Number	Day of Month	In reply to Number	AAA
BM 9			

move	me	my	front	[illegible]
[illegible]	morning	[illegible]	my	right
[illegible]	[illegible]	as	it	[illegible]
my	[illegible]	can	33rd	[illegible]
and	[illegible]	clear	front	line
and	have	[illegible]	intention	of
mopping	up	which	will	make
it	difficult	for	me	to
do	so	although	it	is
important	for	us	to	get
rid	of	the	enemy	[illegible]
between	my	advanced	[illegible]	and
my	original	front	line	

FROM / PLACE & TIME: [illegible] 9.40 AM (10.5 am)

* This line should be erased if not required.

(6334). Wt. W7496/M857. 500,000 Pads. 10/16. D. D. & L. (E 489). Forms C/2123/3.

"C" Form.

Army Form C. 2123.
(In books of 100).

MESSAGES AND SIGNALS.

No. of Message

Prefix Code Words	Received.	Sent, or sent out.	Office Stamp.
£ s. d.	From	At m.	
Charges to collect	By	To	
Service Instructions. Priority		By	

Handed in at Office m. Received 10 m.

TO Hunt

*Sender's Number	Day of Month	In reply to Number	AAA
BM 10	5		

Trust	an	aeroplane	be	sent
to	reconnoitre	the	area	of
WEBBLE	trench	to	ascertain	if
possible	whether	our	men	are
there	or	not	they	will
not	light	flares	until	they
see	an	aeroplane		

10.10 am

FROM PLACE & TIME BMR 9.30 am

* This line should be erased if not required.

(6334). Wt. W7496/M857. 500,000 Pads. 10/16. D. D. & L. (E 489). Forms C/2123/3.

(20)

"A" Form
MESSAGES AND SIGNALS.

Army Form C. 2121
(in pads of 100).

No. of Message..................

Prefix..............Code..................m. | Words. | Charge.

Office of Origin and Service Instructions.

Priority

Sent
At..................m.
To......................
By......................

This message is on a/c of:
...............................*Service.*
....
(Signature of "Franking Officer.")

Recd. at..............m.
Date..................
From..................
By....................

TO 17th Corps

Sender's Number.	Day of Month.	In reply to Number.	AAA
* G698	3		

Could an aeroplane be sent to reconnoitre the area of [illegible] Trench and [illegible] to ascertain if possible whether any men are there or not aaa They will not light flares until they see an aeroplane.

From 9th Division
Place
Time 10.15 am

The above may be forwarded as now corrected. (Z)

.... Censor. | Signature of Addressor or person authorised to telegraph in his name.

* This line should be erased if not required.

(18965.) Wt. W12952/M1294. 187,500 Pads. 1/17 McC. & Co., Ltd. (E. 818.)

21

"C" Form.

Army Form C. 2123.
(In books of 100).

MESSAGES AND SIGNALS.

No. of Message

Prefix Code Words	Received.	Sent, or sent out.	Office Stamp.
£ s. d. Charges to collect	From By	At m. To By	

Service Instructions. Priority

Handed in at JCA Office 9.55 a.m. Received 10.40 a.m.

TO 9 Divn

Sender's Number	Day of Month	In reply to Number	AAA
G 1017	3		

Hourly report 9.30 AM aaa We hold EASTERN EDGE of GAVRELLE to RAILWAY at C19C62 along railway to B24D28 aaa mgs and 2 Coys infantry on hill 80 aaa LEFT Bde. in forming up trenches aaa WINDMILL has changed hands three times and we are at present making a new attack on it aaa It is now known that LEFT Bde. was hung up in their advance through OPPY WOOD by very thick wire thus leaving LEFT OF RIGHT Bde. open aaa This Bde advancing behind barrage

FROM

PLACE & TIME 10.46 am

* This line should be erased if not required.

(6334). Wt. W7495/M857. 500,000 Pads. 10/16. D. D. & L. (E 489). Forms C/2123/3.

* This line should be erased if not required.

(6334). Wt. W7496/M857. 500,000 Pads. 10/16. D. D. & L. (E 489). Forms C/2123/3.

"C" Form.

Army Form C. 2123.
(In books of 100).

MESSAGES AND SIGNALS. No. of Message

Prefix Code Words	Received.	Sent, or sent out.	Office Stamp.
£ s. d. Charges to collect	From By	At m. To By	Y 13.V.17 R TELEGRAPHS
Service Instructions.			

Handed in at Office m. Received 10.40 a m.

TO 11

*Sender's Number	Day of Month	In reply to Number	AAA

was	~~is~~ very	heavily	coun	ter attacked
from	OPPY	WOOD	and	village
after	barrage	had	passed	and
their	LEFT	FLANK	ROLLED	up
aaa	We	are	making	a
strong	front	at	B12C63	to
join	with	2nd	Divn	aaa
Addsd	13	Corps	Repeated	2nd
and	9th	Divns		

1046

FROM 31 Divn

PLACE & TIME 9.50 am

* This line should be erased if not required.

(6334). Wt. W7496/M857. 500,000 Pads. 10/16. D. D. & L. (E 489). Forms C/2123/3.

22

"C" Form.
MESSAGES AND SIGNALS.

Army Form C. 2123.
(In books of 100).
No. of Message

Prefix Code Words
£ s. d.
Charges to collect
Service Instructions. Priority

Received. From By

Sent, or sent out. At m. To By

Office Stamp.

Handed in at R F C Office 10.45 m. Received 10.49 m.

TO 9 Divn

Sender's Number	Day of Month	In reply to Number	AAA
JB472	3		

In	confirmation	telephone	message	
Send	machine	to	call	for
flares	and	reconn	oitre	area
WOBBLE	trench	and	SQUARE	
wood	to	ascertain	if	possible
our	men	there	or	not
aaa	Addressed	13	Sqdn	
RFC	Repeated	9	Divn	

10.54 am

FROM 17 Corps
PLACE & TIME 10.40 am

* This line should be erased if not required.
(5334). Wt. W7496/M857. 500,000 Pads. 10/16. D. D. & L. (E 189). Forms C/2123/3.

"A" Form

Army Form C. 2121 (in pads of 100).

MESSAGES AND SIGNALS.

No. of Message..................

Prefix............Code...............m.	Words.	Charge.	This message is on a/c of:	Recd. at...........m.
Office of Origin and Service Instructions. Priority	Sent At...............m. To.................. By..................		...........................Service. (Signature of "Franking Officer.")	Date.............. From.............. By..............

TO 29th Bde

Sender's Number.	Day of Month.	In reply to Number.	
* 4767	3		AAA

An aeroplane has been told to call for flares and reconnoitre SQUARE Wood and WOBBLE trench to ascertain if our troops are in this area

From 9th Division
Place
Time 11 am

The above may be forwarded as now corrected. (Z)

Censor. Signature of Addressor or person authorised to telegraph in his name.

* This line should be erased if not required.

(18965.) Wt. W12952/M1294. 187,500 Pads. 1/17 McC. & Co., Ltd. (E. 818.)

"C" Form (Duplicate).
MESSAGES AND SIGNALS.

Army Form C. 2123.
(In books of 50's in duplicate.)
No. of Message..................

	Charges to Pay. £ s. d.	Office Stamp.
Service Instructions.		

Handed in at RFC Office 12.35 p m. Received 12.45 p m.

TO 9 Divn

Sender's Number	Day of Month	In reply to Number	AAA
G.B. 474	3/5		

Contact Patrol Aeroplane will fly along Corps front and call for FLARES at two PM today paying special attention to CHEMICAL WORKS aaa Addressed 4th and 9th Divisions Repeated 13 Squadron RFC

12-40

FROM 17th Corps
PLACE & TIME 12.30 PM

Wt. 432—M437 500,000 Pads. H W V 5/16 Forms C.2123.

25

"A" Form

Army Form C. 2121 (in pads of 100).

MESSAGES AND SIGNALS.

No. of Message.................

Prefix.........Code.........m. Office of Origin and Service Instructions.	Words.	Charge.	This message is on a/c of:	Recd. at.........m.
Priority	Sent At.........m. To......... By.........		.........Service. (Signature of "Franking Officer.")	Date......... From......... By.........

TO			
26th Inf Bde	C.R.A.		9th Divn
H.A. 9th Divn	14th Corps		3rd Inf Bde
27th Inf Bde	21st Divn		

Sender's Number.	Day of Month.	In reply to Number.	AAA
* G 791	3		

26th Inf Bde will assault
W.T. Trench between Cross roads
I.2.C. and Northern boundary
of 9th Division at I.1.b.9.8 at
Zero hour to be notified later
aaa O.G.1.P. and W.T. Trenches and
WORBLE Trench North of I.2.a.5.8
will be intensely bombarded from
Zero hour aaa At Zero plus
2 minutes the Artillery fire
will lift off the portion of the
trench to be assaulted aaa
A smoke barrage will be
placed South of the Cross roads
in I.2.C. to conceal the advance
from the high ground on
South aaa Acknowledge

From 9th Division

Place

Time 12.55 pm

The above may be forwarded as now corrected. (Z)

Censor. Signature of Addressor or person authorised to telegraph in his name.

*This line should be erased if not required.

(18965.) Wt. W12952/M1294. 187,500 Pads. 1/17 McC. & Co., Ltd. (E. 818.)

26

......Code......m.	Words.	Charge.	*This message is on a/c of:*	Recd. at......m.
Office of Origin and Service Instructions.	Sent		......Service.	Date......
	At......m.			From......
	To......			
	By......		(Signature of "Franking Officer.")	By......

TO { 9th Division

Sender's Number.	Day of Month.	In reply to Number.	
* G1023	3rd		AAA

We are now in touch with 9th Divn. S. of GAVRELLE aaa addressed 17th Corps repeated 9th Divn

From 51st Divn

Place

Time 12.40 pm

The above may be forwarded as now corrected. (Z)

Censor. Signature of Addressor or person authorised to telegraph in his name.

* This line should be erased if not required.

(18965.) Wt. W12952/M1294. 187,500 Pads. 1/17 McC. & Co., Ltd. (E. 818.)

...de...............m.	Words.	Charge.	This message is on a/c of:	Recd. at..........m.
...n Origin and Service Instructions.	Sent		..........................Service.	Date..................
	At................m.			From..................
	To..................			
	By..................		(Signature of "Franking Officer.")	By..................

TO Eighth Bde

* Sender's Number.	Day of Month.	In reply to Number.	AAA
G774	3		

43rd Divn report that they are now in touch with you

From 7th Divn
Place
Time 1·20 pm

The above may be forwarded as now corrected. (Z)

Censor. Signature of Addressor or person authorised to telegraph in his name.

* This line should be erased if not required.

(18965.) Wt. W12952/M1294. 187,500 Pads. I/17 McC. & Co., Ltd. (E. 818.)

28

Army Form C. 2123.
(In books of 100).

"C" Form.

MESSAGES AND SIGNALS. No. of Message..................

Prefix .... Code .... Words .... £ s. d. Charges to collect	Received. From .... By	Sent, or sent out. At .... m. To .... By	Office Stamp.
Service Instructions.			

Handed in at .... Office .... m. Received .... m.

TO [illegible]

*Sender's Number	Day of Month	In reply to Number	AAA
[illegible]			

			KOSB	
[illegible]	from	OC	[illegible]	[illegible]
[illegible]	[illegible]	[illegible]	[illegible]	[illegible]
[illegible]	in	[illegible]	[illegible]	OC
[illegible]	[illegible]	[illegible]	[illegible]	[illegible]
[illegible]	[illegible]	[illegible]	[illegible]	[illegible]
[illegible]	[illegible]	[illegible]	[illegible]	[illegible]
[illegible]	CYC 32	A [illegible]	[illegible]	[illegible]
[illegible]				

FROM
PLACE & TIME [illegible]

* This line should be erased if not required.

(6334). Wt. W7496/M857. 500,000 Pads. 10/16. D. D. & L. (E 489). Forms C/2123/3.

29

"C" Form (Original).
MESSAGES AND SIGNALS.

Army Form C. 2123.
(In books of 50's in duplicate.)
No. of Message

Prefix Code Words	Received	Sent, or sent out	Office Stamp.
£ s. d.	From	At m.	
Charges to collect	By	To	
Service Instructions.		By	

Handed in at YCH Office 2.15 p m. Received 2.35 p m.

TO 9 Div

*Sender's Number	Day of Month	In reply to Number	AAA
R1128	3.5.17		

enemy is seen in C19B preparing for another attack on GAVRELLE wind mill artillery is engaging him

3 6

FROM 31 Div

PLACE & TIME 2.6 pm.

* This line should be erased if not required.

Wt. 432—M437 500,000 Pads. H W V 5/16 Forms C.2123.

"A" Form
Army Form C. 2121
(in pads of 100).

MESSAGES AND SIGNALS.

No. of Message..................

Prefix.............Code.................m. / Office of Origin and Service Instructions.	Words. Charge. / Sent / At.................m. / To..................... / By.....................	This message is on a/c of: ....Service. / (Signature of "Franking Officer.")	Recd. at.............m. / Date..................... / From..................... / By.....................

TO: Right Inf. Bde

Sender's Number.	Day of Month.	In reply to Number.	
* G446	13		AAA

[illegible] Division [illegible] 2.6 pm [illegible] enemy in [illegible] on C.19.b preparing for another attack on GAVRELLE Windmill Artillery is engaging him

From: [illegible] Division
Place
Time: 3.6 pm

The above may be forwarded as now corrected. (Z)

.... Censor.

.... Signature of Addressor or person authorised to telegraph in his name.

*This line should be erased if not required.

(18965.) Wt. W12952/M1294. 187,500 Pads. 1/17 McC. & Co., Ltd. (E. 818.)

31

"A" Form
MESSAGES AND SIGNALS.

Army Form C. 2121
(in pads of 100).

No. of Message.................

Prefix............Code..............m.	Words.	Charge.	*This message is on a/c of:*	Recd. at...........m.
Office of Origin and Service Instructions.	Sent		........................*Service.*	Date..................
	At..............m.			From..................
	To..................			
	By..................		(Signature of "Franking Officer.")	By....................

TO CRA

Sender's Number.	Day of Month.	In reply to Number.	AAA
* EF2	3		

F.O.O. reports 7.5 pm White lights are being sent up from L.4.a.3.3.

5 Bn. F. Bde

From
Place
Time

The above may be forwarded as now corrected. (Z)

Censor. Signature of Addressor or person authorised to telegraph in his name.

*This line should be erased if not required.

(18965.) Wt. W12952/M1294. 187,500 Pads. 1/17 McC. & Co., Ltd. **(E. 818.)**

32

"C" Form (Duplicate).
MESSAGES AND SIGNALS.

Army Form C. 2123.
(In books of 50's in duplicate.)
No. of Message

Charges to Pay. £ s. d.

Office Stamp.

Service Instructions.

Handed in at YCA Office 2.45 p m. Received 3.10 p m.

TO 9 Dwn

Sender's Number	Day of Month	In reply to Number	AAA
G1032	3		

4th	Counter	attack	on	hill
by	us	successful	but	with
heavy	loss	aaa	hill	now
held	by	us	but	fighting
still	going	on	otherwise	situation
unchanged	aaa	we	are	in
touch	with	Dwn	on	right
aaa	Enemy	heavy	arty	very
active	against	our	left	Bde
aaa	Added	13	Corps	Repld
2	and	9	Dwn	

AL 3 30

FROM
PLACE & TIME 31st Dwn 2.40 pm

Wt. 432—M437 500,000 Pads. H W V 5/16 Forms C.2123.

"A" Form

MESSAGES AND SIGNALS.

No. of Message..................

Prefix.............Code..................m. | Words. | Charge.

Office of Origin and Service Instructions.

Priority

Sent At..................m. To...................... By......................

This message is on a/c of: ....Service.

(Signature of "Franking Officer.")

Recd. at............m. Date...................... From...................... By......................

TO

Gds Bde	CRA	4th Divn	
[illegible] Division	14 Corps	[illegible] Gds Bde.	
[illegible] Bde	56th Divn		

Sender's Number.	Day of Month.	In reply to Number.	AAA
* G 444	3		

With reference my G441 aaa ZERO will be 5 pm aaa acknowledge

From 4th Division

Place

Time 4 pm

The above may be forwarded as now corrected. (Z)

Censor. Signature of Addressor or person authorised to telegraph in his name.

*This line should be erased if not required.

(18965.) Wt. W12952/M1294. 187,500 Pads. 1/17 McC. & Co., Ltd. (E. 818.)

34

MESSAGES AND SIGNALS.

No. of Message..................

Prefix..........Code..........m. Office of Origin and Service Instructions.	Words.	Charge.	This message is on a/c of: ....Service. (Signature of "Franking Officer.")	Recd. at..........m. Date.......... From.......... By..........
	Sent At..........m. To.......... By..........			

TO [illegible] Division

Sender's Number.	Day of Month.	In reply to Number.	AAA
* G61	3		

Situation as far as can be ascertained is as follows aaa We are holding original front line with exception of posts at 1.B. [illegible] on some of enclosures and building near Chateau and possibly in Chemical Works aaa Enemy have been advancing into CRONA Trench and it would appear we now have no troops on Black Line aaa Situation in CLOVER Trench not clear aaa 1 Coy [illegible] and 1 Coy [illegible] have been sent to clear up situation aaa Enemy have made several strong [illegible] attacks aaa Hampshire [illegible] have been placed at disposal of [illegible] are moving to [illegible] this [illegible] 1 Batt in [illegible] Reserve

From [illegible] Division
Place
Time 4.58 pm

The above may be forwarded as now corrected. (Z)

Censor. Signature of Addressor or person authorised to telegraph in his name.

*This line should be erased if not required.

(18965.) Wt. W12952/M1294. 187,500 Pads. 1/17 McC. & Co., Ltd. (E. 818.)

(in pads of 100)

MESSAGES AND SIGNALS. No. of Message..................

Prefix............Code..............m. | Words. | Charge.

Office of Origin and Service Instructions.

Priority

Sent
At..............m.
To..............
By..............

This message is on a/c of:
..........................*Service.*
....
(Signature of "Franking Officer.")

Recd. at..............m.
Date..............
From..............
By..............

TO { 86th Bde | 87th Bde | CRE | GD Pioneers

Sender's Number.	Day of Month.	In reply to Number.	AAA
* G481	3/5/17		

One Field Coy R.E. and two Pioneer Companies will be at the disposal of each Bde tonight for work on the new front line and communication trenches AAA 86. GD Pioneers will arrange to place one additional Company at the disposal of each Bde for the purpose AAA Connection between KISH trench and the Brickfield in CUBA should be made by the construction of intermediate strong points which can subsequently be connected by a continuous trench AAA Acknowledge

From GD Division
Place
Time 6.35 pm

The above may be forwarded as now corrected. (Z)
....
Censor. Signature of Addressor or person authorised to telegraph in his name.

* This line should be erased if not required.

(18965.) Wt. W12952/M1294. 187,500 Pads. 1/17 McC. & Co., Ltd. (E. 818.)

"C" Form.

MESSAGES AND SIGNALS.

Army Form C. 2123.
(In books of 100).

No. of Message

Prefix ... Code ... Words ... £ s. d. Charges to collect	Received. From ... By ...	Sent, or sent out. At ... m. To ... By ...	Office Stamp.

Office Stamp: ARMY ... TELEGRAPHS 3.V.17

Service Instructions.

Handed in at RRC Pronts [illegible] Office ... m. Received ... m.

TO ADO 9th Div

*Sender's Number	Day of Month	In reply to Number	AAA
RB283	3/5		

Divisions will consolidate and improve the positions held aaa Touch will be kept with the enemy by means of patrols aaa Addsd ado 4th And 9th Divns Repted 17th Div CorkA. and 13 Sqdn RFC

7.35pm

FROM
PLACE & TIME 17 Corps [illegible]

* This line should be erased if not required.

(6334). Wt. W7496/M857. 500,000 Pads. 10/16. D. D. & L. (E489). Forms C/2123/3.

"A" Form (in pads of 100).

MESSAGES AND SIGNALS.

No. of Message.................

Prefix..........Code..........m.	Words.	Charge.	This message is on a/c of:	Recd. at..........m.
Office of Origin and Service Instructions.	Sent		..........................Service.	Date..................
	At..............m.			From..................
	To..................			
	By..................		(Signature of "Franking Officer.")	By..................

TO 12th Bde CRE
11th Bde
CRA

Sender's Number.	Day of Month.	In reply to Number.	AAA
* G 783	3		

17th Corps will begin
Divisions will consolidate
and improve the positions
held aaa Touch will be
kept with the enemy by means
of patrols aaa
For information and necessary
action

From 4th Division
Place
Time 7.45 am

The above may be forwarded as now corrected. (Z)

Censor. Signature of Addressor or person authorised to telegraph in his name.

*This line should be erased if not required.

(18965.) Wt. W12952/M1294. 187,500 Pads. 1/17 McC. & Co., Ltd. (E. 318.)

9th Division

Spare Copies

War Diary

For [illegible]

Instructions regarding War Diaries and Intelligence Summaries are contained in F. S. Regs., Part II. and the Staff Manual respectively. Title pages will be prepared in manuscript.

WAR DIARY
or
INTELLIGENCE SUMMARY.
(Erase heading not required.)

Army Form C. 2118.

Place	Date	Hour	Summary of Events and Information	Remarks and references to Appendices
ETRUN	April 9th	3.35am	Message was received from 26th Inf. Bde reporting that they were ready for attack.	
		5.10am	South African Brigade reported verbally on telephone that they were ready for attack.	
		5.15am	Officer Commanding, 9th Seaforth Highlanders reported that all companies had arrived in battle positions and that H.Q. were established in SUNDAY AVENUE G.17.b.1.9.	
		5.26am	Message from 27th Bde (received 5.35 am) reporting that they were ready for attack.	
		5.30am	Barrage opened on German Trenches and assaulting waves left our trenches, enemy put up a number of "golden rain" rockets.	
		5.50am	Report received verbally that attack was well launched, and that all four companies of 8th Black Watch had crossed "No man's land" without a casualty.	
		5.55am	Report received from 52nd Bde. R.F.A. that attack was well launched, our barrage good. Enemy's barrage opened fire five minutes after ours on our front and support trenches.	
		6.17am	S.A. Brigade reported that hostile barrage was slight and that 4th South African Regiment had sent back 30 prisoners.	
		6.24am	27th Infantry Brigade reported that 12th Royal Scots had captured the German third trench	
		6.25am	Message received from 15th Division that they had captured FREDS WOOD.	
		6.30am	Reports were received from F.O.O. to the effect that our troops had been seen on 1st objective (BLACK LINE)	
		6.40am	F.O.O's reported BLACK LINE captured.	
		6.45am	Report sent to XV11 Corps that our troops had occupied BLACK LINE.	
		6.45am	Report received from 34th Division that their attack was progressing satisfactorily.	
		6.55am	51st Brigade R.F.A. reported that a batch of 200 prisoners was being sent back.	
		6.57am	C.R.A. reported that one battery from 29th and 50th Brigades was moving forward - XV11 Corps and 4th Division were informed of this action.	
		7.5 am	26th Infantry Brigade reported Black Watch had gained 1st objective with slight casualties.	
		7.10am	Red flares were reported burning in vicinity of BLACK LINE.	
		7.10am	Enemy commenced to shell BLACK LINE.	
		7.18am	F.O.O. of 52nd Artillery Brigade reported 400 prisoners taken and that a visual signalling station was established at BLANGY CEMETERY. Prisoners reported to be Bavarians and Prussians. The same source reported two Tanks crossing enemy's front line at 6.54 a.m.	
		7.26am	51st Division reported that they had captured BLACK LINE, at same time 34th Division reported that their troops had taken all of MAISON BLANCHE ridge.	
		7.34am	F.O.O. of 52nd Artillery Brigade reported that enemy had ceased firing on our front system.	

A5834 Wt. W4973/M687 750,000 8/16 D. D. & L. Ltd. Forms/C.2118/13.

Instructions regarding War Diaries and Intelligence Summaries are contained in F. S. Regs., Part II. and the Staff Manual respectively. Title pages will be prepared in manuscript.

WAR DIARY
or
INTELLIGENCE SUMMARY.
(Erase heading not required.)

Army Form C. 2118.

Place	Date	Hour	Summary of Events and Information	Remarks and references to Appendices
ETRUN	9th	7.40am	27th Infantry Brigade reported that so far the following prisoners had come in:- 19 of 28th Bavarian Reserve Regt.(belonging 1,2,3 and 4 companies) 4 of 1st M.G. Coy. 26th Bavarian R.I.R. 8th Bavarian Regt. 3rd Reserve Bavarian Pioneer Regt.	
		7.58am	Report received from 14th Brigade R.F.A. timed 7.50 am that our infantry appears to be advancing without difficulty.	
		8.4 am	15th Division reported enemy still holding out in BLANGY.	
		8.11am	C.R.A. reported that at request of left Brigade, 15th Division he was bombarding the Island at BLANGY which was still holding out. The island was eventually cleared by 2/Lieut. BRASH and a party of 7th Seaforth Highlanders. This officer took 20 Prussians prisoners assisted by his servant and another man.	
		8.17am	F.O.O. reported that our Infantry were moving well forward towards BLUE LINE behind our barrage.	
		8.20am	Message received from 15th Division to effect that an N.C.O. captured by 12th Division stated that enemy's main line is on WANCOURT - FEUCHY line and that we are at present dealing with rear guards.	
		8.40am	27th Infantry Brigade report from OBERMEYER GRABEN (BLACK LINE) states that men of 27th Infantry Brigade can be seen on RAILWAY EMBANKMENT (BLUE LINE). Nothing can be seen in cutting. At same time a report was received from C.R.A. that our Infantry were seen on railway bridge at H.8.c.00 northwards along cutting.	
		8.45am	Report received through C.R.A. from CHIMNEY O.P. in ARRAS that our men could be seen moving freely about on BLUE LINE. Capture of BLUE LINE reported by F.O.O. 50th Brigade R.F.A. timed 8.20 a.m.	
		8.50am	26th Infantry Brigade reported that two platoons, front company 7th Seaforth Highlanders are on BLUE LINE, others were advancing. Prisoners state no one escaped from BLUE LINE.	
		9.0 am	26th Infantry Brigade reported that attack was believed to be held up in front of BLUE LINE by heavy Trench Mortar fire from depression through which TEES TRENCH runs. This report was afterwards found to be incorrect.	
		9.15am	Report received from 26th Infantry Brigade to effect that 8th Black Watch had captured its portion of BLUE LINE and was in position on Ridge just East of BLUE LINE. The Regimental Commander of 8th Bavarian Regiment with his Adjutant were captured by 8th Black Watch.	

A5834 Wt. W4973/M687 750,000 8/16 D. D. & L. Ltd. Forms/C.2118/13.

Instructions regarding War Diaries and Intelligence Summaries are contained in F. S. Regs., Part II. and the Staff Manual respectively. Title pages will be prepared in manuscript.

WAR DIARY
or
INTELLIGENCE SUMMARY.
(Erase heading not required.)

Army Form C. 2118.

Place	Date	Hour	Summary of Events and Information	Remarks and references to Appendices
ETRUN	9th	10.16am	52nd Brigade R.F.A. reported that C/52 came into action at ARTILLERY TRENCH at 9.20 a and that 122 Battery had been ordered forward.	
		10.16am	C.R.A. reported that Batteries C/50, A/50,C/52 and 127 were in action at ARTILLERY TRENCH and that 122,126 and B./50 were moving up.	
		10.20am	B.G.,G.S. XVllth Corps informed us that so far we had gone through 2 battalions of 25th Regiment, prisoners reported that 3rd battalion was to have been brought up to RAILWAY (BLUE LINE) last night. If this is the case, we have wiped them out too. It is important to establish this fact, as if correct there would bo no one to oppose us.	
		10.21am.	Divisional Intelligence Officer reports that 17 officers and 650 other ranks have passed through Divisional Cage up to 9.20 a.m.	
		10.28am	Reports received from Artillery and South African Brigade that hostile aeroplanes continually flying low over BLUE LINE.	
		10.40am	The above was repeated to XVllth Corps.	
		11 am	Divisional Intelligence Officer reported that 25 officers and 1000 O.R. had passed through Divisional Cage.	
		11.45am	34th Division reported that their Right Brigade had got BLUE LINE and RAILWAY, Centre Brigade uncertain - men had been seen in B.25.d.9.6., Left Brigade 2 battalions in BLUE LINE, 2 battalions in BLACK LINE. Unable to advance North of GAUL WEG.	
		12.26pm	Following message received " Army Commander congratulates you on your success. Is important to press enemy, leaving any strong points to be dealt with by parties in rear. Time Table should be adhered to". This message was repeated to Brigades and C.R.A.	
		12.28pm	The situation with regards 15th Division was explained to General KENNEDY (26th Infantry Brigade) he was warned to watch hisRight Flank.	
		12.30pm	General KENNEDY (26th Infantry Brigade) asked if 12th Infantry Brigade could cover his advance from BLUE LINE.	
		12.30pm	Report received from 15th Division that they were held up short of the BLUE LINE on their left. Their artillery had been ordered on to line H.20.c.2.0 - H.19.d.5.4 - Eastern Edge of RAILWAY TRIANGLE and along embankment to River SCARPE. Their Infantry was to assault and capture BLUE LINE under cover of barrage at 12.10 pm. C.R.A. 9th Division reported that in view of the check to 15th Division he had arranged for Heavy Artillery to engage FEUCHY REDOUBT during our advance on to BROWN LINE and for a smoke barrage on our Right Flank to screen it from hostile observation from South of River SCARPE.	

Army Form C. 2118.

Instructions regarding War Diaries and Intelligence Summaries are contained in F. S. Regs., Part II. and the Staff Manual respectively. Title pages will be prepared in manuscript.

WAR DIARY
or
INTELLIGENCE SUMMARY.

(Erase heading not required.)

Place	Date	Hour	Summary of Events and Information	Remarks and references to Appendices
ETRUN	9th	12.50pm	27th Bde reported that three of its battalions were 300 strong, 4th battalion 350 strong. In view of this could a 4th Division Brigade support them in their attack on BROWN LINE.	
		12.52pm	C.R.A. reported that our Infantry could be seen advancing to BROWN LINE at 12.32 pm.	
		12.55pm	Sanction obtained from Corps for Brigade of 4th Division to support attack of 27th Brigade on BROWN LINE.	
		12.58pm	27th Infantry Brigade were informed that 12th Infantry Brigade would cover his advance from BLUE LINE.	
		1.8 pm	South African Brigade reported their H.Q. were moving forward to BLACK LINE G.12.d.7.3	
		1.8 pm	15th Division reported enemy retiring in large numbers East of FEUCHY CHAPELLE (H.5.a and H.4.d.) Teams thought to be enemy's guns seen retiring on ATHIES - FAMPOUX Road about 1 pm	
		1.24pm	Orders received from XV11 Corps for one Brigade 4th Division to support our advance on BROWN LINE.	
		1.29pm	26th Inf. Bde reported that our Infantry were past TEES TRENCH.	
		1.29pm	15th Division reported situation 12.40 pm 44th Infantry Brigade reached BLUE LINE South of RAILWAY, 45th Infantry Brigade, Left Battalion East of Railway in H.19.b. right battalion uncertain if east of railway or not, 46th Infantry Brigade will advance from BLUE LINE at 2 pm under artillery barrage as ordered for Zero plus 6 hours 40 minutes.	
		1.35pm	F.O.O. reported all going well, barrage good, good enemy observation obtained from HAYSTACK left (N) of POINT DU JOUR. No enemy retaliation, men very keen inclined to walk into barrage.	
		1.35 pm	32nd Bde. R.F.A. reported that no hostile shelling could be observed	
		1.50 pm	C.R.A. reported our men entering trench at H.9.a.4.0. Advance a little slower on Eastern edge of ATHIES	
		1.50 pm	34th Division reported verbally that from map dropped by aeroplane, flares were burning at H.14.b.9.2 and H.9.c.3.5 on the BROWN LINE.	

A5834 Wt. W4973/M687 750,000 8/16 D. D. & L. Ltd. Forms/C.2118/13.

Instructions regarding War Diaries and Intelligence Summaries are contained in F. S. Regs., Part II. and the Staff Manual respectively. Title pages will be prepared in manuscript.

WAR DIARY
or
INTELLIGENCE SUMMARY.
(Erase heading not required.)

Army Form C. 2118.

Place	Date	Hour	Summary of Events and Information	Remarks and references to Appendices
ETRUN	9th	2.0pm	C.R.A. reported that F.O.O. reported LAUREL, LIMPET and LILAC Trenches taken, the C.R.A. was informed that 11th Brigade was to support 27th Brigade. Barrage to left 4th Division to move through - original programme to be adhered to.	
		2.8pm	32nd Brigade R.F.A. reported enemy seen running from our barrage just West of GREEN LINE in H.10.d. and .c.	
		2.17pm	27th Infantry Brigade reported they had passed BROWN LINE and were now on GREEN LINE.	
		2.20pm	8th Black Watch report our troops have taken ATHIES.	
		2.30pm	XV11 Corps, 15th, 34th and 51st Divisions informed that from reports received it was indicated that BROWN LINE and ATHIES had been captured by 9th Division.	
		2.33pm	C.R.A. reported that enemy were retiring in H.9.d. central and along CAM and EFFIE trenches. G.O.C. instructed C.R.A. to put barrage on to FAMPOUX LINE - GREEN LINE to catch enemy.	
		2.33pm	A message timed 2 pm received from 51st Division stating it was reported they had captured their BROWN LINE. (information incorrect)	
		2.40pm	50th Brigade R.F.A. reported that enemy were retiring. BROWN LINE appeared to be in our possession. Our infantry advancing towards LE POINT DU JOUR. Enemy came into view to right (S) of LE POINT DU JOUR with intent to attack. They turned about and fled. Some of our patrols have now reached POINT DU JOUR	
		3.10pm	34th Division reported that according to map dropped by contact aeroplane at 2.15 pm flares on our front were burning at H.14.b.9.2 to H.9.c.3.5 (BROWN LINE)	
		3.10	26th Infantry Brigade reported verbally that their H.Q. were in SANITAS GRABEN	
		3.25pm	G.O.S. 9th Division handed over command of front to G.O.C. 4th Division on 4th Division passing through BROWN LINE.	
		3.42pm	26th Infantry Brigade instructed by G.S.O.1 not to move back from present positions until ordered and carry on with consolidation of BROWN LINE.	
		3.44"	South African Brigade reported that advance on BROWN LINE commenced at 12.35pm. Enemy barrage weak. Casualties slight. No further news.	
		3.44pm	Orders received from XV11 Corps for all remaining firing battery and first line wagons to move forward at once to wagon lines East of ANZIN. Divisional Ammunition Columns not to move until further orders.	
		4.26pm	15th and 34th Divisions informed that troops of 4th Division having passed through troops of 9th Division on BROWN LINE, G.O.C. 9th Division has handed over command to G.O.C. 4th Division.	
		4.45pm	Message received from XV11 Corps ordering 9th Division to reorganise in BLACK and BLUE lines.	

A5834 Wt. W4973/M687 750,000 8/16 D. D. & L. Ltd. Forms/C.2118/13.

Instructions regarding War Diaries and Intelligence Summaries are contained in F. S. Regs., Part II. and the Staff Manual respectively. Title pages will be prepared in manuscript.

WAR DIARY
or
INTELLIGENCE SUMMARY.
(Erase heading not required.)

Army Form C. 2118.

Place	Date	Hour	Summary of Events and Information	Remarks and references to Appendices
ETRUN	9th	4.50pm	Orders issued to Brigades to withdraw to the BLACK and BLUE lines. Boundaries between Brigades to remain as present.	
		6.10pm	34th Division reported their situation as being 102nd Infantry Brigade report situation as follows 2.40pm. One battalion in Western Trench of BROWN LINEfrom B.27.c.5.0 to B.27.c.5.5, 1 battalion of 101st Infantry Brigade on their immediate right. Enemy holds Eastern trenches of BROWN LINE not in great strength but is being slowly reinforced from BAILLEUL up SUNKEN ROAD. Have asked Heavy Artillery to shell this road and have increased rate of fire of protective barrage. East of Eastern Trench of BROWN LINE. No further information from Right Battalion of Right Brigade or from Left Brigade. 101st Brigade reinforcing his troops on BROWN LINE with one Battn. 102nd Infantry Brigade has no troops available to reinforce his BROWN LINE without unduly weakening BLUE LINE.	
		6.25pm	15th Division reported situation at 5.15pm was as follows. 2 left battalions, 46th Brigade in Northern portion of BROWN LINE, exact limits not known. Reports not received from right battalion which was attacking on front south of H.28.a.3.0 Brigade reports prisoners of 6th Prussian Regt and 30 men of 10th Grenadiers, 3 Trench Mortars, 1 Field Gun and 1 machine gun captured.	
		6.25pm	Message from 4th Division to effect that 11th Brigade has taken all its objectives including HYDERABAD REDOUBT,over 100 prisoners taken. Are being counter attacked by 2 battalions from direction of GAVRELLE. No report from 12th Brigade but a F.O.O. reports enemy now shelling eastern edge of FAMPOUX. Cavalry reported to have been seen at I.19.a.	
		6.35pm	Brigades were instructed to report as early as possible ~~with~~ when they were reorganised and what their approximate fighting strength is, in view of the possibility of being required to assist in repelling counter attack.	
		6.42pm	4th Division stated that F.O.O. 51st Brigade R.F.A. reported that at 4.17 pm our infantry in outskirts of FAMPOUX. Large number of prisoners and several 77 mm guns taken as well as ammunition and stores.	
		6.55pm	O.C. No. 3 Special Company personally reported that his battery of 4" Stokes Mortars fired 130 Thermite shells at Zero this morning.	
		7.45pm	Message from Corps Commander received "Commander in Chief wishes me to convey to you and your troops his hearty congratulations on their success today. This message was repeated to all units of 9th Division	

A5834 Wt. W4973/M687 750,000 8/16 D. D. & L. Ltd. Forms/C.2118/13.

Army Form C. 2118.

WAR DIARY
or
INTELLIGENCE SUMMARY.

(Erase heading not required.)

Instructions regarding War Diaries and Intelligence Summaries are contained in F. S. Regs., Part II. and the Staff Manual respectively. Title pages will be prepared in manuscript.

Place	Date	Hour	Summary of Events and Information	Remarks and references to Appendices
ETRUN	9th	8.7pm	Message from XV11 Corps to effect that contact aeroplane reports flares shown in H.16.d. central to H.11.a.central. Our men seen entering FAMPOUX and Battalion H.Q. established at West end of FAMPOUX. Many of our men seen in H.10.a. and H.10.b. but no flares. Independently of air report 4th Division report their men East of FAMPOUX.	
		8.25pm	Divisional Intelligence Officer reported 2000 prisoners through Divisional Prisoners Cage.	
		8.30pm	Message from Corps Commander received " Army Commander sends warm congratulations to troops XV11th Corps on finr work today. Am proud and delighted to convey these congratulatory messages.	
		9.30pm	Following message giving situation on our front was sent to 3 Infantry Brigades. 11th Infantry Brigade reports HYDERABAD REDOUBT definitely held. Counter attacks ceased. Not in touch with 12th Infantry Brigade on GREEN LINE but have formed defensive flank. Reported FAMPOUX not taken. Enemy reported entrenched South of GAVRELLE road from H.3.d.7.3 to H.4.d.0.1 and thence in trench running due East. Also reported enemy entrenching N. side of GAVRELLE - ROEUX road from I.7.a.1.9 to I.7.c.7.0	
		9.30pm	26th, 27th and S.A. Bdes were informed that 11th Brigade reports that HYDERABAD REDOUBT definitely held, counter attacks ceased. Not in touch with 12th Infantry Brigade on GREEN LINE but have formed defensive flank. reported FAMPOUX not taken. Enemy reported entrenches S. of GAVRELLE Rd from H.3.d.7.3 to H.4.d.0.1 and thence into trench running due East. Also reported enemy entrenching N. side of GAVRELLE- ROEUX road from I-7.a.1.9 to I.7.c.7.0	
		9.35pm	26th Infantry Brigade reported their H.Q. established at FORRESTIER REDOUBT at 9 p.m.	
		9.45pm	South African Brigade was asked if troops had plenty of ammunition and if they were back on BLUE and BLACK lines. Replied "Yes" to both questions.	
		9.50pm	South African Brigade reported their H.Q. established at No. 23 dugout G.11.d.9.2	

A5834 Wt. W4973/M687 750,000 8/16 D. D. & L. Ltd. Forms/C.2118/13.

Instructions regarding War Diaries and Intelligence Summaries are contained in F. S. Regs., Part II. and the Staff Manual respectively. Title pages will be prepared in manuscript.

Army Form C. 2118.

WAR DIARY
or
INTELLIGENCE SUMMARY.
(Erase heading not required.)

Place	Date	Hour	Summary of Events and Information	Remarks and references to Appendices
ETRUN	9th	9.50pm	26th Infantry Brigade were askedif their situation with regards ammunition was satisfactoryy, replied "Yes".	
		11.50pm	Message received from XVIIth Corps to effect that Corps Commander might have to relieve 34th Division by 9th Division, but would not do so if he could possibly help it. Meanwhile 9th Division should press on with repairs of ST LAURENT BLANGY and GAVRELLE Roads. Men to be employed in short shifts so as not to tire them.	
		11.55pm	Corps stating that O.C. TANKS had been instructed to apply to Infantry Brigade for assistance in moving TANK which had got stuck. Only a few men required.	

Instructions regarding War Diaries and Intelligence Summaries are contained in F. S. Regs., Part II. and the Staff Manual respectively. Title pages will be prepared in manuscript.

WAR DIARY
or
INTELLIGENCE SUMMARY.
(Erase heading not required.)

Army Form C. 2118.

Place	Date	Hour	Summary of Events and Information	Remarks and references to Appendices
ETRUN	12th	12.50am	Message received from XV11 Corps saying that 4th Division was to place one Infantry Brigade at disposal of 9th Division for operations on 12th. 4th Division placed 10th Infantry Brigade at our disposal. It snowed heavily during the night and by morning there was about three inches of snow on the ground, this had all disappeared by midday.	
		2.15am	9th Division G.483 giving orders for operations to be carried out tomorrow afternoon issued to all concerned.	
		8.30am	G.O.C. 9th Division met the Brigadiers of the three Infantry Brigades at the H.Q. of 27th Infantry Brigade in OBERMEYER GRABEN. The G.O.C. explained the situation and the plan of operations. The Brigadiers proceeded to reconnoitre the ground.	
		11 am	Message received from XV11 Corps sanctioning the use of a Field Company (9th Division) at present employed on repair of BLANGY road, for operations this afternoon.	
ST. NICHOLAS		11 am	H.Q. 9th Division closed at ETRUN and opened at ST NICHOLAS.	
		11.45am	Message received from South African Brigade stating that men have had no sleep for four nights and no hot food since 8th; with these facts in view it was doubtful if men were in a fit condition for severe operations. The G.O.C. represented the above situation of South African Brigade to the Corps Commander, who replied that if attack was delayed we would not have such a heavy concentration of artillery to support our attack tomorrow.	
		1.26pm	Message received from XV11 Corps timed 12.50 pm saying that ultimate objective of XV11 Corps was GREENLAND HILL and the spur S.W. of PLOUVAIN. If after capture of todays objective it appears possible to secure further objectives, it was important that this should be done as otherwise they would have to be attacked the next day.	
		2.43pm	Message timed 2.43pm from 4th Division giving situation of German trenches on their front as ascertained by aerial reconnaissance.	
		4 pm	Message from 27th Infantry Brigade timed 3.10 pm received stating that as Brigade had to advance 1750 yards in full view before reaching opening line of barrage, might a smoke barrage be put down at Zero - 45 minutes.	

A5834 Wt. W4973/M687 750,000 8/16 D. D. & L. Ltd. Forms/C.2118/13.

Army Form C. 2118.

Instructions regarding War Diaries and Intelligence Summaries are contained in F. S. Regs., Part II. and the Staff Manual respectively. Title pages will be prepared in manuscript.

WAR DIARY
or
INTELLIGENCE SUMMARY.
(Erase heading not required.)

Place	Date	Hour	Summary of Events and Information	Remarks and references to Appendices
			Instructions to this effect was sent to C.R.A. by S.D.R. and verbally by a Staff Officer but these arrived too late for action to be taken.	
			Message from XV11 Corps timed 3.50 pm stating that air reconnaissance at 12.20pm today shows trench newly made on line H.18.c.9.6 - H.18.b.3.4 and H.18.b.8.4 - H.12.b.5.0 - H.12.b.8.0 - H.6.d.5.0 - H.6.c.8.8. This was received too late for any action to be taken.	
		4.23pm	F.O.O. 51st Bde R.F.A. reported a hostile 6 gun battery in action on the road from C.28.d.7.0 to I.4.a.7.5. Corps H.A. were informed.	
		4.50pm	The enemy to whom the forming up of assaulting troops was visible commenced to put down a barrage.	
		5 pm	Zero. - Our artillery opened barrage and infantry advanced. Barrage was thickened by fire from machine gun companies	
		5.45pm	Verbal message from South African Brigade that General DAWSON who was on the GREEN LINE could see no signs of 1st objective having been taken.	
		5.55pm	26th Infantry Brigade reported that Colonel BROWN (5th Cameron Highlanders) on GREEN LINE with General MAXWELL (27th Inf. Bde) can see no signs of the 1st objective being taken and cannot therefore take CAMERONS through.	
		6 pm	C.R.A. reported that message from F.O.O. 51st Bde. R.F.A. timed 5.25 pm states all our Infantry have come back.	
		6.7pm	XV11 Corps were informed of the above report	
		6.15pm	C.R.A. reported that attack apparently failed. Enemy holding trench H.12.b. and .d. parallel to GAVRELLE road. Was starting again at Zero plus 70. Wished slow rate of fire from Heavy Artillery until he knew that second phase had started.	
		6.30pm	Corps H.A. were informed of above	

Army Form C. 2118.

Instructions regarding War Diaries and Intelligence Summaries are contained in F. S. Regs., Part II. and the Staff Manual respectively. Title pages will be prepared in manuscript.

WAR DIARY
or
INTELLIGENCE SUMMARY.
(Erase heading not required.)

Place	Date	Hour	Summary of Events and Information	Remarks and references to Appendices
ST NICHOLAS	12th	6.20pm	51st Bde R.F.A. reported that F.O.O. saw wounded within 10 yards of 1st objective. Thought our troops had gained objective. Could not say if wounded were South Africans, or men of 27th Infantry Brigade. C.R.A. was going to stop bombardment on second objective until situation more certain.	
		6.30pm	27th Inf. Bde and S.A. Bde informed that observers of 17th Division, south of the River report that our men at 6.20pm on north reached GAVRELLE - ROEUX road between CHEMICAL WORKS and cross roads I.7.a.4.4 still advancing, white light sent up from Northern edge of ROUEX. 7.10pm Prisoners coming from direction of GAVRELLE - ROEUX road. Red flares seen at I.7.d.6.5. 11th Brigade also reported that our attack appeared to have progressed on the right and its possible that we have reached ROEUX. - GAVRELLE road. Brigades were to report whether there can be any foundation for these reports.	
		7.10pm	Report from 27th Brigade timed 6.30pm. Attack has not progressed beyond the bottom of the valley. Enemy are firing lights from the new trench the position of which reached me 20 minutes ago. Enemy barrage good, but machine gun fire appears to be holding us up. Do not know what progress the South African Brigade is making, but think that they have not succeeded as enemy lights can be seen fired from a short way in front of FAMPOUX.	
		7.30pm	XV11 Corps and South African Brigade, & C.R.A. informed of above.	
		8 pm	General TUDOR (C.R.A.) reported that Colonel WICKHAM commanding 14th Bde R.H.A. reports at 4.30pm our infantry advanced from H.10 and 11 and immediately came under long range machine gun fire from trench which runs from the curve of the river in front of MOUNT PLEASANT. They lost heavily and appeared to have no chance, only way to deal with this to get close up and pound trench. There are a lot of machine guns.	
		8.20pm	message from South African Brigade timed 7 pm stated that attack had failed. Very many casualties have been caused by machine gun fire from CHEMICAL WORKS and direction of MOUNT PLEASANT WOOD. Attacking troops reached a point slightly in advance of that reached yesterday, but no movement of any kind could be seen at 7.30pm. 3rd S.A.I. report approximate strength 360 still intact and in western edge of FAMPOUX. Asked for instructions regarding further action.	

A5834 Wt. W4973/M687 750,000 8/16 D. D. & L. Ltd. Forms/C.2118/13.

Army Form C. 2118.

Instructions regarding War Diaries and Intelligence Summaries are contained in F. S. Regs., Part II. and the Staff Manual respectively. Title pages will be prepared in manuscript.

WAR DIARY
or
INTELLIGENCE SUMMARY.
(Erase heading not required.)

Place	Date	Hour	Summary of Events and Information	Remarks and references to Appendices
ST NICHOLAS	12th	8.45pm	South African Brigade and 27th Infantry Brigade informed that 26th Infantry Brigade would take over line from HYDERABAD REDOUBT to the RIVER and that on relief these Brigades would come into German 4th line trench system in support. The 26th Infantry Brigade was informed of this order verbally. Reports from 17th Division during the evening that our troops reached the first objective, these reports were incorrect.	
		10.40pm	26th Inf. Bde and South African Brigade informed that 17th Division onour right South of the RIVER SCARPE were sending out patrols to try and gain touch with our right flank, the patrol would cross railway bridge at H.24.a.	
		11 pm	Orders were issued for 26th Infantry Brigade to take over tonight the front line from River SCARPE to HYDERABAD REDOUBT (exclusive). The 4th Division were continuing to hold line from HYDERABAD REDOUBT to H.4.b.8.5 boundary between 4th and 9th Divisions to be HOARY and HECTIC TRENCHES thence a line to cross roads at H.15.a.9.9 thence to ATHIES - ST LAURENT BLANGY Road. South African Brigade on relief to withdraw to FAMPOUX and German 4th system South of the FAMPOUX - ATHIES Road. The 27th Infantry Brigade on relief to withdraw to the German 4th line system North of the FAMPOUX - ATHIES Road where ground has been gained in front of the original front line, the new line to be consolidated provided the troops holding it are not isolated. In cases where troops are isolated, they were to be withdrawn to the best line that would enable connection to be maintained with troops on flanks. Details of relief were to be arranged direct between B.G.O's C. 26th Bde and B.G's C. 27th, S.A. 10th and 12th Brigades. In addition the 26th Brigade was to arrange to place a proportion of vickers guns in the front line to meet and break up any possible counter attack. The 197th Machine Gun Company was placed at the disposal of B.G.C. 26th Infantry Brigade.	
		11.20pm	Instructions were received from XV11 Corps to harry the enemy with incessant machine gun and rifle fire and to interfere with the enemy's consolidation by every means in their power.	

A5834 Wt. W4973/M687 750,000 8/16 D. D. & L. Ltd. Forms/C.2118/13.

Instructions regarding War Diaries and Intelligence Summaries are contained in F. S. Regs., Part II. and the Staff Manual respectively. Title pages will be prepared in manuscript.

Army Form C. 2118.

WAR DIARY
or
INTELLIGENCE SUMMARY.

(Erase heading not required.)

Place	Date	Hour	Summary of Events and Information	Remarks and references to Appendices
ETRUN	12th	12.50am	Message received from XV11 Corps saying that 4th Division was to place one Infantry Brigade at disposal of 9th Division for operations on 12th. 4th Division placed 10th Infantry Brigade at our disposal. It snowed heavily during the night and by morning there was about three inches of snow on the ground, this had all disappeared by midday.	
		2.15am	9th Division G.483 giving orders for operations to be carried out tomorrow afternoon issued to all concerned.	
		8.30am	G.O.C. 9th Division met the Brigadiers of the three Infantry Brigades at the H.Q. of 27th Infantry Brigade in OBERMEYER GRABEN. The G.O.C. explained the situation and the plan of operations. The Brigadiers proceeded to reconnoitre the ground.	
		11 am	Message received from XV11 Corps sanctioning the use of a Field Company (9th Division) at present employed on repair of BLANGY road, for operations this afternoon.	
ST. NICHOLAS		11 am	H.Q. 9th Division closed at ETRUN and opened at ST NICHOLAS.	
		11.45am	Message received from South African Brigade stating that men have had no sleep for four nights and no hot food since 8th; with these facts in view it was doubtful if men were in a fit condition for severe operations. The G.O.C. represented the above situation of South African Brigade to the Corps Commander, who replied that if attack was delayed we would not have such a heavy concentration of artillery to support our attack tomorrow.	
		1.26pm	Message received from XV11 Corps timed 12.50 pm saying that ultimate objective of XV11 Corps was GREENLAND HILL and the spur S.W. of PLOUVAIN. If after capture of todays objective it appears possible to secure further objectives, it was important that this should be done as otherwise they would have to be attacked the next day.	
		2.43pm	Message timed 2.43pm from 4th Division giving situation of German trenches on their front as ascertained by aerial reconnaissance.	
		4 pm	Message from 27th Infantry Brigade timed 3.10 pm received stating that as Brigade had to advance 1750 yards in full view before reaching opening line of barrage, might a smoke barrage be put down at Zero - 45 minutes.	

A5834 Wt. W4973/M687 750,000 8/16 D. D. & L. Ltd. Forms/C.2118/13.

Instructions regarding War Diaries and Intelligence Summaries are contained in F. S. Regs., Part II. and the Staff Manual respectively. Title pages will be prepared in manuscript.

WAR DIARY
or
INTELLIGENCE SUMMARY.
(Erase heading not required.)

Army Form C. 2118.

Place	Date	Hour	Summary of Events and Information	Remarks and references to Appendices
			Instructions to this effect was sent to C.R.A. by S.D.R. and verbally by a Staff Officer but these arrived too late for action to be taken. Message from XV11 Corps timed 3.50 pm stating that air reconnaissance at 12.20pm today shows trench newly made on line H.18.c.9.6 - H.18.b.3.4 and H.18.b.8.4 - H.12.b.5.0 - H.12.b.8.0 - H.6.d.5.0 - H.6.c.8.8. This was received too late for any action to be taken.	
		4.25pm	F.O.O. 51st Bde R.F.A. reported a hostile 6 gun battery in action on the road from C.28.d.7.0 to I.4.a.7.5. Corps H.A. were informed.	
		4.50pm	The enemy to whom the forming up of assaulting troops was visible commenced to put down a barrage.	
		5 pm	Zero. - Our artillery opened barrage and infantry advanced. Barrage was thickened by fire from machine gun companies	
		5.45pm	Verbal message from South African Brigade that General DAWSON who was on the GREEN LINE could see no signs of 1st objective having been taken.	
		5.55pm	26th Infantry Brigade reported that Colonel BROWN (5th Cameron Highlanders) on GREEN LINE with General MAXWELL (27th Inf. Bde) can see no signs of the 1st objective being taken and cannot therefore take CAMERONS through.	
		6 pm	C.R.A. reported that message from F.O.O. 51st Bde. R.F.A. timed 5.25 pm states all our Infantry have come back.	
		6.7pm	XV11 Corps were informed of the above report	
		6.15pm	C.R.A. reported that attack apparently failed. Enemy holding trench H.12.b. and .d. parallel to GAVRELLE road. Was starting again at Zero plus 70. Wished slow rate of fire from Heavy Artillery until he knew that second phase had started.	
		6.30pm	Corps H.A. were informed of above	

A5834 Wt. W4973/M687 750,000 8/16 D. D. & L. Ltd. Forms/C.2118/13.

Army Form C. 2118.

Instructions regarding War Diaries and Intelligence Summaries are contained in F. S. Regs., Part II. and the Staff Manual respectively. Title pages will be prepared in manuscript.

WAR DIARY
or
INTELLIGENCE SUMMARY.
(Erase heading not required.)

Place	Date	Hour	Summary of Events and Information	Remarks and references to Appendices
ST NICHOLAS	12th	6.20pm	51st Bde R.F.A. reported that F.O.O. saw wounded within 10 yards of 1st objective. Thought our troops had gained objective. Could not say if wounded were South Africans, or men of 27th Infantry Brigade. C.R.A. was going to stop bombardment on second objective until situation more certain.	
		6.30pm	27th Inf. Bde and S.A. Bde informed that observers of 17th Division, south of the River report that our men at 6.20pm on north reached GAVRELLE - ROEUX road between CHEMICAL WORKS and cross roads I.7.a.4.4 still advancing, white light sent up from Northern edge of ROUEX. 7.10pm Prisoners coming from direction of GAVRELLE - ROEUX road. Red flares seen at I.7.d.6.5. 11th Brigade also reported that our attack appeared to have progressed on the right and it is possible that we have reached ROEUX. - GAVRELLE road. Brigades were to report whether there can be any foundation for these reports.	
		7.10pm	Report from 27th Brigade timed 6.30pm. Attack has not progressed beyond the bottom of the valley. Enemy are firing lights from the new trench the position of which reached me 20 minutes ago. Enemy barrage good, but machine gun fire appears to be holding us up. Do not know what progress the South African Brigade is making, but think that they have not succeeded as enemy lights can be seen fired from a short way in front of FAMPOUX.	
		7.30pm	XVII Corps and South African Brigade, CRA informed of above.	
		8 pm	General TUDOR (C.R.A.) reported that Colonel WICKHAM commanding 14th Bde R.H.A. reports at 4.30pm our infantry advanced from H.10 and 11 and immediately came under long range machine gun fire from trench which runs from the curve of the river in front of MOUNT PLEASANT. They lost heavily and appeared to have no chance, only way to deal with this to get close up and pound trench. There are a lot of machine guns.	
		8.20pm	message from South African Brigade timed 7 pm stated that attack had failed. Very many casualties have been caused by machine gun fire from CHEMICAL WORKS and direction of MOUNT PLEASANT WOOD. Attacking troops reached a point slightly in advance of that reached yesterday, but no movement of any kind could be seen at 7.30pm. 3rd S.A.I. report approximate strength 280 still intact and in western edge of FAMPOUX. Asked for instructions regarding further action.	

A5834 Wt. W4973/M687 750,000 8/16 D. D. & L. Ltd. Forms/C.2118/13.

Instructions regarding War Diaries and Intelligence Summaries are contained in F. S. Regs., Part II. and the Staff Manual respectively. Title pages will be prepared in manuscript.

WAR DIARY
or
INTELLIGENCE SUMMARY.
(Erase heading not required.)

Army Form C. 2118.

Place	Date	Hour	Summary of Events and Information	Remarks and references to Appendices
ST NICHOLAS	12th	8.45pm	South African Brigade and 27th Infantry Brigade informed that 26th Infantry Brigade would take over line from HYDERABAD REDOUBT to the RIVER and that on relief these Brigades would come into German 4th line trench system in support. The 26th Infantry Brigade was informed of this order verbally. Reports from 17th Division during the evening that our troops reached the first objective, these reports were incorrect.	
		10.40pm	26th Inf. Bde and South African Brigade informed that 17th Division onour right South of the RIVER SCARPE were sending out patrols to try and gain touch with our right flank, the patrol would cross railway bridge at H.24.a.	
		11 pm	Orders were issued for 26th Infantry Brigade to take over tonight the front line from River SCARPE to HYDERABAD REDOUBT (exclusive). The 4th Division were continuing to hold line from HYDERABAD REDOUBT to H.4.b.6.5. boundary between 4th and 9th Divisions to be HOARY and MOCHIC TRENCHES. South African Brigade on relief to withdraw to FAMPOUX and German 4th system South of the FAMPOUX - ATHIES Road. The 27th Infantry Brigade on relief to withdraw to the German 4th line system North of the FAMPOUX - ATHIES Road where ground has been gained in front of the original front line, the new line to be consolidated provided the troops holding it are not isolated. In cases where troops are isolated, they were to be withdrawn to the best line that would enable connection to be maintained with troops on flanks. Details of relief were to be arranged direct between B.G.C's C. 26th Bde and B.G's C. 27th, S.A. 10th and 12th Brigades. In addition the 26th Brigade was to arrange to place a proportion of vickers guns in the front line to meet and break up any possible counter attack. The 197th Machine Gun Company was placed at the disposal of B.G.C. 26th Infantry Brigade.	
		11.20pm	Instructions were received from XV11 Corps to harry the enemy with incessant machine gun and rifle fire and to interfere with the enemy's consolidation by every means in their power.	

A5834 Wt. W4973/M687 750,000 8/16 D. D. & L. Ltd. Forms/C.2118/13.

Instructions regarding War Diaries and Intelligence Summaries are contained in F. S. Regs., Part II. and the Staff Manual respectively. Title pages will be prepared in manuscript.

WAR DIARY
or
INTELLIGENCE SUMMARY.
(Erase heading not required.)

Army Form C. 2118.

Place	Date	Hour	Summary of Events and Information	Remarks and references to Appendices
ETRUN	12th	12.5am	Message received from 17th Corps saying that 4th Division was to place one Infantry Brigade at disposal of 9th Division for operation on 12th. 4th Division placed 10th Infantry Brigade at our disposal. It snowed heavily during the night and by morning there was about 3 inches of snow on the ground, this had all disappeared by midday.	
		2.15am	9th Division G 483 giving orders for operation to be carried out to-morrow afternoon issued to all concerned.	
		8.30am	G.O.C 9th Division met the Brigadiers of the three Infantry Brigades at the Head Quarters of 27th Infantry Brigade in OBERMEYER GRABEN. The G.O.C explained the situation and the plan of operations. The Brigadiers proceeded to reconnoitre the ground.	
		11am	Message received from 17th Corps sanctioning the use of a Field Company (9th Division), at present employed on repair of BLANGY road, for operations this afternoon.	
St NICHOLAS		11am	Head Quarters 9th Division closed at ETRUN and open at St NICHOLAS.	
		11.45	Message received from South African Brigade stating that men have had no sleep for four nights and no hot food since 8th, with these facts in view it was doubtful if men were	

Instructions regarding War Diaries and Intelligence Summaries are contained in F. S. Regs., Part II. and the Staff Manual respectively. Title pages will be prepared in manuscript.

WAR DIARY
or
INTELLIGENCE SUMMARY.
(Erase heading not required.)

Army Form C. 2118.

Place	Date	Hour	Summary of Events and Information	Remarks and references to Appendices
			in a fit condition for severe operations.	
			The G.O.C represented the above situation of South African Brigade to the Corps Commander, who replied that if attack was delayed we would not have ~~should~~ such a heavy concentration of artillery to support our attack to-morrow.	
		1.26	Message received from 17th Corps timed 12.50 a.m saying that ultimate objective of 17th Corps was GREENLAND HILL and the open S.W of PLOUVAIN. If after capture of to-days objective it appears possible to secure further objectives it was important that this should be done as otherwise they would have to be attacked the next day.	
		2.43	Message timed 2.43 from 4th Division giving situation of German trenches on their front as ascertained by aerial reconnaissance.	
		4 pm	Message from 27th Infantry Brigade timed 3.10 pm received stating that as Brigade had to advance 1750 yards in full view before they reached opening line of barrage might a smoke barrage be put down at Zero – 45 minutes. Instructions to this effect were sent to C.R.A & S.D.R and verbally by a Staff Officer but	

A5834 Wt. W4973/M687 750,000 8/16 D. D. & L. Ltd. Forms/C.2118/13.

Army Form C. 2118.

Instructions regarding War Diaries and Intelligence Summaries are contained in F. S. Regs., Part II. and the Staff Manual respectively. Title pages will be prepared in manuscript.

WAR DIARY
or
INTELLIGENCE SUMMARY.
(Erase heading not required.)

Place	Date	Hour	Summary of Events and Information	Remarks and references to Appendices
			but these arrived too late for action to be taken.	
			message from 17th Corps timed 3.50 p.m. stating that air reconnaissance at 12.20 p.m. to-day shows trench newly made on line H.18.c.9.6 – H.19.b.3.4 and H.18.b.8.4 – H.12.b.5.0 – H.12.b.8.0 – H.6.d.5.0 – H.6.c.8.8 this was received too late for any action to be taken.	
		~~5.10~~ 4.23	7.0.0 51st Brigade R.F.A. reported a hostile 6 gun battery in action on the road from C.28.d.7.0 to I.4.a.7.5. Corps Heavy Artillery are informed.	
		4.50	The enemy to whom the forming up of assaulting troops was visible commenced to put down a barrage.	
		5 p.m.	Zero – our artillery opened barrage and infantry advanced. Barrage was thickened by fire from four machine gun companies.	
		5.45	verbal message from South African Brigade that General DAWSON who was on the GREEN LINE could see no signs of 1st objective having been ~~reached~~ taken.	

A5834 Wt. W4973/M687 750,000 8/16 D. D. & L. Ltd. Forms/C.2118/13.

Instructions regarding War Diaries and Intelligence Summaries are contained in F. S. Regs., Part II. and the Staff Manual respectively. Title pages will be prepared in manuscript.

WAR DIARY
or
INTELLIGENCE SUMMARY.
(Erase heading not required.)

Army Form C. 2118.

Place	Date	Hour	Summary of Events and Information	Remarks and references to Appendices
		5.55	26th Infantry Brigade reported that Colonel BROWN (5th Cameron Highlanders) on GREEN LINE with General MAXWELL (27th Inf Bde) can see no signs of the 1st objective having been taken and cannot therefore send Camerons through.	
		6 pm	C.R.A reported that message from F.O.O. 51st Brigade R.F.A ~~[illegible]~~ timed 5.25 pm states our infantry have all come back.	
		6.7	17th Corps were informed of above report.	
		6.15	C.R.A reported that attack apparently failed. Enemy holding trench H.12.b and d parallel to GAVRELLE Road. Was starting again at Zero plus 70. Wished slow rate of fire from Heavy Artillery until he knows that second phase has started.	
		6.30 pm	Corps Heavy Artillery informed of above.	
		6.20	51st Brigade R.F.A reported that F.O.O. saw wounded within 10 yards of 1st Objective. Thought our troops have gained objective. Could not say if wounded were South Africans	

A5834 Wt. W4973/M687 750,000 8/16 D. D. & L. Ltd. Forms/C.2118/13.

Instructions regarding War Diaries and Intelligence Summaries are contained in F. S. Regs., Part II. and the Staff Manual respectively. Title pages will be prepared in manuscript.

WAR DIARY
or
INTELLIGENCE SUMMARY.
(Erase heading not required.)

Army Form C. 2118.

Place	Date	Hour	Summary of Events and Information	Remarks and references to Appendices
			or men of 27th Infantry Brigade. C.R.A. was going to stop bombardment on second objective until situation more certain.	
		6.30	27th and South African Brigades informed that observers of 17th Division, south of the River report that our men at 6.20 pm on north reached GAVRELLE – ROEUX road between CHEMICAL WORKS and cross roads I.7.a.4.4 still advancing, white light sent up from northern edge of ROEUX. 7.10 pm Prisoners coming in from direction of GAVRELLE – ROEUX road. Red flares seen at I.7.d.6.5. 11th Brigade also reported that our attack appeared to have ~~gained~~ progressed on the right and it is probable we have reached ROEUX – GAVRELLE road. Brigades were to report whether there can be any foundation for these reports.	
		7.10	Report from 27th Infantry Brigade timed 6.30 pm " attack has not progressed beyond the bottom of the valley. Enemy are firing lights from the new trench the position of which reached me 20 minutes ago. Enemy's barrage good but machine gun fire appears to be holding us up. Do not know what progress the South African Brigade is making	

A5834 Wt. W4973/M687 750,000 8/16 D. D. & L. Ltd. Forms/C.2118/13.

Instructions regarding War Diaries and Intelligence Summaries are contained in F. S. Regs., Part II. and the Staff Manual respectively. Title pages will be prepared in manuscript.

WAR DIARY
or
INTELLIGENCE SUMMARY.
(Erase heading not required.)

Army Form C. 2118.

Place	Date	Hour	Summary of Events and Information	Remarks and references to Appendices
			but think that they have not succeeded as enemy lights can be seen fired from a short way in front of FAMPOUX.	
		7.30	17th Corps, 26th and South African Brigades informed of above.	
		8pm	General TUDOR (C.R.A.) reported that Colonel WICKHAM commanding 14th Brigade R.H.A. reports at 4.30pm our infantry advanced from H.10 and 11 and immediately came under long range machine gun fire from trench which runs from the curve of the river in front of MOUNT PLEASANT. They lost heavily. Appeared to have no chance. Only way to deal with this to get close up and pound trench. There are a lot of machine guns.	
		8.20pm	Message from South African Brigade, timed 7pm stated that attack had failed. Very many casualties had been caused by machine gun fire from CHEMICAL WORKS and direction of MOUNT PLEASANT WOOD. Attacking troops reached a point slightly in advance of that reached yesterday but no movement of any kind could be seen at 7.30pm. 3rd S.A. Inf report approximate strength 260 still intact and in western edge of FAMPOUX. asked for instructions regarding further action.	

A5834 Wt. W4973/M687 750,000 8/16 D. D. & L. Ltd. Forms/C.2118/13.

Instructions regarding War Diaries and Intelligence Summaries are contained in F. S. Regs., Part II. and the Staff Manual respectively. Title pages will be prepared in manuscript.

WAR DIARY
or
INTELLIGENCE SUMMARY.
(Erase heading not required.)

Army Form C. 2118.

Place	Date	Hour	Summary of Events and Information	Remarks and references to Appendices
		8.45	South African Brigade and 27th Infantry Brigade informed that 26th Infantry Brigade would take over line from HYDERABAD REDOUBT to the RIVER and that on relief these Brigades would come into German 4th Line trench system in support.	
			The 26th Infantry Brigade was informed of this order verbally.	
			Reports from 17th Division during the evening stated that our troops reached the first objective, these reports were incorrect.	
		10.40	26th Infantry Brigade and South African Brigade informed that 17th Division on our right South of the RIVER SCARPE were sending out patrols to try and gain touch with our right flank, the patrol would cross railway bridge at H.24.a.	
		11pm	Orders were issued for 26th Infantry Brigade to take over to night the front line from RIVER SCARPE to HYDERABAD REDOUBT (exclusive). The 4th Division was continuing to hold line from HYDERABAD REDOUBT to H.4.b.8.5. Boundary between 4th and 9th Divisions to be HOARY + HECTIC TRENCHES	

Instructions regarding War Diaries and Intelligence Summaries are contained in F. S. Regs., Part II. and the Staff Manual respectively. Title pages will be prepared in manuscript.

WAR DIARY
or
INTELLIGENCE SUMMARY.
(Erase heading not required.)

Army Form C. 2118.

Place	Date	Hour	Summary of Events and Information	Remarks and references to Appendices
			thence a line to cross roads at H.15.a.9.9 thence the ATHIES - St LAURENT BLANGY road. South African Brigade on relief to withdraw to FAMPOUX and German 4th line system south of the FAMPOUX - ATHIES road. The 27th Infantry Brigade on relief to withdraw to the German 4th line system north of the FAMPOUX - ATHIES road and to ATHIES. Where ground has been gained in front of the original front line the new line to be consolidated provided the troops holding it were not isolated. In cases where troops were isolated they were to be withdrawn to the best line which would enable connection to be maintained with troops on flanks. Details of relief were to be arranged direct between B.G.G.S. 26th B^de and B.G.S.G. 27th, S.A, 10th and 12th Brigades. In addition the 26th Brigade was to arrange to place a proportion of VICKERS guns in the front line to meet and break up any possible counter attack. The 197th Machine Gun Company was placed at disposal of B.G.C 26th Infantry Brigade	
		11.20	Instructions were received from 17th Corps to harry the enemy with incessant machine gun and rifle fire and to interfere with the enemys consolidation by every means in their power.	

A5834 Wt. W4973/M687 750,000 8/16 D. D. & L. Ltd. Forms/C.2118/13.

Instructions regarding War Diaries and Intelligence Summaries are contained in F. S. Regs., Part II. and the Staff Manual respectively. Title pages will be prepared in manuscript.

WAR DIARY
or
INTELLIGENCE SUMMARY.
(Erase heading not required.)

Army Form C. 2118.

Place	Date	Hour	Summary of Events and Information	Remarks and references to Appendices
RAILWAY CUTTING ST. LAURENT BLANGY	3rd May 1917	3.45am	ZERO hour, our artillery put down barrage and assaulting Infantry advanced.	
		4.1am	A message timed 3.30 am was received from 27th Infantry Brigade reporting that movement into assembly area was complete.	
		4.10am	32nd Bde. R.F.A. reported that enemy was putting down heavy barrage all along our front line. The same Brigade reported heavy rifle and machine gun fire on our front about half an hour later.	
		4.15am	F.O.O. reported that there had been no hostile lights for last ten minutes. Heavy M.G. fire from south of RIVER. Enemy barrage commenced about 3 minutes after ZERO.	
		4.55 am	Report from 32nd Bde. R.F.A. (timed 4.35) stated that hostile lights were going up further East.	
		4.55 am	General KENNEDY (26th Inf. Bde) reported that his Brigade observer reported that enemy's Very Lights were being sent up from much further EAST. Hostile barrage had slackened considerably. A certain amount of M.G. fire from RIGHT. It was still too dark for observation.	
		5.3 am	31st Division (on our LEFT) reported our barrage opened at 3.45 am. Enemy appeared slow in replying. Enemy barrage on Right Brigade commenced 10 minutes after ZERO. Coloured lights now ceased.	
		5.15 am	Following report (G.755) was sent to 17th Corps and repeated to 4th and 31st Divisions. Reports that at 4.55 am state that light was not good for observation. Hostile Very Lights being sent up further EAST. Barrage now decreased.	
		5.20 am	A report was received from 4th Division (on our Right) that their Right Brigade was getting on well. Left Company Somerset Light Infantry had got into ROEUX. Right Company was held up.	
		5.50 am	General KENNEDY (26th Inf. Bde) reported that he was unable to give definite information yet, but from reports of wounded it appeared that our assaulting troops were all back in our front line, The casualties being caused by M.G. fire from Right.	

A6945 Wt. W11422/M1160 350,000 12/16 D. D. & L. Forms/C./2118/14.

Instructions regarding War Diaries and Intelligence Summaries are contained in F. S. Regs., Par. II, and the Staff Manual respectively. Title pages will be prepared in manuscript.

Army Form C. 2118.

WAR DIARY
or
INTELLIGENCE SUMMARY.
(Erase heading not required.)

Place	Date	Hour	Summary of Events and Information	Remarks and references to Appendices
RAILWAY CUTTING ST LAURENT BLANGY	3rd May	6.12.	General KENNEDY (26th Inf. Bde) reported an officer of 5th Camerons in CUTHBERT trench, consolidating, has about 40 men with him but appeared to be isolated.	
		6.17am	27th Inf. Bde reported telephone communications forward of old German 3rd system broken. Enemy's barrage reported heavy in front of CUBA. Right Battalion at 5.10 am had reported no definite news but think Battalion is getting on. Left Battalion at 4.40 am reported Battalion and right of 31st Division had reached WIT trench, but was not in touch on Right.	
		6.20am	XVII Corps and Divisions on flanks informed that reports indicate attack of Right Brigade has failed with loss. Left Brigade believed to have made a little progress, but no definite information.	
		6.50am	52nd Bde. R.F.A. reported that CUTHBERT trench was now evacuated by our Infantry.	
		6.50am	32nd Bde. R.F.A. reported that WOBBLE trench had been captured, and advance continued 700 to 800 yards in direction of SQUARE WOOD.	
		6.50 am	General KENNEDY (26th Inf. Bde) reported that cause of the trouble was machine guns in EMBANKMENT, he thought between CUPID and COST. He had told the artillery to bring back barrage to CUTHBERT, but not South of CASH or North of grid line between I.7 and I.1.	
		7.0 am	Map dropped by contact aeroplane showed no flares in advance of our original front line.	
		7.0am	31st Division reported very heavy hostile barrage. Germans putting up many lights, white breaking into two red balls. Attack on OPPY apparently failed. Right and Left Battalions suffered heavily during assembly, which seems to be disorganised the attack.	
		7.20am	52nd Bde. R.F.A. reported that WOBBLE trench had been captured. Patrols out 600 or 700 yards in front of SQUARE WOOD. Slow progress in centre. On enquiry being made Brigade Major 27th Inf. Bde. stated message from F.O.O. regarding capture of WOBBLE trench had been repeated to him. He had no information to confirm this. Germans were reported to be still in WIT trench (West of WOBBLE) firing on our troops in our original front line.	

A6945 Wt. W11422/M1160 350,000 12/16 D. D. & L. Forms/C./2118/14.

Instructions regarding War Diaries and Intelligence Summaries are contained in F. S. Regs., Part II, and the Staff Manual respectively. Title pages will be prepared in manuscript.

WAR DIARY

or

INTELLIGENCE SUMMARY.

(Erase heading not required.)

Army Form C. 2118.

Place	Date	Hour	Summary of Events and Information	Remarks and references to Appendices
RAILWAY CUTTING ST LAURENT BLANGY	3rd May	7.45am	B.G., G.S. XVII Corps informed G.S.O.1 that he had told 4th Division not to renew their attack, Artillery fire was being brought back. The Heavy Artillery to fire on CANDY, CYPRUS, and CARROT trenches and on ROEUX where more than 400 yards from our line.	
		7.45am	General MAXWELL (27th Inf. Bde) reported that three companies of Left Battalion (6th K.O.S.B) are beyond WIT trench somewhere. WIT trench appears to be occupied by the Germans. It is occupied all along its length, and also occupied to North of us. Brigade on his Left does not know where its people are. One company and three machine guns still in old front line. The situation on the right was that 9th Scottish Rifles had got three companies at least/half of this, or three companies in the "BLUE" beyond WISH and perhaps WIT. There was at one time nobody in lower portion of WISH. Behind in CORK trench a conglomeration of men who are the remainder of the Scottish Rifles trickled back, and some of the two companies of the 11th Royal Scots, who were to have taken WISH and WIT trenches, behind the Scottish Rifles. None of these two companies got forward. In CUBA there are 6 platoons 11th Royal Scots and one machine gun in action and one knocked out. Two platoons of the 11th Royal Scots in shell holes in front of 8th Black Watch's Left, all the Black Watch are in CUBA. Three companies of Reserve Battalion (12th Royal Scots) still in the GREEN LINE. Have asked F.O.O. to keep intermittent bombardment on WIT. Our right is entirely swept by enemy, who are holding 26th Inf. Bde's Area. That he did not propose to make any effort to get into WIT for the time being because Lt-Col. SMYTHE (O.C. Left Battn.) reports it would be hopeless to do this until Southern part is cleared and from his own point of view until Brigade on Left takes their part of WIT trench.	
		7.50am	31st Division reported that they had been able to make no progress, and that Right Brigade was back on defensive in original front trench.	
		8.10 am	31st Division reported enemy was counter-attacking whole front of their Right Brigade in force and had taken the MILL at GAVRELLE, Two Battalions from Divisional Reserve had been sent up in support.	

A6945 Wt. W11422/M1160 350,000 12/16 D. D. & L. Forms/C./2118/14.

Instructions regarding War Diaries and Intelligence Summaries are contained in F. S. Regs., Par. II. and the Staff Manual respectively. Title pages will be prepared in manuscript.

WAR DIARY
or
INTELLIGENCE SUMMARY.
(Erase heading not required.)

Army Form C. 2118.

Place	Date	Hour	Summary of Events and Information	Remarks and references to Appendices
RAILWAY CUTTING ST.LAURENT BLANGY	3rd. May	8.39am	Orders received from XVII Corps that general attack was not to be pressed for present. All local successes of 4th Division to be exploited to full, with a view of capturing CEMETERY, CORONA trench, CHEMICAL WORKS, and buildings North of RAILWAY. 9th Division to continue bombardment of points which held up their attack. Heavy Artillery was to bombard ROEUX, CARROT, CYPRUS, and CANDY trenches and RAILWAY East of CUPID. The above order was repeated to 26th and 27th Inf. Bdes and C.R.A.	
		9.10am	The following report was sent to the XVII Corps:- Right Brigade attack has failed and original front line is now held. Left Brigade, three Companies of each of the two leading battalions appear to have crossed WIT trench, but WIT trench is now occupied by Germans, Consequently the companies which passed WIT trench are for the present cut off. It is not intended to attack WIT trench till higher ground to south can be secured, which is out of the question at present. Meanwhile original front line is held.	
		9.50am	Report received from Corps H.A. through Liaison Officer that our men are in SQUARE WOOD. G.S.O.1 informed 27th Inf. Bde and 31st Division and inquired about 31st Divisions barrage going on to SQUARE WOOD. 31st Division were also informed as to situation as far as we knew it.	
		10.5am	27th Inf. Bde. reported that on hearing that 93rd Inf. Bde, on their left, was being counter attacked, General MAXWELL had ordered up one company of Reserve battalion to CIDER trench and was keeping artillery on to WIT trench. 28th M.G. Coy has 8 guns now barraging the ground beyond our objective in the direction of WAIT trench and SQUARE WOOD, the other 8 are barraging all the high ground East of CUTHBERT so as to protect the Right and rear of 27th Inf. Bde troops in the direction of WOBBLE, otherwise no change. 27th Inf. Bde unable to do more on its front until high ground on right is taken as it commands their area. 93rd Inf. Bde. are in their front line and have no intention of reoccupying WIT, which will make it difficult for 27th Inf. Bde to do so although it is important for them to get rid of the enemy interposing between their advance men and original front line.	

Army Form C. 2118.

Instructions regarding War Diaries and Intelligence Summaries are contained in F. S. Regs., Part II. and the Staff Manual respectively. Title pages will be prepared in manuscript.

WAR DIARY
or
INTELLIGENCE SUMMARY.
(Erase heading not required.)

Place	Date	Hour	Summary of Events and Information	Remarks and references to Appendices
RAILWAY CUTTING ST. LAURENT BLANGY	3rd May	10.5am	27th Inf. Bde were informed that Major HAMILTON (90th Field Coy.R.E.) had reported that the Germans were on Hill 80 N.W. of GAVRELLE. General MAXWELL replied that the Germans were towards HILL 80.	
		10.10am	27th Inf. Bde asked if an aeroplane could be sent to reconnoitre area of WOBBLE trench to ascertain if possible whether our men are there or not.	
		10.10am	G.O.C. reported situation verbally to G.O.C. 17th Corps. Our infantry seen in SQUARE WOOD, WIT trench occupied by Germans who came in to it from the North. WIT trench cannot be retaken unless ground is retaken on right, and also unless the Right Brigade of 31st Division could attack on our Left. 31st Division were unable to do this, were only just managing to hold their original line. Smoke was required on right of 27th Inf. Bde.	
		10.50am	XVII Corps were asked if an aeroplane could be sent to reconnoitre the area of WOBBLE trench and SQUARE WOOD to ascertain if possible whether our men are there or not.	
		10.25am	27th Inf. Bde were asked if they were in touch with 31st Division on their Left, the Brigade replied that their Left troops could see troops on Right of 31st Division in original trench. This information was repeated to H.Q. XVII Corps.	
		10.46am	31st Division reported that they were holding Eastern edge of GAVRELLE to RAILWAY. The WINDMILL had changed hands three times. They were then organising a new attack on it. Apparently their Left Brigade was checked in their advance in OPPY WOOD which enabled the enemy to counter attack exposed left flank of Right Brigade and roll it up.	
		10.54am	Information received from 17th Corps that an aeroplane was being sent to call for "flares" and reconnoitre area WOBBLE trench and SQUARE WOOD to ascertain if possible if our men were there or not. 27th Inf. Brigade were informed.	

A6945 Wt. W11422/M1160 350,000 12/16 D. D. & L. Forms/C./2118/14.

Instructions regarding War Diaries and Intelligence Summaries are contained in F. S. Regs., Par. II. and the Staff Manual respectively. Title pages will be prepared in manuscript.

Army Form C. 2118.

WAR DIARY
or
INTELLIGENCE SUMMARY.
(Erase heading not required.)

Place	Date	Hour	Summary of Events and Information	Remarks and references to Appendices
RAILWAY CUTTING ST LAURENT BLANGY	3rd May	11.15am	General KENNEDY (26th Inf. Bde) reported that the approximate strength of his Brigade was now as follows:-	
			8th Black Watch 205 7th Seaforths Hrs. intact 5th Cameron Hrs. 143 10th A. & S. Hrs. 300	
		11.45am	26th Inf. Bde were informed that 4th Division had some men dug in on road West of CHEMICAL WORKS. They were going to push along CORONA trench and try and take the CEMETERY.	
		12.20pm	Instructions were sent to 27th Inf. Bde to establish connection with 31st Division, and to report when touch had been gained.	
		12.40pm	XVII Corps reported that contact patrol aeroplanes would fly along Corps front and call for flares at 2 pm, paying special attention to CHEMICAL WORKS.	
		12.45pm	XVII Corps reported that contact aeroplane called for flares at 11.40 and 11.50 am but none were shown. Apparently there were no troops British or German in WOBBLE trench, but visibility bad owing to smoke. Aeroplane was fired on by hostile machine guns from West end of WEED trench.	
		12.50pm	26th Inf. Bde reported that units in the front trenches state that CHILI trench was being heavily shelled by 4.2 and 5.9 howitzers from N.E., counter battery action required. The necessary arrangements were made made accordingly with Heavy Artillery.	

Instructions regarding War Diaries and Intelligence Summaries are contained in F. S. Regs., Par. II, and the Staff Manual respectively. Title pages will be prepared in manuscript.

WAR DIARY
or
INTELLIGENCE SUMMARY.
(Erase heading not required.)

Army Form C. 2118.

Place	Date	Hour	Summary of Events and Information	Remarks and references to Appendices
RAILWAY CUTTING ST. LAURENT BLANGY	3rd May	12.50	9th Division message G.771 was issued, this ordered 27th Infantry Brigade to assault WIT trench between cross roads I.2.c. and northern boundary of 9th Division at I.1.b.7.8 at an hour to be notified later. WHIP and WIT trenches and WOBBLE trench N. of I.2.a.5.8 will be intensely bombarded from ZERO hour. At ZERO plus 2 minutes the artillery fire will lift off the portion of the trench to be assaulted. A smoke barrage will be placed South of the cross roads in I.2.c. and conceal the advance from the high ground on south.	
		1.25	31st Division reported that their right was now in touch with our left (27th Inf. Bde) S.E. of GAVRELLE.	
		1.27	The above information was reported to 27th Inf. Bde.	
		2.0	27th Inf. Bde reported that 6th K.O.S.B. were now in touch with 15th West Yorkshire Regt (31st Division)	
		3.6	31st Division reported that enemy had been seen in valley N.E. of GAVRELLE (C.19.b.) preparing for another attack on GAVRELLE WINDMILL. Artillery was engaging him. The above information was repeated to 27th Inf. Bde.	
		3.6	Instructions from XVll Corps Artillery for support of attack by 27th Inf. Bde were received.	
		3.28.	F.O.O. 52nd Brigade reported at 2.57 pm white lights were being sent up from CUBA trench I.7.a.3.3. It was ascertained later that these lights were sent up by our troops as our artillery was shooting short.	
		3.30	31st Division reported that they had recaptured WINDMILL at GAVRELLE.	
		4 pm	All concerned were notified that ZERO hour for attack by 27th Inf. Bde would be 8 p.m.	

A6945 Wt. W11422/M1160 350,000 12/16 D. D. & L. Forms/C./2118/14.

Instructions regarding War Diaries and Intelligence Summaries are contained in F. S. Regs., Par. II, and the Staff Manual respectively. Title pages will be prepared in manuscript.

WAR DIARY
or
INTELLIGENCE SUMMARY.
(Erase heading not required.)

Army Form C. 2118.

Place	Date	Hour	Summary of Events and Information	Remarks and references to Appendices
RAILWAY CUTTING ST. LAURENT BLANGY	3rd May	5.55	4th Division reported that they were holding original front line with axception of posts at I.13.central in some enclosures and buildings near CHATEAU and possibly in CHEMICAL WORKS. Enemy have been advancing into CORONA trench. Situation in GLOVER trench not clear. Enemy had made several strong counter attacks. One company Rifle Brigade and one company 9th Division have been sent to clear up situation.	
		6.50	Orders were issued for one Field Company R.E. and two companies Pioneers to be at disposal of each Brigade tonight for work in clearing front line and communication trenches. O.C. 9th Seaforths to arrange to place one additional company at disposal of each Brigade for the purpose. Connection between WISH trench and the BRICKFIELD in CUBA to be made by the construction of intermediate strong points which can be subsequently connected by a continuous trench.	
		7,35	Orders received from XVII Corps for Divisions to consolidate and improve the positions held. Touch to be kept with the enemy by means of patrols. The above order was repeated to C.R.A., C.R.E. 26th and 27th Infantry Brigades.	
		8.0pm	27th Bde attacked WIT trench with 12th Royal Scots (two companies)	
		9.15	General MAXWELL reported verbally that both companies got into the trench. The right company was knocked out by hostile machine gun fire after getting into the trench. The Left company had not yet returned. No further news. Afraid attack has failed.	
		10.25 pm	27th Inf. Bde was asked if the Brigade Commander wished for a Battalion of 52nd Inf. Bde (17th Division) to be moved forward to the GREEN LINE on account of the attacking companies having suffered heavy casualties. General MAXWELL replied that he did not need this. He asked that the artillery should not fire on trench immediately in front of his Brigade as men of 6th K.O.S.B. and 9th Scottish Rifles might be returning.	

A6945 Wt. W11422/M1160 350,000 12/16 D. D. & L. Forms/C./2118/14.

Army Form C. 2118.

WAR DIARY
or
INTELLIGENCE SUMMARY.
(Erase heading not required.)

Instructions regarding War Diaries and Intelligence Summaries are contained in F. S. Regs., Part II. and the Staff Manual respectively. Title pages will be prepared in manuscript.

Place	Date	Hour	Summary of Events and Information	Remarks and references to Appendices
RAILWAY CUTTING ST. LAURENT BLANGY	3rd May 1917	3.45am	ZERO hour, our artillery put down barrage and assaulting Infantry advanced.	
		4.1 am	A message timed 3.30 am was received from 27th Infantry Brigade reporting that movement into assembly area was complete.	
		4.10am	32nd Bde. R.F.A. reported that enemy was putting down heavy barrage all along our front line. The same Brigade reported heavy rifle and machine gun fire on our front about half an hour later.	
		4.15am	F.O.O. reported that there had been no hostile lights for last ten minutes. Heavy M.G. fire from South of RIVER. Enemy barrage commenced about 3 minutes after ZERO.	
		4.55 am	Report from 32nd Bde. R.F.A. (timed 4.35) stated that hostile lights were going up further East.	
		4.55 am	General KENNEDY (26th Inf. Bde) reported that his Brigade observer reported that enemy's Very Lights were being sent up from much further EAST. Hostile barrage had slackened considerably. A certain amount of M.G. fire from RIGHT. It was still too dark for observation.	
		5.3 am	31st Division (on our LEFT) reported our barrage opened at 3.45 am. Enemy appeared slow in replying. Enemy barrage on Right Brigade commenced 10 minutes after ZERO. Coloured lights now ceased.	
		5.15 am	Following report (G.755) was sent to 17th Corps and repeated to 4th and 31st Divisions. Reports that at 4.55 am state that light was not good for observation. Hostile Very Lights being sent up further EAST. Barrage now decreased.	
		5.20 am	A report was received from 4th Division (on our Right) that their Right Brigade was getting on well. Left Company Somerset Light Infantry had got into ROEUX. Right Company was held up.	
		5.50 am	General KENNEDY (26th Inf. Bde) reported that he was unable to give definite information yet, but from reports of wounded it appeared that our assaulting troops were all back in our front line, the casualties being caused by M.G. fire from Right.	

Instructions regarding War Diaries and Intelligence Summaries are contained in F. S. Regs., Par. II, and the Staff Manual respectively. Title pages will be prepared in manuscript.

WAR DIARY
or
INTELLIGENCE SUMMARY.
(Erase heading not required.)

Army Form C. 2118.

Place	Date	Hour	Summary of Events and Information	Remarks and references to Appendices
RAILWAY CUTTING ST LAURENT BLANGY	3rd May	6.12.	General KENNEDY (26th Inf. Bde) reported an officer of 5th Camerons in CUTHBERT trench, consolidating, has about 40 men with him but appeared to be isolated.	
		6.17am	27th Inf. Bde reported telephone communications forward of old German 3rd system broken. Enemy's barrage reported heavy in front of CUBA. Right Battalion at 5.10 am had reported no definite news but think Battalion is getting on. Left Battalion at 4.40 am reported Battalion and right of 31st Division had reached WIT trench, but was not in touch on Right.	
		6.20am	XVII Corps and Divisions on flanks informed that reports indicate attack of Right Brigade has failed with loss. Left Brigade believed to have made a little progress, but no definite information.	
		6.30am	52nd Bde. R.F.A. reported that CUTHBERT trench was now evacuated by our Infantry.	
		6.30am	52nd Bde. R.F.A. reported that WOBBLE trench had been captured, and advance continued 700 to 800 yards in direction of SQUARE WOOD.	
		6.50 am	General KENNEDY (26th Inf. Bde) reported that cause of the trouble was machine guns in EMBANKMENT, he thought between CUPID and COST. He had told the artillery to bring back barrage to CUTHBERT, but not South of CASH or North of grid line between I.7 and I.1.	
		7.0 am	Map dropped by contact aeroplane showed no flares in advance of our original front line.	
		7.0am	31st Division reported very heavy hostile barrage. Germans putting up many lights, white breaking into two red balls. Attack on OPPY apparently failed. Right and Left Battalions suffered heavily during assembly, which seems to be disorganised the attack.	
		7.20am	52nd Bde. R.F.A. reported that WOBBLE trench had been captured. Patrols out 600 or 700 yards in front of SQUARE WOOD. Slow progress in centre. On enquiry being made Brigade Major 27th Inf. Bde. stated message from F.O.O. regarding capture of WOBBLE trench had been repeated to him. He had no information to confirm this. Germans were reported to be still in WIT trench (West of WOBBLE) firing on our troops in our original front line.	

A6945 Wt. W11422/M1160 350,000 12/16 D. D. & L. Forms/C./2118/14.

Instructions regarding War Diaries and Intelligence Summaries are contained in F. S. Regs., Part II, and the Staff Manual respectively. Title pages will be prepared in manuscript.

WAR DIARY
or
INTELLIGENCE SUMMARY.
(Erase heading not required.)

Army Form C. 2118.

Place	Date	Hour	Summary of Events and Information	Remarks and references to Appendices
RAILWAY CUTTING ST LAURENT BLANGY	3rd May	7.45am	B.G., G.S. XVII Corps informed G.S.O.1 that he had told 4th Division not to renew their attack, Artillery fire was being brought back. The Heavy Artillery to fire on CANDY, CYPRUS, and CARROT trenches and on ROEUX where more than 400 yards from our line.	
		7.45am	General MAXWELL (27th Inf. Bde) reported that three companies of Left Battalion (6th K.O.S.B) are beyond WIT trench somewhere. WIT trench appears to be occupied by the Germans. It is occupied all along its length, and also occupied to North of us. Brigade on his Left does not know where its people are. One company and three machine guns still in old front line. The situation on the right was that 9th Scottish Rifles had got three companies at least, half of this, or three companies in the "BLUE" beyond WISH and perhaps WIT. There was at one time nobody in lower portion of WISH. Behind in CORK trench a conglomeration of men who are the remainder of the Scottish Rifles trickled back, and some of the two companies of the 11th Royal Scots, who were to have taken WISH and WIT trenches, behind the Scottish Rifles. None of these two companies got forward. In CUBA there are 6 platoons 11th Royal Scots and one machine gun in action and one knocked out. Two platoons of the 11th Royal Scots in shell holes in front of 8th Black Watch's Left, all the Black Watch are in CUBA. Three companies of Reserve Battalion (12th Royal Scots) still in the GREEN LINE. Have asked F.O.O. to keep intermittent bombardment on WIT. Our right is entirely swept by enemy, who are holding 26th Inf. Bde's Area. That he did not propose to make any effort to get into WIT for the time being because Lt-Col. SMYTHE (O.C. Left Battn.) reports it would be hopeless to do this until Southern part is cleared and from his own point of view until Brigade on Left takes their part of WIT trench.	
		7.50am	31st Division reported that they had been able to make no progress, and that Right Brigade was back on defensive in original front trench.	
		8.10 am	31st Division reported enemy was counter-attacking whole front of their Right Brigade in force and had taken the MILL at GAVRELLE, Two Battalions from Divisional Reserve had been sent up in support.	

A6945 Wt. W11422/M1160 350,000 12/16 D. D. & L. Forms/C./2118/14.

Instructions regarding War Diaries and Intelligence Summaries are contained in F. S. Regs., Par. II. and the Staff Manual respectively. Title pages will be prepared in manuscript.

WAR DIARY
or
INTELLIGENCE SUMMARY.
(Erase heading not required.)

Army Form C. 2118.

Place	Date	Hour	Summary of Events and Information	Remarks and references to Appendices
RAILWAY CUTTING ST.LAURENT BLANGY	3rd. May	8.30am	Orders received from XVII Corps that general attack was not to be pressed for present. All local successes of 4th Division to be exploited to full, with a view of capturing CEMETERY, CORONA trench, CHEMICAL WORKS, and buildings North of RAILWAY. 9th Division to continue bombardment of points which held up their attack. Heavy Artillery was to bombard ROEUX, CARROT, CYPRUS, and CANDY trenches and RAILWAY East of CUPID. The above order was repeated to 26th and 27th Inf. Bdes and C.R.A.	
		9.10am	The following report was sent to the XVII Corps:- Right Brigade attack has failed and original front line is now held. Left Brigade, three companies of each of the two leading battalions appear to have crossed WIT trench, but WIT trench is now occupied by Germans. Consequently the companies which passed WIT trench are for the present cut off. It is not intended to attack WIT trench till higher ground to South can be secured, which is out of the question at present. Meanwhile original front line is held.	
		9.50am	Report received from Corps H.A. through Liaison Officer that our men are in SQUARE WOOD. G.S.O.1 informed 27th Inf. Bde and 31st Division and inquired about 31st Division's barrage going on to SQUARE WOOD. 31st Division were also informed as to situation as far as we knew it.	
		10.5am	27th Inf. Bde. reported that on hearing that 93rd Inf. Bde, on their left, was being counter attacked, General MAXWELL had ordered up one company of Reserve battalion to CIDER trench and was keeping artillery on to WIT trench. 28th M.G. Coy has 8 guns now barraging the ground beyond our objective in the direction of WAIT trench and SQUARE WOOD, the other 8 are barraging all the high ground East of CUTHBERT so as to protect the Right and rear of 27th Inf. Bde troops in the direction of WOBBLE, otherwise no change. 27th Inf. Bde unable to do more on its front until high ground on right is taken as it commands their area. 93rd Inf. Bde. are in their front line and have no intention of reoccupying WIT, which will make it difficult for 27th Inf. Bde to do so although it is important for them to get rid of the enemy interposing between their advance men and original front line.	

A6945 Wt. W11422/M1160 350,000 12/16 D. D. & L. Forms/C./2118/14.

Instructions regarding War Diaries and Intelligence Summaries are contained in F. S. Regs., Part II, and the Staff Manual respectively. Title pages will be prepared in manuscript.

WAR DIARY
or
INTELLIGENCE SUMMARY.
(*Erase heading not required.*)

Army Form C. 2118.

Place	Date	Hour	Summary of Events and Information	Remarks and references to Appendices
RAILWAY CUTTING ST.LAURENT BLANGY	3rd May	10.5am	27th Inf. Bde were informed that Major HAMILTON (90th Field Coy.R.E.) had reported that the Germans were on Hill 80 N.W. of GAVRELLE. General MAXWELL replied that the Germans were towards HILL 80.	
		10.10am	27th Inf. Bde asked if an aeroplane could be sent to reconnoitre area of WOBBLE trench to ascertain if possible whether our men are there or not.	
		10.10am	G.O.C. reported situation verbally to G.O.C. 17th Corps. Our infantry seen in SQUARE WOOD, WIT trench occupied by Germans who came in to it from the North. WIT trench cannot be retaken unless ground is retaken on right, and also unless the Right Brigade of 31st Division could attack on our Left. 31st Division were unable to do this, were only just managing to hold their original line. Smoke was required on right of 27th Inf. Bde.	
		10.50am	XVII Corps were asked if an aeroplane could be sent to reconnoitre the area of WOBBLE trench and SQUARE WOOD to ascertain if possible whether our men are there or not.	
		10.25am	27th Inf. Bde were asked if they were in touch with 31st Division on their Left, the Brigade replied that their Left troops could see troops on Right of 31st Division in original trench. This information was repeated to H.Q. XVII Corps.	
		10.46am	31st Division reported that they were holding Eastern edge of GAVRELLE to RAILWAY. The WINDMILL had changed hands three times. They were then organising a new attack on it. Apparently their Left Brigade was checked in their advance in OPPY WOOD which enabled the enemy to counter attack exposed left flank of Right Brigade and roll it up.	
		10.54am	Information received from 17th Corps that an aeroplane was being sent to call for "flares" and reconnoitre area WOBBLE trench and SQUARE WOOD to ascertain if possible if our men were there or not. 27th Inf. Brigade were informed.	

A6945 Wt. W11422/M1160 350,000 12/16 D. D. & L. Forms/C./2118/14.

Instructions regarding War Diaries and Intelligence Summaries are contained in F. S. Regs., Par. II. and the Staff Manual respectively. Title pages will be prepared in manuscript.

WAR DIARY
or
INTELLIGENCE SUMMARY.
(Erase heading not required.)

Army Form C. 2118.

Place	Date	Hour	Summary of Events and Information	Remarks and references to Appendices
RAILWAY CUTTING ST LAURENT BLANGY	3rd May	11.15am	General KENNEDY (26th Inf. Bde) reported that the approximate strength of his Brigade was now as follows:- 8th Black Watch 205 7th Seaforth Hrs. intact 5th Cameron Hrs. 145 10th A. & S. Hrs. 300	
		11.45am	26th Inf. Bde were informed that 4th Division had some men dug in on road West of CHEMICAL WORKS. They were going to push along CORONA trench and try and take the CEMETERY.	
		12.20pm	Instructions were sent to 27th Inf. Bde to establish connection with 31st Division, and to report when touch had been gained.	
		12.40pm	XVII Corps reported that contact patrol aeroplanes would fly along Corps front and call for flares at 2 pm, paying special attention to CHEMICAL WORKS.	
		12.45pm	XVII Corps reported that contact aeroplane called for flares at 11.40 and 11.50 am but none were shown. Apparently there were no troops British or German in WOBBLE trench, but visibility bad owing to smoke. Aeroplane was fired on by hostile machine guns from West end of WEED trench.	
		12.50pm	26th Inf. Bde reported that units in the front trenches state that CHILI trench was being heavily shelled by 4.2 and 5.9 howitzers from N.E., counter battery action required. The necessary arrangements were made made accordingly with Heavy Artillery.	

Instructions regarding War Diaries and Intelligence Summaries are contained in F. S. Regs., Part II, and the Staff Manual respectively. Title pages will be prepared in manuscript.

WAR DIARY
or
INTELLIGENCE SUMMARY.
(Erase heading not required.)

Army Form C. 2118.

Place	Date	Hour	Summary of Events and Information	Remarks and references to Appendices
RAILWAY CUTTING ST. LAURENT BLANGY	3rd May	12.50	9th Division message G.771 was issued, this ordered 27th Infantry Brigade to assault WIT trench between cross roads I.2.c. and northern boundary of 9th Division at I.1.b.7.3 at an hour to be notified later. WHIP and WIT trenches and WOBBLE trench N. of I.2.a.5.8 will be intensely bombarded from ZERO hour. At ZERO plus 2 minutes the artillery fire will lift off the portion of the trench to be assaulted. A smoke barrage will be placed South of the cross roads in I.2.c. and conceal the advance from the high ground on south.	
		1.25	31st Division reported that their right was now in touch with our left (27th Inf. Bde) S.E. of GAVRELLE.	
		1.27	The above information was reported to 27th Inf. Bde.	
		2.0	27th Inf. Bde reported that 6th K.O.S.B. were now in touch with 15th West Yorkshire Regt (31st Division)	
		3.6	31st Division reported that enemy had been seen in valley N.E. of GAVRELLE (C.19.b.) preparing for another attack on GAVRELLE WINDMILL. Artillery was engaging him. The above information was repeated to 27th Inf. Bde.	
		3.6	Instructions from XVII Corps Artillery for support of attack by 27th Inf. Bde were received.	
		3.38.	F.O.O. 52nd Brigade reported at 2.57 pm white lights were being sent up from CUBA trench I.7.a.3.3. It was ascertained later that these lights were sent up by our troops as our artillery was shooting short.	
		3.30	31st Division reported that they had recaptured WINDMILL at GAVRELLE.	
		4 pm	All concerned were notified that ZERO hour for attack by 27th Inf. Bde would be 8 p.m.	

A6945 Wt. W11422/M1160 350,000 12/16 D. D. & L. Forms/C./2118/14.

Instructions regarding War Diaries and Intelligence Summaries are contained in F. S. Regs., Par. II. and the Staff Manual respectively. Title pages will be prepared in manuscript.

WAR DIARY
or
INTELLIGENCE SUMMARY.
(Erase heading not required.)

Army Form C. 2118.

Place	Date	Hour	Summary of Events and Information	Remarks and references to Appendices
RAILWAY CUTTING ST. LAURENT BLANGY	3rd May	5.55	4th Division reported that they were holding original front line with exception of posts at I.13.central in some enclosures and buildings near CHATEAU and possibly in CHEMICAL WORKS. Enemy have been advancing into CORONA trench. Situation in CLOVER trench not clear. Enemy had made several strong counter attacks. One company Rifle Brigade and one company 9th Division have been sent to clear up situation.	
		6.50	Orders were issued for one Field Company R.E. and two companies Pioneers to be at disposal of each Brigade tonight for work in clearing front line and communication trenches. O.C. 9th Seaforths to arrange to place one additional company at disposal of each Brigade for the purpose. Connection between WISH trench and the BRICKFIELD in CUBA to be made by the construction of intermediate strong points which can be subsequently connected by a continuous trench.	
		7.35	Orders received from XVII Corps for Divisions to consolidate and improve the positions held. Touch to be kept with the enemy by means of patrols. The above order was repeated to C.R.A., C.R.E. 26th and 27th Infantry Brigades.	
		8.0pm	27th Bde attacked WIT trench with 12th Royal Scots (two companies)	
		9.15	General MAXWELL reported verbally that both companies got into the trench. The right company was knocked out by hostile machine gun fire after getting into the trench. The Left company had not yet returned. No further news. Afraid attack has failed.	
		10.25 pm	27th Inf. Bde was asked if the Brigade Commander wished for a Battalion of 52nd Inf. Bde (17th Division) to be moved forward to the GREEN LINE on account of the attacking companies having suffered heavy casualties. General MAXWELL replied that he did not need this. He asked that the artillery should not fire on trench immediately in front of his Brigade as men of 6th K.O.S.B. and 9th Scottish Rifles might be returning.	

Instructions regarding War Diaries and Intelligence Summaries are contained in F. S. Regs., Par. II, and the Staff Manual respectively. Title pages will be prepared in manuscript.

WAR DIARY
or
INTELLIGENCE SUMMARY.
(*Erase heading not required.*)

Army Form C. 2118.

Place	Date	Hour	Summary of Events and Information	Remarks and references to Appendices
ST NICHOLAS.	June. 5th.	8 pm.	Situation during day in trenches normal.	
			27th Infantry Brigade were informed that an aeroplane would go up at 3.35 a.m. on June 6th for a few hours to ascertain if the enemy were massing, if they were it would fire "white" "red" "white" lights.	
		8 pm.	Zero hour our barrage opened and after a few seconds our Infantry advanced.	
		8.10 pm.	General Lukin (G.O.C. 9th Division) on FAMPOUX line rang up to say that he was watching the barrage and could see nothing on account of the dust. He suggested that artillery fire should cease for 20 minutes, commencing from 8.20 pm. The matter was referred to H.Q. 17th Corps but Corps Commander said he could not sanction any change in programme at this time.	
		8.15 pm.	23rd F.A. Brigade reported that our Infantry were in CUPID trench; this information was passed on to 27th Infantry Brigade H.Q.	
		8.29 pm.	29th Bde. R.F.A. reported that German barrage started at 8.8 pm. No German S.O.S. rockets had gone up. Hostile barrage was said to be in our back trenches and FAMPOUX.	
		8.34 pm.	Hostile aeroplane brought down by one of our planes and fell near FEUCHY.	
		8.41 pm.	C.R.A. reported that hostile heavy guns opened at 8.6 pm but observation was difficult owing to smoke. Hostile Machine Gun fire could now be heard; it was impossible to tell direction on	

A6945 Wt. W11422/M1160 350,000 12/16 D. D. & L. Forms/C./2118/14.

Instructions regarding War Diaries and Intelligence Summaries are contained in F. S. Regs., Par. II, and the Staff Manual respectively. Title pages will be prepared in manuscript.

WAR DIARY
or
INTELLIGENCE SUMMARY.
(Erase heading not required.)

Army Form C. 2118.

Place	Date	Hour	Summary of Events and Information	Remarks and references to Appendices
			from which it was firing.	
		8.50 pm.	27th Infantry Brigade reported that 12th Royal Scots captured CUPID trench at 8.20 pm.	
		8.51 pm.	17th Corps and 34th Division were informed of capture of CUPID trench.	
		9 pm.	27th Infantry Brigade asked if protective barrage could be stopped and were informed that it could not be done as artillery had to fire as per programme.	
		9.30 pm.	27th Infantry Brigade were informed that flares had been seen in the forward trench that had to be dug at I.14.a.7.2., I.14.a.9.3. A golden rain rocket had been seen at I.14.c.8.8.	
		9.30 pm.	Report from 34th Division (timed 9 pm) stated that centre battalion 102nd Brigade reported that one Company had got first objective. Another Company was progressing alright. A certain number of prisoners were coming in.	
		9.45 pm.	27th Infantry Brigade reported that left Battalion (12th Royal Scots) held CUPID trench except near CAMBRIAN trench where enemy still holds trench preventing them from getting into touch with 34th Division. Post on right now established in right place about 200 yards East. The left post was reported to be in correct place in shell holes about I.8.c.5.0. Flares reported at I.14.a.7.2., placed right Battalion (11th Royal Scots) on right line but flare reported at I.14.a.9.3. was rather in advance of line intended but might have gone forward to	

Instructions regarding War Diaries and Intelligence Summaries are contained in F. S. Regs., Par. II, and the Staff Manual respectively. Title pages will be prepared in manuscript.

WAR DIARY
or
INTELLIGENCE SUMMARY.
(Erase heading not required.)

Army Form C. 2118.

Place	Date	Hour	Summary of Events and Information	Remarks and references to Appendices
			deal with hostile machine guns at that point. Hostile barrage had been very servere on the line of CHRMICAL WORKS, all telephone lines to front Battalionswere cut; all communication at present done by runner.	
		10 pm.	Information was received from 17th Corps that aeroplane observer reported as follows:-	
			8.20 pm. Golden rain rocket seen from near BIACHE about I.7.c.7.4.	
			8.21 and 8.35. Several flares lit before being called for between I.8.c.00.85 and I.7.b.8.3. along CUTHBERT trench.	
			8.32 pm. Red rocket at I.8.c.20.55.	
			8.45 pm. Called for flares. Green flares seen at I.7.a.5.7., I.7.a.50.85., one red flare seen at I.7.b.4.7. also one green flare at I.7.b.50.95.	
			8.45 and 8.50. One green flare lit twice at I.14.a.85.25.	
			20 other flares seen south of railway and 20 flares lit along RAILWAY. No moveme t of troops to be seen owing to smoke and dust of barrage. Our barrage very good, hostile barrage very feeble. Our shelling of HAUSA and DELBAR WOOD very accurate also the guns or batteries which were walking the RAILWAY.	
		10.20 pm.	Information recd ved from 17th Corps that contact aerpplanes would call for flares at 4.30 am.	

A6945 Wt. W11422/M1160 350,000 12/16 D. D. & L. Forms/C./2118/14.

Instructions regarding War Diaries and Intelligence Summaries are contained in F. S. Regs., Par. II, and the Staff Manual respectively. Title pages will be prepared in manuscript.

WAR DIARY
or
INTELLIGENCE SUMMARY.
(Erase heading not required.)

Army Form C. 2118.

Place	Date	Hour	Summary of Events and Information	Remarks and references to Appendices
			6th. 27th Infantry Brigade informed.	
		11 pm.	27th Infantry Brigade reported that right Battalion (11th Royal Scots) reports objective reached but a pocket of enemy still in organised shell holes about I. 14.c.5.9. These are being dealt with. Some prisoners including one Officer have come in from both our Battalions. They say surprise was complete. Our casualties not yet known but do not think they are severe so far. No enemy barrage on our old front and support trenches up to 10 pm., but heavy barrage in CHEMIVAL WORKS line and West of it though very late in coming. Latter died down with our own bombardment. Communication from front is by runner only back to RAILWAY Brigade wires having been cut. Prisoners so far counted 34. They have passed our advanced H.Q's. Barrage at present heavy in FAMPOUX.	
		11.5 pm.	27th Infantry Brigade reported that 11th Royal Scots reported there is occasional sniping and machine gun fire from HAUSA WOOD.	
		11.15 pm.	Report from 34th Division states that their right Company on right Battalion has not reached objective. Troops on right had not got in. Right Company centre battalion got first objective. No news about second objective.	
		11.40 pm.	Report from 34th Division states that 102nd Infantry Brigade (34th Division) report centre	

A6945 Wt. W11422/M1160 350,000 12/16 D. D. & L. Forms/C./2118/14.

Instructions regarding War Diaries and Intelligence Summaries are contained in F. S. Regs., Par. II, and the Staff Manual respectively. Title pages will be prepared in manuscript.

WAR DIARY
or
INTELLIGENCE SUMMARY.
(Erase heading not required.)

Army Form C. 2118.

Place	Date	Hour	Summary of Events and Information	Remarks and references to Appendices
			Company left Battalion in position in both objectives and in touch on both flanks in CHARLIE, CHARLIE TRENCH held up to 20 yards N.E. of its junction with CUTHBERT. R.E. party has been sent out to make strong point at about I. 1.d.85.20. and a party of pioneers to dig C.T. from CUBA to CHARLIE at I. 7.b.1.2.	
	June 6th.	12 mdnt.	Corps Headquarters stated verbally that the 34th Division did not want the pre-arranged bombardment at 3.30 am. 27th Infantry Brigade were accordingly asked if they wanted bombardment cancelled. General Maxwell replied that he wishes 3.30 am. bombardment to hold good but would like present artillery fire to cease. Corps Headquarters were informed accordingly. Arrangements were made with C.R.A. for harassing fire to cease.	
		12.45 am.	C.R.A. reported that under instructions received from Corps the 3.30 am. bombardment was cancelled. 27th Infantry Brigade and 26th Infantry Brigade were informed accordingly.	
		1.10 am.	27th Infantry Brigade forwarded following report from Officer Commanding left assaulting Battalion (12th Royal Scots):- "Officer Commanding left assaulting Company reports that all objectives are gained and being held. One platoon of 34th Division is occupying CUPID for 20 yards to North of CAMBRIAN but there are Germans between it and rest of Division who are bombing hard. A platoon from our support Company has been ordered to attack these Germans	

Instructions regarding War Diaries and Intelligence Summaries are contained in F. S. Regs., Par. II, and the Staff Manual respectively. Title pages will be prepared in manuscript.

WAR DIARY
or
INTELLIGENCE SUMMARY.
(Erase heading not required.)

Army Form C. 2118.

Place	Date	Hour	Summary of Events and Information	Remarks and references to Appendices
			across the open from CAMBRIAN".	
		1.45 am.	Report from 34th Division (timed 11.55 pm June 5th) stated that situation at 11.45 pm was as follows;- Right Battalion holds portions of CHARLIE astride CASH. Centre Battalion establishedin CHARLIE on their proper frontage and have posts in CUTHBERT. Left Battalion established in CHARLIE and CUTHBERT and have post 20 yards N.E. of junction. Right of 103rd Brigade in touch with left of 102nd Brigade at that point. Two Companies support Battalion of 102nd Brigade with Stokes Motar have been ordered to pass through centre Battalion and down to the right (south) to assist right Battalion. Right of 102nd Brigade is not in touch with 9th Division.	
		2.15 am.	34th Division reported that their right was definately in touch with 27th Brigade at East end of CAMBRIAN. CURLY and Cash appear to be held by the enemy. These are being attacked from South and West and Stokes Mortars are co-operating.	
		4.20 am.	26th Infantry Brigade morning report timed 2.40 am. "Situation forward satisfactory CEYLON trench being heavily shelled. FAMPOUX has been shelled intermittently during night. Enemy shrapnelling roads and tow path just west of FAMPOUX at intervals.	

Instructions regarding War Diaries and Intelligence Summaries are contained in F. S. Regs., Par. II, and the Staff Manual respectively. Title pages will be prepared in manuscript.

WAR DIARY
or
INTELLIGENCE SUMMARY.
(Erase heading not required.)

Army Form C. 2118.

Place	Date	Hour	Summary of Events and Information	Remarks and references to Appendices
		5.20 am.	Aeroplane dripped map showing flares at I. 1.d.7.½., I. 7.b.4.7., I. 7.b.4.3., I. 7.b.5.½., I. 7.d.5.8., I. 7.d.8.3., I. 14.a.0.9., I. 14.a.6.8., I. 7.b.4.5. Two at I. 14.a.6.4. and new trench from this point to I. 14.a.9.6., with communication trench from I. 14.a. to this trench at I. 14.a.5.2. Signalling lamp was used from this trench and though to send O.K.	
		6.30 am.	17th Corps and 34th and 3rd Divisions were informed that situation on 9th Division front was now fairly quiet. We hold following line - North of Railway CUPOD trench, with two posts about 200 yards to East of it. One near RAILWAY and the other further North believed to be about I. 8.c.5.0. Out left is in touch with party of 34th Division, North of whom there are still some Germans. South of Railway new trench shown on aeroplane map is held with two posts in front on line of original German shell hole line. The new trench is shown on aeroplane map to have joined up with our original front line but no information is yet to hand as to whether this trench hasbeen completed.	

A6945 Wt. W11422/M1160 350,000 12/16 D. D. & L. Forms/C./2118/14.

OFFICE COPY.

GENERAL STAFF

9th (SCOTTISH) DIVISION.

WAR DIARY.

JUNE 5th/6th 1917.

(6202) W 11186/M1151 350,000 12/16 McA. & W., Ltd. (Est. 731) Forms/W 3091/3. Army Form W. 3091.

Cover for Documents.

Nature of Enclosures.

Notes, or Letters written.

Instructions regarding War Diaries and Intelligence Summaries are contained in F. S. Regs., Part II, and the Staff Manual respectively. Title pages will be prepared in manuscript.

WAR DIARY
or
INTELLIGENCE SUMMARY.
(Erase heading not required.)

Army Form C. 2118.

Place	Date	Hour	Summary of Events and Information	Remarks and references to Appendices
ST NICHOLAS.	June. 5th.	8 pm.	Situation during day in trenches normal.	
			27th Infantry Brigade were informed that an aeroplane would go up at 3.35 a.m. on June 6th for a few hours to ascertain if the enemy were massing, if they were it would fire "white" "red" "white" lights.	
		8 pm.	Zero hour our barrage opened and after a few seconds our Infantry advanced.	
		8.10 pm.	General Lukin (G.O.C. 9th Division) on FAMPOUX line rang up to say that he was watching the barrage and could see nothing on account of the dust. He suggested that artillery fire should cease for 20 minutes, commencing from 8.20 pm. The matter was referred to H.Q. 17th Corps but Corps Commander said he could not sanction any change in programme at this time.	
		8.15 pm.	23rd F... Brigade reported that our Infantry were in CUPID trench; this information was passed on to 27th Infantry Brigade H.Q.	App 1, 2
		8.29 pm.	29th Bde. R.F.A. reported that German barrage started at 8.8 pm. No German S.O.S. rockets had gone up. Hostile barrage was said to be in our back trenches and FAMPOUX.	App 3, 4, 5
		8.35 pm.	Hostile aeroplane brought down by one of our planes and fell near FEUCHY.	
		8.41 pm.	C.R.A. reported that hostile heavy guns opened at 8.6 pm but observation was difficult owing to smoke. Hostile Machine Gun fire could now be heard; it was impossible to tell direction on	App 6

Instructions regarding War Diaries and Intelligence Summaries are contained in F. S. Regs., Part II, and the Staff Manual respectively. Title pages will be prepared in manuscript.

WAR DIARY
or
INTELLIGENCE SUMMARY.
(Erase heading not required.)

Army Form C. 2118.

Place	Date	Hour	Summary of Events and Information	Remarks and references to Appendices
			from which it was firing.	
		8.50 pm.	27th Infantry Brigade reported that 12th Royal Scots captured CUPID trench at 8.20 pm.	
		8.51 pm.	17th Corps and 34th Division were informed of capture of CUPID trench.	
		9 pm.	27th Infantry Brigade asked if protective barrage could be stopped and were informed that it could not be done as artillery had to fire as per programme.	
		9.30 pm.	27th Infantry Brigade were informed that flares had been seen in the forward trench that had to be dug at I.14.a.7.2., I.14.a.9.3. A golden rain rocket had been seen at I.14.c.8.8.	
		9.30 pm.	Report from 34th Division (timed 9 pm) stated that centre battalion 102nd Brigade reported that one Company had got first objective. Another Company was progressing alright. A certain number of prisoners were coming in.	
		9.45 pm.	27th Infantry Brigade reported that left Battalion (12th Royal Scots) held CUPID trench except near CAMBRIAN trench where enemy still holds trench preventing them from getting into touch with 34th Division. Post on right now established in right place about 200 yards East. The left post was reported to be in correct place in shell holes about I.8.c.5.0. Flares reported at I.14.a.7.2., placed right Battalion (11th Royal Scots) on right line but flare reported at I.14.a.9.3. was rather in advance of line intended but might have gone forward to	

A6945 Wt. W11422/M1160 350,000 12/16 D. D. & L. Forms/C./2118/14.

Instructions regarding War Diaries and Intelligence Summaries are contained in F. S. Regs., Par. II. and the Staff Manual respectively. Title pages will be prepared in manuscript.

WAR DIARY
or
INTELLIGENCE SUMMARY.
(Erase heading not required.)

Army Form C. 2118.

Place	Date	Hour	Summary of Events and Information	Remarks and references to Appendices
			deal with hostile machine guns at that point. Hostile barrage had been very servere on the	
			line of CHEMICAL WORKS, all telephone lines to front Battalionswere cut; all communication	
			at present done by runner.	
		10 pm.	Information was received from 17th Corps that aeroplane observer reported as follows:-	
			8.20 pm. Golden rain rocket seen from near BIACHE about I.7.c.7.4.	
			8.21 and 8.35. Several flares lit before being called for between I.8.c.00.85 and I.7.b.8.3.	
			along CUTHBERT trench.	
			8.32 pm. Red rocket at I.8.c.20.55.	
			8.45 pm. Called for flares. Green flares seen at I.7.a.5.7., I.7.a.0.85., one red flare	
			seen at I.7.b.4.7. also one green flare at I.7.b.50.95.	
			8.45 and 8.50. One green flare lit twice at I.14.a.85.25.	
			20 other flares seen south of railway and 20 flares lit along RAILWAY. No movement of tropps	
			to be seen owing to smoke and dust of barrage. Our barrage very good, hostile barrage very	
			feeble. Our shelling of HAUSA and DELBAR WOOL very accurate also the guns or batteries	
			which were walking the RAILWAY.	
		10.20 pm.	Information received from 17th Corps that contact aerpplanes would call for flares at 4.30 am.	

A6945 Wt. W11422/M1160 350,000 12/16 D. D. & L. Forms/C./2118/14.

Army Form C. 2118.

Instructions regarding War Diaries and Intelligence Summaries are contained in F. S. Regs., Par. II. and the Staff Manual respectively. Title pages will be prepared in manuscript.

WAR DIARY
or
INTELLIGENCE SUMMARY.
(Erase heading not required.)

Place	Date	Hour	Summary of Events and Information	Remarks and references to Appendices
			6th. 27th Infantry Brigade informed.	
		11 pm.	27th Infantry Brigade reported that right Battalion (11th Royal Scots) reports objective reached but a pocket of enemy still in organised shell holes about I. 14.c.5.9. These are being dealt with. Some prisoners including one Officer have come in from both our Battalions. They say surprise was complete. Our casualties not yet known but do not think they are severe so far. No enemy barrage on our old front and support trenches up to 10 pm., but heavy barrage in CHEMICAL WORKS line and West of it though very late in coming. Latter died down with our own bombardment. Communication from front is by runner only back to RAILWAY Brigade wires having been cut. Prisoners so far counted 34. They have passed our advanced H.Q's. Barrage at present heavy in FAMPOUX.	
		11.5 pm.	27th Infantry Brigade reported that 11th Royal Scots reported there is occasional sniping and machine gun fire from HAUSA WOOD.	
		11.15 pm.	Report from 34th Division states that their right Company on right Battalion has not reached objective. Troops on right had not got in. Right Company centre battalion got first objective. No news about second objective.	App 8
		11.40 pm.	Report from 34th Division states that 102nd Infantry Brigade (34th Division) report centre	

A6945 Wt. W11422/M1160 350,000 12/16 D. D. & L. Forms/C./2118/14.

Instructions regarding War Diaries and Intelligence Summaries are contained in F. S. Regs., Par. II. and the Staff Manual respectively. Title pages will be prepared in manuscript.

WAR DIARY
or
INTELLIGENCE SUMMARY.
(Erase heading not required.)

Army Form C. 2118.

Place	Date	Hour	Summary of Events and Information	Remarks and references to Appendices
			Company left Battalion in position in both objectives and in touch on both flanks in CHARLIE. CHARLIE TRENCH held up to 20 yards N.E. of its junction with CUTHBERT. R.E. party has been sent out to make strong point at about I. 1.d.85.20. and a party of pioneers to dig C.T. from CUBA to CHARLIE at I. 7.b.1.2.	
	June 6th.	12 mdnt.	Corps Headquarters stated verbally that the 34th Division did not want the pre-arranged bombardment at 3.30 am. 27th Infantry Brigade were accordingly asked if they wanted bombardment cancelled. General Maxwell replied that he wishes 3.30 am. bombardment to hold good but would like present artillery fire to cease. Corps Headquarters were informed accordingly. Arrangements were made with C.R.A. for harassing fire to cease.	
		12.45 am.	C.R.A. reported that under instructions received from Corps the 3.30 am. bombardment was cancelled. 27th Infantry Brigade and 26th Infantry Brigade were informed accordingly.	
		1.10 am.	27th Infantry Brigade forwarded following report from Officer Commanding left assaulting Battalion (12th Royal Scots):- "Officer Commanding left assaulting Company reports that all objectives are gained and being held. One platoon of 34th Division is occupying CUPID for 20 yards to North of CAMBRIAN but there are Germans between it and rest of Division who are bombing hard. A platoon from our support Company has been ordered to attack these Germans	

A6945 Wt. W11422/M1160 350,000 12/16 D. D. & L. Forms/C./2118/14.

Instructions regarding War Diaries and Intelligence Summaries are contained in F. S. Regs., Par. II. and the Staff Manual respectively. Title pages will be prepared in manuscript.

WAR DIARY
or
INTELLIGENCE SUMMARY.
(*Erase heading not required.*)

Army Form C. 2118.

Place	Date	Hour	Summary of Events and Information	Remarks and references to Appendices
			across the open from CAMBRIAN".	
		1.45 am.	Report from 34th Division (timed 11.55 pm June 5th) stated that situation at 11.45 pm was as follows;- Right Battalion holds portions of CHARLIE astride CASH. Centre Battalion establishedin CHARLIE on their proper frontage and have posts in CUTHBERT. Left Battalion established in CHARLIE and CUTHBERT and have post 20 yards N.E. of junction. Right of 103rd Brigade in touch with left of 102nd Brigade at that point. Two Companies support Battalion of 102nd Brigade with Stokes Motar have been ordered to pass through centre Battalion and down to the right (south) to assist right Battalion. Right of 102nd Brigade is not in touch with 9th Division.	App 9
		2.15 am.	34th Division reported that their right was definately in touch with 27th Brigade at East end of CAMBRIAN. CURLY and Cash appear to be held by the enemy. These are being attacked from South and West and Stokes Mortars are co-operating.	App 10
		4.20 am.	26th Infantry Brigade morning report timed 2.40 am. "Situation forward satisfactory CEYLON trench being heavily shelled. FAMPOUX has been shelled intermittently during night. Enemy shrapnelling roads and tow path just west of FAMPOUX at intervals.	App 11

Army Form C. 2118.

Instructions regarding War Diaries and Intelligence Summaries are contained in F. S. Regs., Par. II, and the Staff Manual respectively. Title pages will be prepared in manuscript.

WAR DIARY
or
INTELLIGENCE SUMMARY.
(Erase heading not required.)

Place	Date	Hour	Summary of Events and Information	Remarks and references to Appendices
		5.20 am.	Aeroplane dropped map showing flares at I. 1.d.7.½., I. 7.b.4.7., I. 7.b.4.3., I. 7.b.5.½., I. 7.d.5.8., I. 7.d.8.3., I. 14.a.0.9., I. 14.a.6.8., I. 7.b.4.5. Two at I. 14.a.6.4. and new trench from this point to I. 14.a.9.6., with communication trench from I. 14.a. to this trench at I. 14.a.5.2. Signalling lamp was used from this trench and though to send O.K.	
		6.30 am.	17th Corps and 34th and 3rd Divisions were informad that situation on 9th Division front was now fairly quiet. We hold following line - North of Railway CUPOD trench, with two posts about 200 yards to East of it. One near RAILWAY and the other further North believed to be about I. 8.c.5.0. Our left is in touch with party of 34th Division, North of whom there are still some Germans. South of Railway new trench shown on aeroplane map is held with two posts in front on line of original German shell hole line. The new trench is shown on aeroplane map to have joined up with our original front lire but no information is yet to hand as to whether this trench hasbeen completed.	App. 12

A6945 Wt. W11422/M1160 350,000 12/16 D. D. & L. Forms/C./2118/14.

App 1

"A" Form.
MESSAGES AND SIGNALS.

Army Form C.2121
(in pads of 100).
No. of Message

Prefix ... Code ... m.	Words	Charge	This message is on a/c of:	Recd. at ... m.
Office of Origin and Service Instructions.	Sent		... Service.	Date
	At ... m.			From
	To			
	By		(Signature of "Franking Officer.")	By

TO BM. RA.

Sender's Number.	Day of Month.	In reply to Number.	AAA
* W.14	5		

23rd Bde. RFA. OP. reports infantry have reached Cpid Trench

From 23rd Bde.
Place
Time 8.10 pm.

The above may be forwarded as now corrected. (Z)

Censor. Signature of Addressor or person authorised to telegraph in his name.

* This line should be erased if not required.

750,000. W 2186—M509. H. W. & V., Ld. 6/16.

App. 2.

"A" Form. Army Form C.2121 (In pads of 100).

MESSAGES AND SIGNALS. No. of Message

Prefix .... Code .... m. | Words | Charge | This message is on a/c of: .... Service. | Recd. at .... m.

Office of Origin and Service Instructions.

Copy

Sent At .... m. To .... By ....

(Signature of "Franking Officer.")

Date .... From .... By ....

TO 7th Brigade

Sender's Number.	Day of Month.	In reply to Number.	AAA
* G 255	5		

23rd Bde O.P. report infantry have reached Cross trench

From 7th Division

Place

Time 8.20pm

The above may be forwarded as now corrected. (Z)

Censor. Signature of Addressor or person authorised to telegraph in his name.

* This line should be erased if not required.

750,000. W 2186—M509. H. W. & V., Ld. 6/16.

App 3

"A" Form.
MESSAGES AND SIGNALS.

Army Form C.2121 (In pads of 100).
No. of Message..........

Prefix ....Code..........m. | Words | Charge | This message is on a/c of: ....Service. | Recd. at..........m.
Office of Origin and Service Instructions. Copy
Sent At..........m. To.......... By..........
(Signature of "Franking Officer.")
Date..........
From..........
By..........

TO CRA

Sender's Number.	Day of Month.	In reply to Number.	AAA
*	5		

German barrage started at 8-8 pm.

From 7th Bde RFA
Place
Time 8-10 pm

The above may be forwarded as now corrected. (Z)
Censor. Signature of Addressor or person authorised to telegraph in his name.
* This line should be erased if not required.

750,000. W 2186—M509. H. W. & V., Ld. 6/16.

App. 4

"A" Form.

Army Form C.2121 (In pads of 100).

No. of Message

MESSAGES AND SIGNALS.

Prefix .... Code .... m. | Words | Charge

Office of Origin and Service Instructions.

Copy

Sent

At .... m.

To ....

By ....

This message is on a/c of: .... Service.

(Signature of "Franking Officer.")

Recd. at .... m.

Date ....

From ....

By ....

TO CRA

Sender's Number.	Day of Month.	In reply to Number.	AAA
*	5		

No German S.O.S. rocket seen

From 29th Bde RFA

Place

Time 8.14 pm

The above may be forwarded as now corrected. (Z)

Censor. Signature of Addressor or person authorised to telegraph in his name.

* This line should be erased if not required.

750,000. W 2186—M509. H. W. & V., Ld. 6/16.

App. 5

"A" Form.

Army Form C.2121
(in pads of 100).

MESSAGES AND SIGNALS.

No. of Message ....

Prefix .... Code .... m. Office of Origin and Service Instructions. Copy	Words / Charge Sent At ....m. To .... By	*This message is on a/c of:* ....*Service.* (Signature of "Franking Officer.")	Recd. at ....m. Date .... From .... By ....

TO 9th Division

* Sender's Number.	Day of Month.	In reply to Number.	AAA
	5		

27th Bde report barrage opened well at 8-2 pm, our infantry could be seen lining up at 8-3 pm. nothing more could be seen on account of smoke aaa Hostile barrage opened at 8-4 pm on our back trenches and FAMPOUX aaa Timed 8-20 pm

From 9th D.A.
Place
Time 8-20 pm

The above may be forwarded as now corrected. (Z)

.... *Censor.* Signature of Addressor or person authorised to telegraph in his name.

* This line should be erased if not required.

750,000. W 2186—M509. H. W. & V., Ld. 6/16.

App 6

"A" Form.
MESSAGES AND SIGNALS.

Army Form C.2121 (in pads of 100).
No. of Message ....

Prefix .... Code .... m.	Words	Charge	This message is on a/c of:	Recd. at .... m.
Office of Origin and Service Instructions. Copy	Sent		.... Service.	Date ....
	At .... m.			From ....
	To			
	By		(Signature of "Franking Officer.")	By ....

TO { 9th Division

Sender's Number.	Day of Month.	In reply to Number.	AAA
*			

Enemy heavy guns opened at 8-6 pm. Bad observation apparently owing to smoke aaa Smoke now clearing aaa Hostile MG can now be heard impossible to tell direction from which firing aaa Above received from 23rd Bde at 8 40 pm

From 9th D.A.
Place
Time 8 41 pm

The above may be forwarded as now corrected. (Z)

Censor. Signature of Addressor or person authorised to telegraph in his name.

* This line should be erased if not required.

750,000. W 2186—M509. H. W. & V., Ld. 6/16.

App. 7

"C" Form.
MESSAGES AND SIGNALS.

Army Form C. 2123.
(In books of 100.)

No. of Message

Prefix ... Code ... Words ...	Received.	Sent, or sent out.	Office Stamp.
£ s. d.	From	At ... m.	
Charges to Collect	By	To	
Service Instructions		By	

Handed in at ... Office 9.44 p.m. Received ... m.

TO 98 Bde
Divn

*Sender's Number	Day of Month	In reply to Number	AAA
G K 28	2		

Verbal report liason officer RA with centre Bn 102 Bde begins aaa 1 Company got first objective aaa another company proceeding all right aaa certain number of prisoners returning aaa ends

9.30 pm

FROM
PLACE & TIME
34 Divn
G. Armn

*This line should be erased if not required.

(27892) Wt. W1481? M'523. [E 930] 100,000 Pads 3/17. M.R.Co.,Ltd. Forms C/2123.

App 8.

"C" Form. Army Form C. 2123.
(In books of 100.)

MESSAGES AND SIGNALS. No. of Message............

Prefix...... Code...... Words...... £ s. d. Charges to Collect	Received. From [illegible] By......	Sent, or sent out. At......m. To...... By......	Office Stamp. -3.VI.17

Service Instructions Priority

Handed in at .... Office......m. Received......m.

TO 9 Divn

*Sender's Number	Day of Month	In reply to Number	AAA
G 62	3rd		

Situation aaa Right Battn 8.45
pm right coy not reached
objective troops on their right
not got on aaa Centre Battn
8.55 pm right coy got
first objective aaa Left Battn
8.40 pm got first objective
no news as to 2nd
objective aaa Prisoners being
sent back from Centre & left
Battns aaa Protective Barrage
still kept on whole front at
Round a gun every 4 mins
at request of Brigadier aaa
Addsd 17 Corps reptd 17
Corps HA 9th Div 101 & 103
Bdes & CRA

FROM 34 Div
PLACE & TIME 11 15 pm 10 pm

*This line should be erased if not required.

(27802) Wt. W14832/M1523. [E 930] 100,000 Pads—3/17. M.R.Co.,Ltd. Forms C./2123.

App. 9.

"C" Form
Army Form C. 2123
(In books of 100.)

MESSAGES AND SIGNALS.

No. of Message ....

Prefix .... Code .... Words ....

£ s. d.

Charges to collect

Service Instructions.

Received From HCO By MA

Sent, or sent out — At ......m. To ...... By ......

Office Stamp. [-9 IV 17]

Handed in at YCD Office 12.14 am. Received 1.24 am.

TO 9 Divn

*Sender's Number	Day of Month	In reply to Number	AAA
FA65	3/6	—	

Situation at 11.45 pm aaa Right Battalion holds portions of CHARLIE astride CASH aaa Centre Battalion established in CHARLIE on their proper frontage and have posts in CUTHBERT aaa Left Battn established in CHARLIE and CUTHBERT and have post 20 yards NE of junction aaa Right of 103rd Bde in touch with left of 102nd Bde at that point aaa 2 Coys support battalion of 102nd Bde with Stokes Mortar have been ordered to push through Centre Battalion & work down to the right to

FROM

PLACE & TIME

* This line should be erased if not required.

(B 8188) Wt. w. 7496—M857 250,000 Pads. 1/17 H & S (E489.) Forms/C.2123/3.

FROM 34 Div

PLACE & TIME 11.53 pm

* This line should be erased if not required.

(B 8188) Wt. w. 7496—M857 250,000 Pads. 1/17 H & S (E489.) Forms/C.2123/3.

"C" Form

Army Form C. 2123.
(In books of 100.)

MESSAGES AND SIGNALS.

No. of Message.....................

Prefix.........Code.........Words.........	Received	Sent, or sent out	Office Stamp.
£ s. d. / Charges to collect	From..................	At.... -5.VI.17 ....m.	YI
	By..................	To..................	
Service Instructions.		By..................	

Handed in at......................Office..........m. Received..........m.

TO (2)

*Sender's Number	Day of Month	In reply to Number	AAA	
Right	Right	Battn	aaa	Right
of	103rd	Bde	in	touch
with	9	Div	aaa	Added
17	Corps	17	Corps	HA
103rd	Bde	101st	Bde	9th
and	63rd	Divns		

1.45 am

FROM 34 Div

PLACE & TIME 11.53 pm

* This line should be erased if not required.

(B 8188) Wt. w. 7496—M857 250,000 Pads. 1/17 H & S (E489.) Forms/C.2123/3.

App 10.

"C" Form
Army Form C. 2123.
(In books of 100.)

MESSAGES AND SIGNALS. No. of Message.........

Prefix......... Code......... Words.........

£ s. d.

Charges to collect

Service Instructions.

Received From......... By W.A.

Sent, or sent out At.........m. To......... By.........

Office Stamp. 6.VI.17 TELEGRAPHS

Handed in at 9 D Office 1.33 a.m. Received 2.11 a.m.

TO 9th Divn

*Sender's Number	Day of Month	In reply to Number	AAA
GL 67	6		

102nd Bde wires that his Right Battn reported at 1220 am that it is apparently in touch with 27 Bde at East End of CAMBRIAN aaa CURLY and CASH appear to be held by the enemy aaa These are being attacked from south & west respectively & Stokes mortars are cooperating too aaa Generally the situation about this quarter is not yet clear aaa Ends aaa Addsd 17 Corps reptd 9 Divn

repeated [illegible]

CRA + 27 Bde

FROM 34 Divn

PLACE & TIME 1.15 am

* This line should be erased if not required.

(B 8188) Wt. W. 7496 M857 250,000 ... /17 H & S (E420.) Forms/C.2123/2.

App 11

"C" Form
Army Form C. 2123.
(In books of 100.)

MESSAGES AND SIGNALS.

No. of Message..........

Prefix SM Code RE Words 40	Received From 8BT By [illegible]	Sent, or sent out At.....m. To..... By.....	Office Stamp.
£ s. d. Charges to collect			
Service Instructions.			

Handed in at MG Office 2.45 am. Received 3.10 am.

TO: 9th Div

*Sender's Number	Day of Month	In reply to Number	AAA
BM/24	6		

Situation forward satisfactory aaa CEYLON being heavily shelled FAMPOUX has been shelled intermittently during night aaa Enemy shrapnelling road and towpath just west of Fampoux at intervals aaa Wind NE very light aaa

Repeated Corps & 27 Bde

4.20 am

FROM: Meet
PLACE & TIME: 2.40 am

* This line should be erased if not required.

(B 8188) Wt. w. 7496—M857 250,000 Pads 1/17 H & S (E489.) Forms/C.2123/3.

App 12

"A" Form.

Army Form C.2121 (in pads of 100).

MESSAGES AND SIGNALS.

No. of Message ....

Prefix ...... Code ...... m. Office of Origin and Service Instructions. Copy	Words / Charge; Sent At ..... m. To ..... By	This message is on a/c of: ...... Service. (Signature of "Franking Officer.")	Recd. at ..... m. Date ..... From ..... By .....

TO 14 Corps
3rd Divn
3rd Divn

Sender's Number.	Day of Month.	In reply to Number.	
* G 242	6		AAA

Situation now fairly quiet aaa
We hold following line aaa
North of Railway CORD trench with
two posts about 200 yards in front
one near railway and the
other further North behind to
about I.8.C.5.0 aaa Our left in
touch with party of 3rd Div
beyond whom there are still
some Germans aaa South of
Railway new trench shown on
aeroplane map is held with two
posts in front on line of original
German shell holes line aaa
The new trench is shown on
aeroplane map to have been
joined up with our original front

From

Place

Time

The above may be forwarded as now corrected. (Z)

Censor. Signature of Addressor or person authorised to telegraph in his name.

* This line should be erased if not required.

750,000. W 2186—M509. H. W. & V., Ld. 6/16.

"A" Form.

Army Form C.2121
(in pads of 100).

MESSAGES AND SIGNALS.

No. of Message..........

Prefix .... Code .... m. | Words | Charge

Office of Origin and Service Instructions.

Sent
At.................m.
To ....
By ....

This message is on a/c of:
....................*Service.*
....
(Signature of "Franking Officer.")

Recd. at.................m.
Date..................
From..................
By ....

TO

Sender's Number. | Day of Month. | In reply to Number. | AAA

Line has no information yet as to whether this trench has been completed

Addressed 14th Corps repeated 34th and 3rd Division

From 9th Division
Place
Time 6-30 am

The above may be forwarded as now corrected. (Z)

....
Censor.

....
Signature of Addressor or person authorised to telegraph in his name.

* This line should be erased if not required.

750,000. W 2186—M509. H. W. & V., Ld. 6/16.

S E C R E T.

Copy No. 12.

9th (SCOTTISH) DIVISION.

DEFENCE SCHEME

(Provisional)

GENERAL STAFF,
9th (SCOTTISH) DIVISION.

1st June, 1917.

9th (SCOTTISH) DIVISION.

DEFENCE SCHEME.

(Provisional).

=*=*=*=*=*=*=*=*=*=*=*=*=*=*=*=

1. <u>General Description of the front line.</u>

The front held by the 9th Division (Right Division 17th Corps) extends from RIVER SCARPE about I.20.c.5.6. to the junction of CINEMA and CAMBRIAN Trenches (inclusive to 9th Division) about I.7.d.4.1.

The VI Corps holds the line on the South of the RIVER SCARPE from I.25.central almost due South, and the 34th Division (Left Division XVII Corps) continues the line on the North as far as XVII Corps Boundary about I.1.b.0.8.

2. <u>Organization of front line.</u>

For the present the 9th Division front will be divided into 2 sectors, each held by one Brigade.

The Right Brigade Sub-sector will be known as "A" Sub-sector, and the Left Brigade Sub-sector as "B" Sub-sector.

3. <u>Boundaries in the forward area.</u>

(a) Between VI Corps and 9th Division - The River SCARPE.

(b) Between 9th Division and 34th Division. - Junction of CINEMA and CAMBRIAN Trenches (inclusive to 9th Division) Communication Trench from CALABAR to CUTE Trench at I.13.a.80.95 (inclusive to 34th Division) - junction of CAMEL and CADIZ trenches at H.18.b.45.70 (inclusive to 9th Division) - thence CAMEL Trench (inclusive to 9th Division) as far as road junction H.17.a.80.95. thence Sunken Road to junction with GAVRELLE SWITCH at H.10.d.75.55, thence to RAILWAY BRIDGE H.8.c.0.0. and due West along grid line to old British Line at G.11.d.9.0.

(c).....

(c) Between "A" and "B" Sub-sectors -
The boundary between 26th and 27th Inf. Bdes. after completion of relief will be -
Post at I.20.a.45.95. (inclusive to 26th Brigade) - junction of CORONA and CABBAGE Trenches at I.20.a.2.9. (inclusive to 27th Brigade) - junction of CUSP and CORFU Trenches I.13.a.7.1. (inclusive to 26th Brigade) thence CORFU Trench (inclusive to 27th Brigade) as far as its junction with CRETE Trench - thence Northwards to road junction H.18.d.6.1. - thence along road to Railway Bridge H.18.d.2.1.

4. General description of tactical features.

The main physical feature on the immediate front of the Division is the Spur running from what is known as GREENLAND HILL on the North of the Railway to HAUSA WOOD. The highest point of this spur is immediately South of the Railway about I.14.b.6.9. From HAUSA WOOD the ground falls fairly steeply to the River SCARPE, and HAUSA WOOD stands up as a stronghold facing sub-sector "A". Elsewhere the slope of the ground from our front line to this spur is very gradual.

The whole of this high ground can be observed from the front line, and from the GAVRELLE - FAMPOUX Line in H.16.b.

The tactical points within our lines are - ROEUX and the CHEMICAL WORKS and the general line of the ROEUX - GAVRELLE Road.

During the counter attack on this line on the 16th May, the enemy approached on the South along the River Bank, and on the North along the Railway. These two lines of approach are now sufficiently guarded.

The CHEMICAL WORKS and ROEUX might still form the objective of a local counter attack.

The line of the ROEUX Cemetery - CHEMICAL WORKS is intermittently shelled by day and night and no troops are stationed in the vicinity.

5.......

5. Defensive organisation.

The defences within the Divisional Area consist of -

(a) Front system. Consisting of firing line, support line, and reserve line.

(b) Corps Line. Consisting for the present of firing line only, sited along the trenches just West of FAMPOUX and continued to POINT du JOUR along EFFIE Trench.

(c) GAVRELLE SWITCH. Consisting of old German FAMPOUX - GAVRELLE Line organized for fire Eastwards

6. The front system of the Division consists of -

(a) Front Line. COLOMBO Trench, covered by a line of strong points, the positions of which are approximately I.14.c.5.2., I.20.a.4.9., I.20.a.4.4., I.20.a.9.2., I.20.c.80.75. (There is a belt of wire about 10 feet deep in front of these posts from the River to I.20.a.4.4.). From junction of COLOMBO with CORONA, front line is continued along CORONA and CROW to I.13.b.55.50, thence due North to I.7.d.4.1.

(b) Support Line. CORONA (South of its junction with COLOMBO with three strong points in the village of ROEUX on the line of the ROEUX - GAVRELLE Road, CORONA SUPPORT, CUBA.

(c) Reserve Line. CUSP, CORDITE and CADIZ Trenches.

7. Organization and duvelopment of trenches.

(a) As a principle the front system will be developed by consolidating tho two most Easterly trenches as firing and support lines. Work, especially as regards wiring, will be concentrated on the support line first. The reserve line will be developed along the general line CEYLON, CAWDOR, CADIZ Trenches.

Battalion Headquarters will be constructed on the general line of the reserve line.

Brigade Headquarters will be established in the general line of the FAMPOUX - GAVRELLE Trench system.

(b)...

(b) The Corps Line will for the present be organised as a single fire trench, fire-stepped and wired, and will consist of the FAMPOUX - GAVRELLE Trench system as far as its junction with EFFIE thence along EFFIE to POINT DU JOUR.

(c) GAVRELLE SWITCH consists of the old German FAMPOUX - GAVRELLE line organized for fire Eastwards.

8. Dispositions.

"A" Sub-sector is held by:-

1 Battalion	Front Line.
1 Battalion	In support.
2 Battalions	In reserve.

"B" Sub-sector is held by:-

2 Battalions	Front Line. (finding own supports)
2 Battalions	In reserve.

The third Brigade and 197th Machine Gun Company are in ARRAS in Divisional Reserve.

9. Headquarters.

Divisional Headquarters.	G.16.b.7.7. (Div. Battle H.Q. H.14.a.0.8)
Right Brigade H.Q.	H.14.a.0.8. (Bde. Battle H.Q. H.23.b.4.0)
Right front Battn.	I.19.c.95.45.
Support "	H.23.c.8.9.
Left Bde. H.Q.	H.16.d.2.7.
Right front Battn.	H.18.d.2.1.
Left "	QUARRY, I.13.a.2.2.
Reserve Bde. H.Q.	ARRAS (1, Rue d'Ancre)
9th Seaforths (Pnrs)	G.18.c.5.5.
197th Machine Gun Coy.	ARRAS.

10. Machine Gun Defence.

Each line from the support line inclusive Westwards will have a definite scheme of machine gun defence so arranged that the whole of each line is covered by flanking gun fire.

Machine guns....

Machine guns will always be in position in the support and reserve lines.

The dispositions of the guns are as follows:-

(i)	For defence of Front Line	5 guns.
	COLOMBO Trench	3 guns.
	CORONA Trench	1 gun.
	CROOK Trench	1 gun.
(ii)	For defence of support line	5 guns.
	CORONA Trench	2 guns.
	CORONA Support	1 gun
	CUBA Trench	1 gun
	CROOK Trench	1 gun.
(iii)	For defence of Reserve Line	6 guns.
	CUSP Trench	2 guns.
	QUARRY	2 guns.
	CRUMP Trench	2 guns.

(The last two guns are kept in CRUMP Trench as CUSP Trench between CEYLON and the Railway is very heavily shelled. They are always kept in readiness to push forward to CUSP Trench in case of necessity).

(iv)	In immediate reserve.	12 guns.
	FAMPOUX, H.17.d.90.95.	4 guns.
	Embankment, H.23.c.6.8.	8 guns.
(v)	In ARRAS.	16 guns (197th Machine Gun Coy.)

The Machine guns of the Reserve Bde. are reserved for manning positions in the GAVRELLE SWITCH.

11. Artillery.

(a) The front is covered by two groups as under:-

"A" Sub-sector - 255th Brigade R.F.A.
32nd Brigade R.F.A.

"B" Sub-sector - 29th Brigade R.F.A.
256th Brigade R.F.A.

The S.O.S. Barrage Line is CUPID Trench - thence Southwards about 200 yards East of the Sunken Road in I.14.a. and c., continuing to the River SCARPE about 200 yards East of the Eastern end of ROEUX.

(b)....

(b) The Corps Heavy Artillery is prepared to concentrate Artillery fire on the Right or Left of the Corps front on an S.O.S. being sent up.

The Signal to be employed for this Division is - "S.O.S. RIGHT" by telephone - Light Signal - Two RED Lights.

12. Action in case of attack.

Eastern end of ROEUX - COLOMBO - CORONA ~~and~~ CROW + CINEMA Trenches are the main line of resistance in the event of advanced posts in Sunken Road being driven in.

In the event of the line East of ROEUX - GAVRELLE Road being driven in, an immediate counter attack will be delivered.

Brigades will move up their Brigade Reserves to the Railway Cutting (H.23) and FAMPOUX - OPPY Line.

Divisional Reserve will be moved according to situation.

13. Signal Communication.

(a) Brigade Headquarters are in telephone communication with Divisional Headquarters, Artillery, Artillery O.P., Battalion Headquarters and Brigades on Right and Left.

There is visual signalling by lamp from forward Battalion Headquarters to Brigade Headquarters.

(b) There is a Power Buzzer in COLOMBO Trench.

(c) There is a wireless installation at the Right front Battalion Headquarters.

(d) Pigeon communication is also available.

(e) There is a Contact Aeroplane Dropping Station at G.16.b.5.8. operated by the Division.

14.....

14. Dumps.

Main R.E. Dump is situated at G.23.b.5.3.

Adv. R.E. Dump is situated at H.15.d.3.3.

Divisional Reserve Magazine - BRASSERIE, ST NICHOLAS.

Advanced Grenade Dump - H.13.b.8.3.

Water Dump - H.13.c.2.2. (1000 gallons in Tanks).

15. Medical arrangements for evacuation of wounded.

From Regimental Aid Posts by hand or wheeled stretchers to Bearer Post, FAMPOUX, thence by Ambulance Car to Advanced Dressing Station, ~~ST NICHOLAS~~, L'ABBAYETTE or by Pontoon from FAMPOUX Lock to ATHIES Lock, and then by Ambulance Car.

Main Dressing Station is at ~~HAUTE AVESNES~~. Deaf and Dumb Institute ARRAS.

16. Notes on the River SCARPE.

(i) The C.R.E. of the Right Division is responsible for regulating the level of water between FAMPOUX and ATHIES. Sluices at FAMPOUX MILL are employed for this purpose.

(ii) Bridges. There are four bridges over the river in the forward Area -

at H.24.a.4.7.	Wooden	- to take Infantry in file and pack animals.
H.24.a.6.4.	Wooden	- to take Infantry in file.
H.24.central.	"	- to take Infantry in file and pack animals.
H.24.d.65.70.	"	- to take infantry in file and pack animals.

There is a Bridge ready on the bank at H.22.a.75.25.

(iii) Pontoons. There are 9 pontoons used for the conveyance of R.E. material and other stores and for the evacuation of wounded. These are supplemented by five punts.

Traffic....

Traffic is from ATHIES to FAMPOUX Lock, which is out of repair. Material etc., is trans-shipped round the Lock by means of a tramway supplied with derricks. Pontoons and punts proceed thonce at present as far as H.24.d.5.8.

(iv) Tow-path. The tow-path has been repaired as far as H.24.d.5.8.

(v) Piers. There are piers - one above and one below FAMPOUX Lock, and one at H.24.d.5.8. and one at H.24.a.4.7.

Stewart.
Lieutenant Colonel,
General Staff,
9th (Scottish) Division.

1st June, 1917.

A P P E N D I C E S.

==*=*=*=*=*=*=*=*=*=*=*=*=*=*=*

May 1917

W. 15517—M. 141. 250,000. 1/16. L. S. & Co. Forms/W 3091/2. Army Form W. 3091.

Cover for Documents.

Nature of Enclosures.

Notes, or Letters written.

(1)

AB Cg 9 Lz4 Thes

Charges to Pay. £ s. d.

Office Stamp. ARMY Y1 -9.IV.17. TELEGRAPHS

Service Instructions. Priority Lz4

Handed in at .... Office 5.30 a m. Received 5.3.. m.

TO Hunt

Sender's Number	Day of Month	In reply to Number	AAA
JB39	9th		

YYV 120

All ready for attack.

FROM Meet

PLACE & TIME 3.30 am

Wt. 432—M437 500,000 Pads. H W V 5/16 Forms C.2123.

2

"A" Form.

MESSAGES AND SIGNALS.

Army Form C.2121
(in pads of 100).
No. of Message ....

Prefix .... Code .... m. Office of Origin and Service Instructions.	Words | Charge Sent At .... m. To .... By	*This message is on a/c of:* .... *Service.* .... (Signature of "Franking Officer.")	Recd. at .... m. Date .... From .... By ....

TO: 9th Division

Sender's Number.	Day of Month.	In reply to Number.	AAA
* [illegible]	9th		

All Companies 9th Seaforths Pioneers arrived in battle position. Headquarters Sunday Avenue G.16.b.1.9

From: C.O. Pioneers

Place: Sunday Avenue

Time:

The above may be forwarded as now corrected.

.... *Censor.*

(Z)

.... Signature of Addressor or person authorised to telegraph in his name.

* This line should be erased if not required.

750,000. W 2186—M509. H. W. & V., Ld. 6/16.

Army Form C. 2123.
(In books of 50's in duplicate.)

"C" Form (Original).
MESSAGES AND SIGNALS.

No. of Message ....

Prefix .... Code .... Words ....

£ s. d.

Charges to collect

Service Instructions.

Received

From ....

By ....

Sent, or sent out

At ....

To ....

By ....

Office Stamp.

9.IV.17.

TELEGRAPHS

Handed in at .... Office .... m. Received .... m.

TO

*Sender's Number	Day of Month	In reply to Number	AAA
	9		

YYY AAA 109

all ready for attack

5 – 39

FROM
PLACE & TIME

Covey

5·26 am

* This line should be erased if not required.

Wt. 492—M437 500,000 Pads. H W V 5 16 Forms C.2123.

4

"A" Form.

Army Form C.2121
(In pads of 100).

MESSAGES AND SIGNALS.

No. of Message ....

Prefix .... Code .... m.	Words	Charge	This message is on a/c of:	Recd. at .... m.
Office of Origin and Service Instructions.	Sent		.... Service.	Date ....
Copse	At .... m.			From ....
	To			
	By		(Signature of "Franking Officer.")	By ....

TO CRA

Sender's Number.	Day of Month.	In reply to Number.	AAA
* AD 34	9/4		

5 40 am FOO reports attack well launched aaa Our barrage good aaa Enemy barrage opened fire five minutes after ours

From Blasers (52nd Bde)
Place
Time

The above may be forwarded as now corrected.

(Z)

Censor. Signature of Addressor or person authorised to telegraph in his name.

* This line should be erased if not required.

750,000. W 2186—M509. H. W. & V., Ld. 6/16.

5

"C" Form. Army Form C. 2123. (In books of 100).

MESSAGES AND SIGNALS. No. of Message

Prefix SB Code JC Words 37	Received. From [illegible] By Miller	Sent, or sent out. At To By	Office Stamp. 9.IV.17
Charges to collect £ s. d.			
Service Instructions. Priority			

Handed in at G 7 Office 6.15 a m. Received 6.17 m.

TO G 9 Div.

*Sender's Number	Day of Month	In reply to Number	AAA
BM 909	9		

Enemy barrage slight and caused very few casualties at starting aaa BROOK reports at 6.5 am thirty prisoners passing back

14

FROM G 7 [illegible] Bde
PLACE & TIME 6.15 am

* This line should be erased if not required.

(6834). Wt. W7496/M857. 500,000 Pads. 10/16. D. D. & L. (E 489). Forms C/2123/3.

6

"C" Form.

MESSAGES AND SIGNALS.

Army Form C. 2123.
(In books of 100).

No. of Message

Prefix Am Code FBS Words 30

Received. From FZ2 By Thos

Charges to collect £ s. d.

Service Instructions.

Sent, or sent out. At ... m. To ... By ...

Office Stamp. ARMY TELEGRAPHS YI 9.IV.17.

Handed in at FZ2 Office 5.13am. Received 5.22am.

TO Hunt

Sender's Number	Day of Month	In reply to Number	AAA
Bm 301	9th		

German third trench taken by 12th Royal Scots and telephone communication established to their temporary hd qrs which are in a shell hole

20

FROM
PLACE & TIME
Over
5.55 am

* This line should be erased if not required.

(6334). Wt. W7496/M857. 500,000 Pads. 10/16. D. D. & L. (E 489). Forms C/2123/3.

4

"A" Form.
Army Form C.2121
(In pads of 100).

MESSAGES AND SIGNALS.

No. of Message ....

Prefix .... Code .... m.	Words / Charge	*This message is on a/c of:*	Recd. at ....m.
Office of Origin and Service Instructions.	Sent	..........*Service.*	Date ....
....	At..........m.		From ....
....	To	....	
....	By	(Signature of "Franking Officer.")	By ....

TO { 9th Division

Sender's Number.	Day of Month.	In reply to Number.	AAA
*			

R.F. [illegible] report that they
have taken FREDS Wood
[illegible] [illegible] [illegible] [illegible] on
Black line but cannot be
relieved by 9th Div. Troops

From Corps [illegible]
Place
Time 6.29am

The above may be forwarded as now corrected. (Z)

.... *Censor.* Signature of Addressor or person authorised to telegraph in his name.

* This line should be erased if not required.

750,000. W 2186—M509. H. W. & V., Ld. 6/16.

8

"A" Form.

Army Form C.2121
(In pads of 100).

No. of Message ....

MESSAGES AND SIGNALS.

Prefix ..... Code ..... m. / Office of Origin and Service Instructions.	Words	Charge	This message is on a/c of: ..... Service. (Signature of "Franking Officer.")	Recd. at ..... m.
	Sent			Date .....
	At ..... m.			From .....
	To			
	By			By .....

TO 9th Division

* Sender's Number.	Day of Month.	In reply to Number.	AAA

Foo reports we have captured Black Line

Phone

From
Place
Time 6.40 am

The above may be forwarded as now corrected. (Z)

Censor. Signature of Addressor or person authorised to telegraph in his name.

* This line should be erased if not required.

750,000. W 2186—M509. H. W. & V., Ld. 6/16.

9

To

17th Corps.
15th Division.
34th Division.
4th Division.

No.G.397. 9/4.

Right Battalion, 27th Infantry Brigade reported in German Third Trench telephonic communication established.a.a.a. F.O.O. with 26th Infantry Brigade reports that Brigade has occupied BLACK LINE.

9th Division.

6.45 a.m.

(11)

"A" Form.
MESSAGES AND SIGNALS.

Army Form C.2121
(In pads of 100).
No. of Message..........

Prefix ....Code..........m. | Words | Charge | This message is on a/c of: | Recd. at..........m.

Office of Origin and Service Instructions.
Copy

Sent
At..........m.
To..........
By..........

..........Service.
(Signature of "Franking Officer.")

Date..........
From..........
By..........

TO 9th Division

Sender's Number.	Day of Month.	In reply to Number.	AAA
* 93			

29th Bde is sending one Battery forward 6-50 am.

From Bde 9
Place
Time 6-52 am

The above may be forwarded as now corrected.
....
Censor.

(Z) (sd) S.K. Hayden
Signature of Addressor or person authorised to telegraph in his name.

* This line should be erased if not required.

750,000. W 2186—M509. H. W. & V., Ld. 6/16.

"A" Form.

Army Form C.2121
(In pads of 100)

MESSAGES AND SIGNALS.

No. of Message ....

Prefix .... Code .... m. / Office of Origin and Service Instructions.	Words / Charge	This message is on a/c of:	Recd. at ....m.
	Sent	.... Service.	Date ....
	At .... m.		From ....
	To		
	By	(Signature of "Franking Officer.")	By ....

TO 9th Division

Sender's Number.	Day of Month.	In reply to Number.	
* 15	9		AAA

OC 50th Bde reports he is moving 6/50 forward and that the enemy is offering very little resistance aaa [illegible] 11.35 am

From RA 9
Place
Time 6 am

The above may be forwarded as now corrected.

Censor.

(Z) (sd) [illegible]

Signature of Addressor or person authorised to telegraph in his name.

* This line should be erased if not required.

750,000. W 2186—M509. H. W. & V., Ld. 6/16.

13

To.

XVII Corps.
4th Division.

No.G.398. 9/4.

One Battery of 50th Brigade and one battery 29th Brigade are moving forward a.a.a. Addressed 17th Corps, repeated 4th. Division.

9th Division.

7 a.m.

14

"A" Form.
Army Form C.2121
(in pads of 100).

MESSAGES AND SIGNALS.

No. of Message ....

Prefix ....Code..........m.	Words	Charge	This message is on a/c of:	Recd. at..........m.
Office of Origin and Service Instructions.	Sent		..........Service.	Date ....
	At..........m.			From ....
	To			
	By		(Signature of "Franking Officer.")	By ....

TO 9th Divn

Sender's Number.	Day of Month.	In reply to Number.	
*	9/4		AAA

Black Watch on Black Line
few casualties
A Coy 9th Seaforths on their
objective C Coy held up by
bombing attacks from [illegible]

From 26th Bde
Place
Time 7.5 am

The above may be forwarded as now corrected. (Z)

.... Censor. Signature of Addressor or person authorised to telegraph in his name.

* This line should be erased if not required.

750,000. W 2186—M509. H. W. & V., Ld. 6/16.

(15)

"A" Form.

MESSAGES AND SIGNALS.

Army Form C.2121
(in pads of 100).
No. of Message ....

Prefix .... Code .... m.	Words	Charge	This message is on a/c of:	Recd. at .... m.
Office of Origin and Service Instructions.	Sent		.... Service.	Date ....
	At .... m.			From ....
	To			
	By		(Signature of "Franking Officer.")	By ....

TO 7th Division

Sender's Number.	Day of Month.	In reply to Number.	AAA
* 14			

14th Bde reports our [illegible] are right in Black Line approximately H 7 a 8 0 [illegible] up H 7 a and G 12 a aaa Enemy barrage not heavy [illegible] shelling Eastern approaches to ARRAS. Message received 6 55 am

From Bde 7th

Place

Time 6 59 am

The above may be forwarded as now corrected.

(Z)

Censor. Signature of Addressor or person authorised to telegraph in his name.

* This line should be erased if not required.

750,000. W 2186—M509. H. W. & V., Ld. 6/16.

15

"A" Form.

MESSAGES AND SIGNALS.

Army Form C.2121
(In pads of 100).
No. of Message ....

Prefix .... Code .... m. Office of Origin and Service Instructions.	Words / Charge Sent At .... m. To .... By	*This message is on a/c of:* .... *Service.* .... (Signature of "Franking Officer.")	Recd. at .... m. Date .... From .... By ....

TO { CRA

Sender's Number.	Day of Month.	In reply to Number.	
*			AAA

Battle progressing favourably About 40 prisoners have come down since 6 am. A visual signalling post has been established at [illegible] [illegible] Cemetery aaa German [illegible] appears to come from Blue Line Our infantry visible on crest in G 12 b & D aaa Red [illegible] visible in front line in G 18 b

Recd 7.15 am

From	Fr.	2nd Bde
Place		
Time		

The above may be forwarded as now corrected. (Z)

.... *Censor.* .... Signature of Addressor or person authorised to telegraph in his name.

* This line should be erased if not required.

750,000. W 2185—M509. H. W. & V., Ld. 6/16.

16

"A" Form.
Army Form C.2121
(In pads of 100).

MESSAGES AND SIGNALS.

No. of Message ....

Prefix ....Code..........m. / Office of Origin and Service Instructions.	Words	Charge	This message is on a/c of:	Recd. at..........m.
....	Sent		..........Service.	Date..........
....	At..........m.			From ....
....	To			
....	By		(Signature of "Franking Officer.")	By ....

TO { [illegible]

Sender's Number.	Day of Month.	In reply to Number.	AAA
* KA34	9th		

L.O. report that prisoners are Bavarians and Prussians and two Battns are in reserve at ROEUX

Recd 9 [illegible]

From 1st Bde RA [illegible]
Place
Time

The above may be forwarded as now corrected.
(Z)
.... Censor.
.... Signature of Addressor or person authorised to telegraph in his name.

* This line should be erased if not required.

750,000. W 2186—M509. H. W. & V., Ld. 6/16.

14

Army Form C. 2123
(In books of 100.)

"C" Form.

MESSAGES AND SIGNALS.

No. of Message

Prefix [illegible] Code [illegible] Words [illegible]	Received. From [illegible] By [illegible]	Sent, or sent out. At m. To By	Office Stamp. ARMY TELEGRAPHS Y I -9.IV.17.
£ s. d. Charges to collect			
Service Instructions.			

Handed in at [illegible] Office [illegible] m. Received [illegible] m.

TO 9th Div

*Sender's Number	Day of Month	In reply to Number	AAA
[illegible]	9		

Observers from left brigade OP report BLACK LINE captured aaa Addsd 17 Corps repeated 5th Div 1st Canadian Div 4 and 2 Div

42

7-20 am

FROM PLACE & TIME 51st Div 6.55 am

* This line should be erased if not required.

(6334). Wt. W7496/M857. 500,000 Pads. 10/16. D. D. & L. (E489). Forms C/2123/3.

(18)

"C" Form.

Army Form C. 2123.
(In books of 100).

MESSAGES AND SIGNALS.

No. of Message

Prefix SM Code GCK Words 39	Received. From RLC By Rlk	Sent, or sent out. At m. To By	Office Stamp. ARMY TELEGRAPHS 9 IV 17
£ s. d. Charges to collect			
Service Instructions.			

Handed in at AJLR Office 7.45 a.m. Received 7.50 a.m.

TO 9th Divn

*Sender's Number	Day of Month	In reply to Number	AAA
G 8	9		

Our Gunners report that our troops have taken all of MAISON BLANCHE Ridge / G 6 D area Enemy putting up barrage in old NO MANS LAND also smoke barrage eastern side of above ridge

(A)

G 7.55

H. S.

FROM 34 Div

PLACE & TIME

* This line should be erased if not required.

(6334). Wt. W7496/M857. 500,000 Pads. 10/16. D. D. & L. (E 489). Forms C/2123/3.

19

"A" Form.

Army Form C.2121
(In pads of 100).

MESSAGES AND SIGNALS.

No. of Message ....

Prefix .... Code .... m. / Office of Origin and Service Instructions.	Words	Charge	This message is on a/c of: .... Service. (Signature of "Franking Officer.")	Recd. at .... m.
	Sent			Date ....
	At .... m.			From ....
	To			
	By			By ....

TO CRA

Sender's Number.	Day of Month.	In reply to Number.	
*	9th		AAA

Enemy have practically ceased firing on our front system only occasional 77 mm landing in the Mons Farm

Recd 7.34 am

From Tras Bde

Place

Time

The above may be forwarded as now corrected.

(Z)

Censor.

Signature of Addressor or person authorised to telegraph in his name.

* This line should be erased if not required.

750,000. W 2180—M509. H. W. & V., Ld. 6/16.

20

"C" Form.
MESSAGES AND SIGNALS.

Army Form C. 2123.
(In books of 100).
No. of Message

Prefix Am Code JJ2 Words 58
£ s. d.
Charges to collect
Service Instructions.
JJ2

Received.
From 132
By Sus

Sent, or sent out
At m.
To
By

Office Stamp.
ARMY ... 9 II 17 ... GRAPHS

Handed in at JJ2 Office 7.3 m. Received 7.? m.

TO Hunt

*Sender's Number	Day of Month	In reply to Number	AAA
JC 2	9		

following	further	number	prisoners	received
aaa	25th	Bavarian	Reserve	Regt
19	belonging	to	companies	1
2	3	4	also	4
men	of	1st	machine	Gun
Coy	same	regt	aaa	8th
Bavarian	Infantry	8	belonging	to
companies	6	and	8	aaa
3rd	Reserve	bavarian	pioneer	regt
2	belonging	one	and	reserve
companies				

7.40 am

FROM Cover
PLACE & TIME 7.20 am

* This line should be erased if not required.
(6334). Wt. W7496/M857. 500,000 Pads. 10/16. D. D. & L. (E 489). Forms C/2123/3.

21

"A" Form.
Army Form C.2121
(In pads of 100).

MESSAGES AND SIGNALS.

No. of Message..........

Prefix ....Code............m. | Words | Charge | This message is on a/c of: | Recd. at..............m.

Office of Origin and Service Instructions.

Sent
At..............m.
To..............
By..............

..................Service.

(Signature of "Franking Officer.")

Date..............
From..............
By..............

TO { 9th Division

Sender's Number.	Day of Month.	In reply to Number.	AAA
*			

746 14th Bde reports our Infantry are advancing without difficulty

From 9th Bde
Place
Time 7.50 am

L Rose Major

The above may be forwarded as now corrected.

(Z)

..........................Censor.

Signature of Addressor or person authorised to telegraph in his name.

* This line should be erased if not required.

750,000. W 2186—M509. H. W. & V., Ld. 6/16.

22

MESSAGES AND SIGNALS.

(In books of 100). No. of Message

Prefix XYS Code GKX Words 29	Received. From YO By Payne	Sent, or sent out. At To By
£ s. d. Charges to collect		Office Stamp. ARMY TELEGRAPHS 9.IV.17.
Service Instructions. Priority		

Handed in at .... Office 7.54 A m. Received 7.58 m.

TO 9th Divn

*Sender's Number	Day of Month	In reply to Number	AAA
G561	9		

Enemy still holding out in BLANGY about G.24a 5.5 being dealt with aaa added corps corps Arty 9th 12th 37th Divns

8.4 am

FROM PLACE & TIME 15 Divn 7.45am

* This line should be erased if not required.

(6334). Wt. W7406/M857. 500,000 Pads. 10/16. D. D. & L. (E480). Forms C/2123/3.

23

"A" Form.

MESSAGES AND SIGNALS.

Army Form C.2121
(In pads of 100).
No. of Message..........

Prefix ....Code............m. | Words | Charge

Office of Origin and Service Instructions.

Sent
At...............m.
To...............
By...............

This message is on a/c of:
.................*Service.*
(Signature of "Franking Officer.")

Recd. at...............m.
Date...............
From...............
By...............

TO { G.W. Division

Sender's Number. | Day of Month. | In reply to Number. | AAA

The 18th W.B. report that at the request of the left Bde they have put heavy TMs on the Island

From G.W. Bde
Place
Time 8 am

(sd) J. Rose
Major

The above may be forwarded as now corrected. (Z)

Censor. Signature of Addressor or person authorised to telegraph in his name.

* This line should be erased if not required.

750,000. W 2186—M509. H. W. & V., Ld. 6/16.

24

"A" Form.

Army Form C.2121
(In pads of 100).

MESSAGES AND SIGNALS.

No. of Message ....

Prefix ....Code..........m. Office of Origin and Service Instructions.	Words / Charge — Sent At..........m. To .... By	This message is on a/c of: ....Service. (Signature of "Franking Officer.")	Recd. at..........m. Date .... From .... By ....

TO CRA

Sender's Number. *	Day of Month.	In reply to Number.	AAA

Infantry moving well forward towards Blue Line behind our barrage

From 100 32nd Bat
Place
Time

The above may be forwarded as now corrected. (Z)

Censor. Signature of Addressor or person authorised to telegraph in his name.

* This line should be erased if not required.

750,000. W 2186—M509. H. W. & V., Ld. 6/16.

25

Army Form C. 2123.
(In books of 100).

"C" Form.

MESSAGES AND SIGNALS.

No. of Message

Prefix [illegible] Code Words 40	Received.	Sent, or sent out.	Office Stamp.
£ s. d. Charges to collect	From YG By Hnd	At m.	ARMY YI-9.IV.17. TELEGRAPHS
Service Instructions. YG priority		To	
		By	8/15

Handed in at YG Office 8/15a m. Received m.

TO 9th Div

*Sender's Number	Day of Month	In reply to Number	AAA
563	9th		

NCO captured by 12th Div states that enemy main line is on WANCOURT FEUCHY line & that we are at present dealing with rearguards aaa added Bdes HA & 9th Div

8 20 Hd

FROM 9th Div
PLACE & TIME 8.15 am

* This line should be erased if not required.

(6334). Wt. W7496/M857. 500,000 Pads. 10/16. D. D. & L. (E 489). Forms C/2123/3.

26

"C" Form.

MESSAGES AND SIGNALS.

Army Form C. 2123.
(In books of 100).

No. of Message

Prefix HM Hex 26 Code .... Words ....

£ s. d.

Charges to collect

Received. From .... By ....

Sent, or sent out. At .... To .... By ....

Office Stamp.

Service Instructions.

Handed in at .... Office .... m. Received 8-35 m.

TO 9 Divn

*Sender's Number	Day of Month	In reply to Number	AAA
BM 304	9		

Report from OBERMEYER says COVER
can be seen on railway
embankment and nothing can be
seen in cutting aaa

8.40am

FROM
PLACE & TIME Cover 8.2am

* This line should be erased if not required.

(6334). Wt. W7496/M857. 500,000 Pads. 10/16. D. D. & L. (E 489). Forms C/2123/3.

24

"A" Form.

MESSAGES AND SIGNALS.

Army Form C.2121
(in pads of 100).
No. of Message ....

Prefix .... Code .... m. | Words | Charge

Office of Origin and Service Instructions.

Sent
At .... m.
To ....
By ....

This message is on a/c of:
.... *Service.*
....
(Signature of "Franking Officer.")

Recd. at .... m.
Date ....
From ....
By ....

TO 9th Division

Sender's Number.	Day of Month.	In reply to Number.	AAA
*			

Left Regiment at Chimney OP reports he can see men moving about freely on the railway at 8-35 am

Rec'd 8-45 am

From RA 9th
Place
Time 8-40 am

The above may be forwarded as now corrected. (Z)

.... *Censor.* Signature of Addressor or person authorised to telegraph in his name.

* This line should be erased if not required.

750,000. W 2186—M509. H. W. & V., Ld. 6/16.

28

"A" Form.

MESSAGES AND SIGNALS.

Army Form C.2121 (In pads of 100).

No. of Message ....

Prefix ....Code..........m. | Words | Charge

Office of Origin and Service Instructions.

Sent

At..........m.

To ....

By ....

This message is on a/c of:

..........*Service.*

(Signature of "Franking Officer.")

Recd. at..........m.

Date..........

From ....

By ....

TO 9th Division

Sender's Number.	Day of Month.	In reply to Number.	AAA
*	9th		

[illegible] 10th [illegible] reports Blue Line Captured at 8-20 am Confirmed by Liaison Officer of 27th Bde

[illegible]

From 9th Da

Place

Time

The above may be forwarded as now corrected.

Censor.

(Z)

Signature of Addressor or person authorised to telegraph in his name.

* This line should be erased if not required.

750,000. W 2186—M509. H. W. & V., Ld. 6/16.

29

"A" Form. Army Form C.2121 (In pads of 100).

MESSAGES AND SIGNALS.

No. of Message ....

Prefix .... Code .... m.	Words	Charge	This message is on a/c of:	Recd. at .... m.
Office of Origin and Service Instructions.	Sent		.... Service.	Date ....
	At .... m.			From ....
	To			
	By		(Signature of "Franking Officer.")	By ....

TO 9th Division

Sender's Number.	Day of Month.	In reply to Number.	AAA
*	9th		

8.50 am 9th Seaforths 2 Platoons front Coy reported on Blue Line Others are advancing Prisoners say no one escaped from Blue Line British on Railway Line

From 26th Brigade
Place
Time 8.50 am.

The above may be forwarded as now corrected. (Z)

Censor. Signature of Addressor or person authorised to telegraph in his name.

* This line should be erased if not required.

760,000. W 2186—M509. H. W. & V., Ld. 6/16.

30

"A" Form.

MESSAGES AND SIGNALS.

Army Form C.2121
(In pads of 100).
No. of Message ....

Prefix ....Code.............m. | Words | Charge

Office of Origin and Service Instructions.

Sent
At..................m.
To ....
By ....

This message is on a/c of:
..........................*Service.*
....
(Signature of "Franking Officer.")

Recd. at..............m.
Date..................
From ....
By ....

TO 9th Division

Sender's Number. | Day of Month. 9 | In reply to Number. | AAA

Report 9am. that attack believed held up just in front of Blue line. Heavy trench mortar fire from depression through which TEES trench runs

From 26th Bde
Place
Time 9 am.

The above may be forwarded as now corrected. (Z)

Censor. Signature of Addressor or person authorised to telegraph in his name.

* This line should be erased if not required.

750,000. W 2186—M509. H. W. & V., Ld. 6/16.

31

"A" Form.
Army Form C.2121
(In pads of 100).

MESSAGES AND SIGNALS.

No. of Message ....

Prefix .... Code .... m.	Words	Charge	This message is on a/c of:	Recd. at .... m.
Office of Origin and Service Instructions.	Sent		.... Service.	Date ....
	At .... m.			From ....
	To			
	By		(Signature of "Franking Officer.")	By ....

TO 9th Division

Sender's Number.	Day of Month.	In reply to Number.	AAA
*	9/4		

Coy of Seaforths at HERON Farm very weak. C.O. 7th Seaforths sent for reinforcements to enable him to attack that part of Blue line. 26th Bde have used up 3 Battns and General Kennedy does not consider Camerons strong enough to attack Brown line

From 26th Brigade
Place
Time 9.15 am.

The above may be forwarded as now corrected. (Z)

.... Censor. Signature of Addressor or person authorised to telegraph in his name.

* This line should be erased if not required.

750,000. W 2186—M509. H. W. & V., Ld. 6/16.

32

"C" Form.

MESSAGES AND SIGNALS.

Army Form C. 2123.
(In books of 100).

No. of Message

Prefix ... Code ... Words ... £ s. d. Charges to collect	Received. From ... By ...	Sent, or sent out. Office Stamp. At ... To ... By ...
Service Instructions.		

Handed in at ... Office ... m. Received ... m.

TO

*Sender's Number	Day of Month	In reply to Number	AAA

9.29 am

FROM

PLACE & TIME

* This line should be erased if not required.

(6334). Wt. W7496/M857. 500,000 Pads. 10/16. D. D. & L. (E 489). Forms C/2123/3.

"C" Form.

Army Form C. 2123.
(In books of 100).

MESSAGES AND SIGNALS. No. of Message..................

Prefix.......... Code.......... Words.......... £ s. d. Charges to collect Service Instructions.	Received. From.......... By..........	Sent, or sent out. At..........m. To.......... By..........	Office Stamp. ARMY TELEGRAPHS 9.IV.17

Handed in at [illegible] Office [illegible] m. Received 10 [illegible] m.

TO [illegible]

*Sender's Number	Day of Month	In reply to Number	AAA
KIM 306	9th		

Information from OBERMEYER confirms taking of BLUE LINE by H. L. Bde aaa same officer reports he can see South Africans also on this line but smoke too heavy to see anything on left aaa He reports enemy shelling OBERMEYER to left of 27th Bde.

10.2 am

FROM 27th Bde

PLACE & TIME 8.55 am

* This line should be erased if not required.

(6334). Wt. W7496/M857. 500,000 Pads. 10/16. D. D. & L. (E 489). Forms C/2123/3.

34

"A" Form.
Army Form C.2121
(In pads of 100).

MESSAGES AND SIGNALS.

No. of Message..........

Prefix ....Code..........m. Office of Origin and Service Instructions.	Words / Charge — Sent: At..........m. To.......... By..........	This message is on a/c of: ....Service. (Signature of "Franking Officer.")	Recd. at..........m. Date.......... From.......... By..........

TO: CRA

Sender's Number.	Day of Month.	In reply to Number.	AAA
*	9		

One of our Tanks can be seen approaching blue line at [illegible] [illegible] top speed

Recd 9 40 am

From	FOO	C/32 HA [illegible]
Place		
Time		6.50 am

The above may be forwarded as now corrected. (Z)

Censor. Signature of Addressor or person authorised to telegraph in his name.

* This line should be erased if not required.

750,000. W 2186—M509. H. W. & V., Ld. 6/16.

36

"C" Form.

Army Form C. 2123.
(In books of 100).

MESSAGES AND SIGNALS. No. of Message

Prefix ... Code ... Words ...	Received.	Sent, or sent out.	Office Stamp.
£ s. d. Charges to collect	From ... By [illegible]	At ... m.	ARMY Y1 – 9.IV.17 TELEGRAPHS
Service Instructions.		To ... By ...	

Handed in at [illegible] Office 8.45 m. Received 9.44 m.

TO 9 Divn.

*Sender's Number	Day of Month	In reply to Number	AAA
	9		

About	400	prisoners	all	normal
aaa	taken	in	front	system
and	black	line	aaa	know
nothing	about	troops	behind	them
aaa	Do	not	appear	to
have	put	up	fight	

9-47am

FROM PLACE & TIME O 9 Divn 8-0 am

* This line should be erased if not required.

(6334). Wt. W7496/M857. 500,000 Pads. 10/16. D. D. & L. (E 489). Forms C/2123/3.

37

"C" Form. Army Form C. 2123.
(In books of 100).

MESSAGES AND SIGNALS. No. of Message

Prefix SB Code 9.38 Words 53

£ s. d.

Charges to collect

Received. From 9th By SM

Service Instructions. Priority

Sent, or sent out. At m. To By

Office Stamp. ARMY TELEGRAPHS 9.IV.17

Handed in at 15th Office 9.37 m. Received m.

TO 9th Div

*Sender's Number	Day of Month	In reply to Number	AAA
G568	9th		

Situation 9.25 am aaa On Right reports conflicting aaa OP reports our troops in FEUCHY SWITCH east of HARTS WORK at 9.37 am aaa Left Bde OP reports they have blue line aaa BLANGY is cleared aaa [illegible] Corps [illegible] 9th 12th and 37th Divns

9.58 a

FROM 15th Divn

PLACE & TIME 9.35 am

* This line should be erased if not required.

(6334). Wt. W7496/M857. 500,000 Pads. 10/16. D. D. & L. (E 489). Forms C/2123/3.

"C" Form.

Army Form C. ...
(In books of 100).

MESSAGES AND SIGNALS.

No. of Message ....

Prefix ...... Code ...... Words	Received.	Sent, or sent out.	Office Stamp.
Charges to collect £ s. d.	From	At ...... m.	ARMY YI-9.IV.17 TELEGRAPHS
Service Instructions. Priority	By	To	
		By	

Handed in at ...... Office 9.50 am. Received ...... m.

TO 9th Divn

*Sender's Number	Day of Month	In reply to Number	AAA
G 3888	9		

4 Divn will advance in accordance with their orders aaa addsd 4th Divn Repeated 9th Divn 34th Divn 6th Corps 3rd Army

Bdes informed

9.58 am

FROM 17 Corps

PLACE & TIME 9-45 am

* This line should be erased if not required.

(6334). Wt, W7496/M857. 500,000 Pads. 10/16. D. D. & L. (E 489). Forms C/2123/3.

39

"C" Form.

Army Form C. 2123.
(In books of 100).

MESSAGES AND SIGNALS.

No. of Message

Prefix Code Words

£ s. d.

Charges to collect

Service Instructions.

Received.
From
By

Sent, or sent out.
At m.
To
By

Office Stamp.
Y1 -9.IV.17. ARMY TELEGRAPHS

Handed in at YCDR Office 9.50 am m. Received 10.2 a m.

TO 9 Divn

*Sender's Number S14 | Day of Month 9 | In reply to Number | AAA

Aeroplane Flares show Blue Line H1C and H1B captured by 101st Bde aaa No flares yet seen north of Railway B25A B25D aaa Observer adds aaa Can see lots of our men in the Railway addressed 17th Corps repeated 9th 51st and 4th Divns

10.5am

FROM
PLACE & TIME 34 Divn 9am

* This line should be erased if not required.

(6334). Wt. W7496/M857. 500,000 Pads. 10/16. D. D. & L. (E 489). Forms C/2123/3.

40

"A" Form.

MESSAGES AND SIGNALS.

Army Form C.2121
(In pads of 100).
No. of Message ....

Prefix .... Code .... m. Office of Origin and Service Instructions.	Words	Charge	This message is on a/c of: .... Service. (Signature of "Franking Officer.")	Recd. at .... m.
	Sent			Date ....
	At .... m.			From ....
	To			
	By			By ....

TO { 9th Div

Sender's Number.	Day of Month.	In reply to Number.	AAA
*			

S O S 72nd Bde in NTE Trench
reports it does not appear that
15th Div South of Scarpe
have got on as far as we
have MG fire from South
coming over NTE Trench

From RA 9th Div
Place
Time 10.3 am

The above may be forwarded as now corrected. (Z)
.... *Censor.* Signature of Addressor or person authorised to telegraph in his name.

* This line should be erased if not required.

750,000. W 2186—M509. H. W. & V., Ld. 6/16.

41

"C" Form.
MESSAGES AND SIGNALS.

Army Form C. 2123.
(In books of 100).

No. of Message

Prefix Code YT Words 32

Received. From Y6 By

Sent, or sent out. At To By

Office Stamp. Y1 9.IV.17. TELEGRAPHS

Charges to collect £ s. d.

Service Instructions.

Handed in at Y6DR Office 9.30a m. Received m.

TO 9 Divn

Sender's Number	Day of Month	In reply to Number	AAA
G15	9		

Map dropped By aeroplane these Hdqrs shows flares Railway cutting H7B and D. your front aaa addsd 9th Divn aaa Repld 17 Corps

H7B

10.16 am

FROM PLACE & TIME 34 Divn 9-25am

* This line should be erased if not required.

(6334). Wt. W7496/M857. 500,000 Pads. 10/16. D. D. & L. (E 489). Forms C/2123/3.

42

"A" Form.

Army Form C.2121
(in pads of 100).

MESSAGES AND SIGNALS.

No. of Message ....

Prefix .... Code .... m.	Words	Charge	This message is on a/c of:	Recd. at .... m.
Office of Origin and Service Instructions.	Sent		.... Service.	Date ....
....	At .... m.			From ....
....	To		....	
....	By		(Signature of "Franking Officer.")	By ....

TO { CRA

* Sender's Number.	Day of Month.	In reply to Number.	
6028	9th		AAA

A/40 opened fire from forward position at 9.30 am CRA then sending [illegible] forward

Recd 10.16 am

From 50th Bde
Place
Time 10 am

The above may be forwarded as now corrected.

(Z)

.... *Censor.*

.... Signature of Addressor or person authorised to telegraph in his name.

* This line should be erased if not required.

750,000. W 2186—M509. H. W. & V., Ld. 6/16.

42

"A" Form.

Army Form C.2121
(In pads of 100).

MESSAGES AND SIGNALS.

No. of Message ....

Prefix .... Code .... m. | Words | Charge | *This message is on a/c of:* .... *Service.* (Signature of "Franking Officer.") | Recd. at .... m. Date .... From .... By ....

Office of Origin and Service Instructions.

Sent At .... m. To .... By ....

TO [illegible]

Sender's Number.	Day of Month.	In reply to Number.	AAA
* AB 38	9th		

C Battery in action Artillery [illegible] [illegible] 122 Battery have orders to move forward aaa 9.20 am

From 5 [illegible] Brigade

Place

Time 9.30 am

The above may be forwarded as now corrected. (Z)

.... *Censor.* .... Signature of Addressor or person authorised to telegraph in his name.

* This line should be erased if not required.

760,000. W 2186—M509. H. W. & V., Ld. 6/16.

(44)

"A" Form.

MESSAGES AND SIGNALS.

Army Form C.2121
(In pads of 100).
No. of Message ....

Prefix .... Code .... m.

Office of Origin and Service Instructions.

Words	Charge

Sent
At .... m.
To ....
By ....

This message is on a/c of:
.... *Service.*

(Signature of "Franking Officer.")

Recd. at .... m.
Date ....
From ....
By ....

TO 9th Division

Sender's Number.	Day of Month.	In reply to Number.	AAA
*			

Batteries in action in [illegible] Artillery Trench C/50 A/50 C/52 124 & moving forward 122 126 and B/50 [illegible] 10.15 am

From RA 9th Divn
Place
Time 10.15 am

The above may be forwarded as now corrected.

(Z)

Censor.

Signature of Addressor or person authorised to telegraph in his name.

* This line should be erased if not required.

750,000. W 2186—M509. H. W. & V., Ld. 6/16.

45

"A" Form.

Army Form C.2121
(In pads of 100).

MESSAGES AND SIGNALS.

No. of Message ....

Prefix ....Code..........m. Office of Origin and Service Instructions.	Words	Charge	This message is on a/c of:	Recd. at..........m.
	Sent		..........Service.	Date..........
	At..........m.			From..........
	To..........			
	By..........		(Signature of "Franking Officer.")	By..........

TO 9th Division.

Sender's Number.	Day of Month.	In reply to Number.	AAA
*	9/4		

Have been through 2 Battalions 4th Regt. Reported that 3rd Bn was to have been brought up to Railway Cutting last night. If this was so we had wiped it out. Important to establish this fact as if correct we would have its one in front of us

From ~~[illegible]~~ HQrs 17th Corps
Place
Time 10.20 a.m.

The above may be forwarded as now corrected.

(Z)

Censor. Signature of Addressor or person authorised to telegraph in his name.

* This line should be erased if not required.

750,000. W 2186—M569. H. W. & V., Ld. 6/16.

46

"C" Form.
MESSAGES AND SIGNALS.

Army Form C. 2123.
(In books of 100.)

No. of Message

Prefix SM Code KAW Words 25	Received	Sent, or sent out	Office Stamp
£ s. d.	From YBK	At	Y m. 9. IV. 17. – D TELEGRAPHS
Charges to collect	By Thu	To	
Service Instructions.		By	

Handed in at YBK Office 10.8 m. Received 10.10 m.

TO 9th Div

*Sender's Number	Day of Month	In reply to Number	AAA
	9th	—	

About 17 officers and 650 OR all of 14 Bav Div have passed through here aaa 9.20 am

10.21a

FROM
PLACE & TIME I O 9th Div

* This line should be erased if not required.

(S.O. 1065) Wt. 7496—M 857 125,000 Pads. McC. & Co., Ltd. 10/16 (E 489) Forms C/2123

44

"A" Form.
MESSAGES AND SIGNALS.

Army Form C.2121
(in pads of 100).
No. of Message ....

Prefix ....Code..........m. | Words | Charge | This message is on a/c of: | Recd. at..........m.
Office of Origin and Service Instructions.

Sent
At..........m.
To ....
By ....

..........Service.

(Signature of "Franking Officer.")

Date ....
From ....
By ....

TO { CRA

Sender's Number.	Day of Month.	In reply to Number.	AAA
*	9		

G
Enemy aircraft very active
over our front

Recd 10-18 am

From 100 D/52 RFA
Place
Time 10 am

The above may be forwarded as now corrected. (Z)
.... Censor. Signature of Addressor or person authorised to telegraph in his name.

* This line should be erased if not required.

750,000. W 3186—M509. H. W. & V., Ld. 6/16.

47

"C" Form.

MESSAGES AND SIGNALS.

Army Form C. 2123.
(In books of 100).

No. of Message

Prefix SM Code Kg Words 18

£ s. d.

Charges to collect

Service Instructions.

Received. From By

Sent, or sent out. Office Stamp.

At m. To By

ARMY TELEGRAPHS Y1-9.IV.17.

Handed in at 3 A Bde Office m. Received m.

TO 9 Divn

*Sender's Number	Day of Month	In reply to Number	AAA
SM 954	9		

BROOK reports ENEMY PLANE continually flying very low over BLUE LINE

10.59 am

H.T.L.

Corps informed

FROM PLACE & TIME 3 A Bde 10.55 am

* This line should be erased if not required.

(6384). Wt. W7496/M857. 500,000 Pads. 10/16. D. D. & L. (E 489). Forms C/2123/3.

48

To.

17th Corps.

No.G.410. 9/4.

Infantry report enemy planes continually flying very low over BLUE LINE.

9th Division.

10.40 a.m.

49

Army Form C. 2123.
(In books of 100.)

"C" Form.

MESSAGES AND SIGNALS.

No. of Message.........

Prefix [illegible] Code [illegible] Words [illegible]

£ s. d.

Charges to collect

Received From JSK By Moran

Sent, or sent out At ......m. To ...... By ......

Office Stamp. ARMY Y- 9.IV.17.-D TELEGRAPHS

Service Instructions.

Handed in at JSK [illegible] Fields 10.57 Office ......m. Received ......m.

TO 9th Div ~~[illegible]~~

*Sender's Number	Day of Month	In reply to Number	AAA
	9th		

25 officers 1000 O.R. have passed through cage aaa still none of resting batt aaa 10.25 am aaa

11 am

FROM PLACE & TIME J.O. 9th Div

* This line should be erased if not required.

(S.O. 1065) Wt. 7406—M 857 125,000 Pads. McC. & Co., Ltd. 10/16 (E 489) Forms C/2123

50

"A" Form. Army Form C.2121 (In pads of 100).

MESSAGES AND SIGNALS.

No. of Message ....

Prefix .... Code .... m.	Words	Charge	This message is on a/c of:	Recd. at .... m.
Office of Origin and Service Instructions.	Sent		.... Service.	Date ....
	At .... m.			From ....
	To			
	By		(Signature of "Franking Officer.")	By ....

TO 9th Division

Sender's Number.	Day of Month.	In reply to Number.	AAA
*	9/4		

Right Bde have got Blue line
and Railway
Centre Brigade a bit uncertain
men seen in I 35 d 9.6.
Left Bde 2 Battns in Blue line
and 2 in Black. Cannot go
across open N of GAVRELLE
Right Bde [illegible] Dvn held up
Aeroplanes report flares [illegible]
and [illegible] 19 c leaving
gap to the South

From 34th Division
Place
Time 11.45 am

The above may be forwarded as now corrected. (Z)

Censor. Signature of Addressor or person authorised to telegraph in his name.

* This line should be erased if not required.

750,000. W 2186—M509. H. W. & V., Ld. 6/16.

5-1

"A" Form.

MESSAGES AND SIGNALS.

Army Form C.2121
(In pads of 100).
No. of Message..........

Prefix .... Code .... m. | Words | Charge

Office of Origin and Service Instructions.

Sent
At .... m.
To ....
By ....

This message is on a/c of:
.... *Service.*
....
(Signature of "Franking Officer.")

Recd. at .... m.
Date ....
From ....
By ....

TO 9th Division

Sender's Number.	Day of Month.	In reply to Number.	AAA
*	9/4		

Can we use 12th Bde to cover advance from their line

[illegible]

From [illegible]
Place
Time 12-30pm

The above may be forwarded as now corrected.
....
Censor.

(Z)
....
Signature of Addressor or person authorised to telegraph in his name.

* This line should be erased if not required.

750,000. W 9186—M509. H. W. & V., Ld. 6/16.

59

"C" Form.

Army Form C. 2123.
(In books of 100).

MESSAGES AND SIGNALS. No. of Message..........

Prefix...... Code...... Words...... £ s. d. Charges to collect	Received. From...... By......	Sent, or sent out. At......m. To...... By......	Office Stamp. ARMY TELEGRAPHS Y1-9.IV.17
Service Instructions. [illegible]			

Handed in at...... Office......m. Received......m.

TO [illegible]

*Sender's Number	Day of Month	In reply to Number	AAA
[illegible]			

[illegible] H2 [illegible] H [illegible] along [illegible] and along embankment [illegible]

12 30

FROM
PLACE & TIME [illegible]

* This line should be erased if not required.

(6334). Wt. W7496/M857. 500,000 Pads. 10/16. D. D. & L. (E 489). Forms C/2123/3.

53

Army Form C. 2121.
(In books of 100).

"C" Form.

MESSAGES AND SIGNALS.

No. of Message..........

Prefix.......... Code.......... Words..........	Received.	Sent, or sent out.	Office Stamp.
£ s. d.	From..........	At..........m.	ARMY TELEGRAPHS YI 9.IV.17
Charges to collect	By..........	To..........	
Service Instructions.		By..........	

Handed in at.......... Office..........m. Received..........m.

TO

*Sender's Number	Day of Month	In reply to Number	AAA

229 12-48 pm

FROM

PLACE & TIME

* This line should be erased if not required.

(6334). Wt. W7496/M857. 500,000 Pads. 10/16. D. D. & L. (E 489). Forms C/2123/3.

54

"A" Form.

Army Form C.2121
(in pads of 100).
No. of Message ....

MESSAGES AND SIGNALS.

Prefix .... Code .... m. | Words | Charge | This message is on a/c of: | Recd. at .... m.
Office of Origin and Service Instructions. | Sent | At .... m. | To .... | By .... | .... Service. | (Signature of "Franking Officer.") | Date .... | From .... | By ....

TO 9th Division

Sender's Number.	Day of Month.	In reply to Number.	AAA
*	9		

11th Brigade reports at 12.32 pm our infantry were seen moving towards [illegible] face apparently without much opposition.

From RA 9th Divn
Place
Time 12.46 pm

The above may be forwarded as now corrected. (Z)

Censor. Signature of Addressor or person authorised to telegraph in his name.

* This line should be erased if not required.

750,000. W 2186—M509. H. W. & V., Ld. 6/16.

55

Prefix..............Code..............m.	Words	Charge.	This message is on a/c of:	Recd. at ....m.
Office of Origin and Service Instructions.	Sent		..............Service.	Date
	At..............m.			From
	To			
	By		(Signature of "Franking Officer.")	By

TO ~~11th Bde.~~ Corps.

Sender's Number.	Day of Month.	In reply to Number.	AAA
*			

11.50 G.S.O.1 rang up Corps and asked for authority to use 11th Bde to support 27th Bde in their attack on Brow Line. This was given by B.G.G.S.

From Verbal
Place
Time 12.55 pm.

The above may be forwarded as now corrected. (Z)

Censor. Signature of Addressor or person authorised to telegraph in his name.

* This line should be erased if not required.

(S.O. 1919). Wt. W 5148/M 791 50,000 Pads. 8/16. McC. & Co., Ltd., London.

56

"C" Form.

Army Form C. 2123.
(In books of 100).

MESSAGES AND SIGNALS. No. of Message

Prefix Code Words
£ s. d.
Charges to collect
Service Instructions.

Received. From By

Sent, or sent out. At To By

Office Stamp. ARMY TELEGRAPHS 9 IV 17

Handed in at L22 Office 1.50 p m. Received m.

TO Hunt

*Sender's Number	Day of Month	In reply to Number	AAA
BM/95	9th	—	

am now leaving present head quarters for advanced head quarters at G12d7.3 and no reports through yet from DITCH or JUMP

1.8 pm

FROM
PLACE & TIME Chice 1.55 pm

* This line should be erased if not required.

(6334). Wt. W7496/M857. 500,000 Pads, 10/16. D. D. & L. (E489). Forms C/2123/3.

54

"C" Form (Duplicate).
MESSAGES AND SIGNALS.

Army Form C. 2123.
(In books of 50's in duplicate.)

No. of Message

Charges to Pay. £ s. d.

Office Stamp. YT 9.IV.17. TELEGRAPHS

Service Instructions. Priority

Handed in at YO Office 1.41 m. Received 1.50 p.m.

TO 9th Div

Sender's Number	Day of Month	In reply to Number	AAA
G 580	9		

Information received 1.20 pm aaa Enemy reported retiring in large numbers in N5A and N4D aaa Seen thought to be enemys guns seen retiring on ATHIES FAMPOUX road about 1 pm aaa added Corps 9th 12th 37th Divns Bdes and 15th DA

1-8 pm

FROM 15th Div

PLACE & TIME 1.40 pm

Wt. 432—M437 500,000 Pads. H W V 5/16 Forms C.2123.

58

"C" Form. Army Form C. 2123. (In books of 100).

MESSAGES AND SIGNALS. No. of Message

Prefix ~ Code AX Words 31

£ s. d.

Charges to collect

Received. From RLO By ack

Sent, or sent out. At m. To By

Office Stamp. [stamp] 9.IV.17

Service Instructions.

Handed in at RLO Office 1.4p m. Received 1.4p m.

TO 9th Divn 249

*Sender's Number	Day of Month	In reply to Number	AAA
G 895	9		

One infantry brigade 4th Division will support 9th Division closely in attack of Brown line aaa addsd 4th Divn repld 9th Divn

1.24pm

HL

FROM PLACE & TIME 17 Corps 12.55pm

* This line should be erased if not required.

(6334). Wt. W7493/M857. 500,000 Pads. 10/16. D. D. & L. (E489). Forms C/2123/3.

59

"A" Form.

Army Form C.2121
(In pads of 100).

MESSAGES AND SIGNALS.

No. of Message..........

Prefix ....Code............m. Office of Origin and Service Instructions.	Words / Charge Sent At..................m. To .... By	This message is on a/c of: ....Service. .... (Signature of "Franking Officer.")	Recd. at...............m. Date.................. From .... By ....

TO { 9th Division

Sender's Number.	Day of Month.	In reply to Number.	
*	9/4		AAA

FOOs report that our Infantry have entered TEES trench and passed it

From 26th Brigade
Place
Time 1-22pm

The above may be forwarded as now corrected. (Z)

.... Censor. Signature of Addressor or person authorised to telegraph in his name.

* This line should be erased if not required.

750,000. W 2186—M509. H. W. & V., Ld. 6/16.

60

"C" Form (Duplicate).
MESSAGES AND SIGNALS.

Army Form C. 2123.
(In books of 50's in duplicate.)
No. of Message ....

	Charges to Pay. s. d.	Office Stamp.
Service Instructions.		ARMY TELEGRAPHS

Handed in at .... Office ....m. Received ....m.

TO G Bn 280

Sender's Number	Day of Month	In reply to Number	AAA
575	9		

Eighth	11.40			
Inf	Bde			BLUE
LINE			RAILWAY	
		railway		
E		railway		
			Inf	Bde
			BLUE	
				artillery
			for	6.40
				Bn
				AR

FROM
PLACE & TIME 15th DIVN

12.55 pm

129/b

Wt. 482—M437 500,000 Pads. H W V 5/16 Forms C.2123.

61

"A" Form.

MESSAGES AND SIGNALS.

Army Form C.2121
(In pads of 100).
No. of Message ....

Prefix .... Code .... m.	Words	Charge	This message is on a/c of:	Recd. at .... m.
Office of Origin and Service Instructions.	Sent		.... *Service.*	Date ....
....	At .... m.			From ....
....	To		....	
....	By		(Signature of "Franking Officer.")	By ....

TO { AH

Sender's Number.	Day of Month.	In reply to Number.	AAA
*	9/4		

Everything is going well.
[illegible] going [illegible]
enemy observation. From the
[illegible] distances from the haystack
left of [illegible] one can
still see enemy position in our
advance. The men appear
to be rather done and are
inclined to hold what we
have got

From D/[illegible]
Place
Time 12-25 [illegible]

The above may be forwarded as now corrected. (Z)

.... *Censor.* | Signature of Addressor or person authorised to telegraph in his name.

* This line should be erased if not required.

750,000. W 2086—M509. H. W. & V., Ld. 6/16.

62

"A" Form.

MESSAGES AND SIGNALS.

Army Form C.2121
(In pads of 100).
No. of Message..........

Prefix ....Code..........m.	Words	Charge	This message is on a/c of:	Recd. at..........m.
Office of Origin and Service Instructions.	Sent		..........Service.	Date..........
....	At..........m.			From ....
....	To		....	
....	By		(Signature of "Franking Officer.")	By ....

TO CRA

Sender's Number.	Day of Month.	In reply to Number.	AAA
*	9/4		

1.12 pm the [illegible] [illegible]
can be observed

1.35 pm

From D/3rd Bde
Place
Time 1.44 pm

The above may be forwarded as now corrected.
(Z)
.... Censor.
Signature of Addressor or person authorised to telegraph in his name.

* This line should be erased if not required.

750,009. W 2186—M509. H. W. & V., Ld. 6/16.

63

"A" Form.
MESSAGES AND SIGNALS.

Army Form C.2121
(In pads of 100).
No. of Message..........

Prefix ....Code.............m. | Words | Charge
Office of Origin and Service Instructions.

Sent
At.....................m.
To ....
By ....

This message is on a/c of:
.................................*Service.*
(Signature of "Franking Officer.")

Recd. at................m.
Date...........................
From ....
By ....

TO { 9th Division

Sender's Number.	Day of Month.	In reply to Number.	AAA.
*	9		

FOO 52nd [illegible] RFA reports that
he saw six men entering
trench at H.9.a.4.0 [illegible]
was a [illegible] [illegible] on Eastern
edge of ATHIES

Recd 1.51 pm

From Rd. 9th Division
Place
Time 1.47 pm

The above may be forwarded as now corrected.
(Z)
Censor.
Signature of Addressor or person authorised to telegraph in his name.

* This line should be erased if not required.

750,000. W 2186—M509. H. W. & V., Ld. 6/16.

64

"A" Form. Army Form C.2121
(In pads of 100).

MESSAGES AND SIGNALS.

No. of Message..............

Prefix ....Code..........m.	Words / Charge	This message is on a/c of:	Recd. at..............m.
Office of Origin and Service Instructions.	Sent At..............m. To.............. By..............	..................Service. (Signature of "Franking Officer.")	Date.............. From.............. By..............

TO { 9th Division

* Sender's Number.	Day of Month.	In reply to Number.	AAA
	9th		

54th Division reports that
four spies dropped by aeroplane
have been seen at
H14 b 92 & H 9 c 50

From 54th Division
Place
Time 1.30 pm

The above may be forwarded as now corrected. (Z)

Censor. Signature of Addressor or person authorised to telegraph in his name.

* This line should be erased if not required.

750,000. W 2186—M509. H. W. & V., Ld. 6/16.

65

"A" Form

Army Form C. 2121

MESSAGES AND SIGNALS.

No. of Message..............

Prefix..........Code..........m. Office of Origin and Service Instructions.	Words / Charge. Sent At..........m. To.......... By..........	*This message is on a/c of:* ....*Service.* (Signature of "Franking Officer.")	Recd. at..........m. Date.......... From.......... By..........

TO 9th Division

Sender's Number.	Day of Month.	In reply to Number.	AAA
*	9th		

LAUREL, LIMPET and LILAC trenches taken

From Cha

Place

Time 2pm

The above may be forwarded as now corrected.

(Z)

.... *Censor.*

Signature of Addressor or person authorised to telegraph in his name.

* This line should be erased if not required.

(S.O. 1019). Wt. W 5148/M 701 50,000 Pads. 8/16. McC. & Co., Ltd., London.

65

"A" Form
MESSAGES AND SIGNALS.

Army Form C. 2121

No. of Message..........

Prefix.......Code.......m.	Words	Charge.	This message is on a/c of:	Recd. at ....m.
Office of Origin and Service Instructions.	Sent		..........Service.	Date..........
	At.........m.			From..........
	To..........			
	By..........		(Signature of "Franking Officer.")	By..........

TO C.R.A.

Sender's Number.	Day of Month.	In reply to Number.	AAA
*	9th		

11th Bde is going to support 12th Bde. Ready to let 4th Division to go through. Original programme to be adhered to.

From 9th Division
Place
Time 2 pm

The above may be forwarded as now corrected. (Z)

Censor. Signature of Addressor or person authorised to telegraph in his name.

* This line should be erased if not required.

(S.O. 1019). Wt. W 5148/M 701 50,000 Pads. 8/16. McC. & Co., Ltd., London.

66

"A" Form
Army Form C. 2121

MESSAGES AND SIGNALS.

No. of Message..............

Prefix..........Code..........m.	Words	Charge.	This message is on a/c of:	Recd. at ....m.
Office of Origin and Service Instructions.	Sent		..........Service.	Date..........
....	At..........m.			From..........
....	To..........			
....	By..........		(Signature of "Franking Officer.")	By..........

TO 9th Division

Sender's Number.	Day of Month.	In reply to Number.	AAA
*	9th		

9th Div Patrol report our troops have taken ATHIES

From 9th Division
Place
Time 1.20 Am.

The above may be forwarded as now corrected. (Z)

....
Censor. Signature of Addressor or person authorised to telegraph in his name.

* This line should be erased if not required.

(S.O. 1019). Wt. W 5148/M 701 50,000 Pads. 8/16. McC. & Co., Ltd., London.

64

To.

17th Corps.
15th Division.
34th Division.
51st Division.

No.G.424. 9/4.

Reports indicate that ATHIES and BROWN LINE have been captured.
Addressed 17th Corps, repeated 15th Division, 34th and 51st
Divisions .

9th Division.

2.30 p.m.

68

"A" Form
MESSAGES AND SIGNALS.

Army Form C. 2121

No. of Message..........

Prefix..........Code..........m. | Words | Charge.
Office of Origin and Service Instructions.

Sent
At..........m.
To..........
By..........

This message is on a/c of:
.... *Service.*
(Signature of "Franking Officer.")

Recd. at ....m.
Date..........
From..........
By..........

TO 9th Division

Sender's Number.	Day of Month.	In reply to Number.	AAA
*	9th		

Enemy are retiring in H9a central and along CAM and EFFY.
C.O.C. ordered General Tudor to put barrage on to FAMPOUX Line to catch them

From CRA
Place
Time 2.33 pm.

The above may be forwarded as now corrected. (Z)

Censor. Signature of Addressor or person authorised to telegraph in his name.

* This line should be erased if not required.

(S.O. 1019). Wt. W 5148/M 701 50,000 Pads. 8/16. McC. & Co., Ltd., London.

69

"A" Form
MESSAGES AND SIGNALS.

Army Form C. 2121

No. of Message..............

Prefix.............Code.............m. Office of Origin and Service Instructions.	Words / Charge. Sent At..........m. To.......... By..........	This message is on a/c of: ....Service. (Signature of "Franking Officer.")	Recd. at..........m. Date.......... From.......... By..........

TO CRA

Sender's Number.	Day of Month.	In reply to Number.	AAA
* EO41	9		

Arras observer message begins aaa 1.45 pm Brown line seems to be in our possession aaa ends aaa This is not confirmed yet by F.O.O. or Infy. Bde.

Recd 2.40 pm.

From 50th Bde RGA
Place
Time

The above may be forwarded as now corrected. (Z)

Censor. Signature of Addressor or person authorised to telegraph in his name.

* This line should be erased if not required.

(S.O. 1019). Wt. W 5148/M 701 50,000 Pads. 8/16. McC. & Co., Ltd., London.

69

"A" Form

Army Form C. 2121

MESSAGES AND SIGNALS.

No. of Message..........

Prefix..........Code..........m. | Words | Charge.

Office of Origin and Service Instructions.

Sent
At..........m.
To..........
By..........

This message is on a/c of:
..........Service.
(Signature of "Franking Officer.")

Recd. at..........m.
Date..........
From..........
By..........

TO CRA

Sender's Number.	Day of Month.	In reply to Number.	
* E0 42	9		AAA

ARRAS observer message begins at 12.30pm ane infantry advancing to Point du Jour in H.14.a & troops on crest on H.8.A and H.2.C.

2.45pm

From 50th Bde RGA
Place
Time

The above may be forwarded as now corrected.

(Z)

Censor. Signature of Addressor or person authorised to telegraph in his name.

* This line should be erased if not required.

(S.O. 1019). Wt. W 5148/M 701 50,000 Pads. 8/16. McC. & Co., Ltd., London.

"A" Form
MESSAGES AND SIGNALS.

Army Form C. 2121

No. of Message............

Prefix......Code......m.	Words	Charge.	This message is on a/c of:	Recd. at ......m.
Office of Origin and Service Instructions.	Sent		..........Service.	Date..........
	At......m.			From..........
	To..........			
	By..........		(Signature of "Franking Officer.")	By..........

TO CHQ

Sender's Number.	Day of Month.	In reply to Number.	
* E0 43	9		AAA

ARRAS observer reports 1-36 pm. The enemy came into view to the [illegible] of POINT du JOUR with the intent to attack but did not appear to have much confidence. They turned about and fled over the crest. They were in open order [illegible]

Rec 7.40 P.M.

From 50th Bde HQ
Place
Time

The above may be forwarded as now corrected. (Z)

Censor. Signature of Addressor or person authorised to telegraph in his name.

* This line should be erased if not required.

(S.O. 1019). Wt. W 5148/M 701 50,000 Pads. 8/16. McC. & Co., Ltd., London.

MESSAGES AND SIGNALS. No. of Message

Prefix Code Words 1

Received. From 40 By Crisp

Sent, or sent out. At m. To By

Office Stamp.

Charges to collect £ s. d.

Service Instructions. Priority

Handed in at York Office 2.37 p.m. Received 2.58 p.m.

TO 9th Div.

Sender's Number	Day of Month	In reply to Number	AAA
G 36	9th		

Flares shown 1-40 pm from H14B9.2 to H9b3.5 added 17th Corps 9th Divn reptd 51st and 4th Divns

Uey

3-10 pm

FROM PLACE & TIME 34 Divn 2.15 pm

* This line should be erased if not required.

(6334). Wt. W7496/M857. 500,000 Pads. 10/16. D. D. & L. (E 489). Forms C/2123/3.

40

71

"C" Form.

Army Form C. 2123.
(In books of 100).

MESSAGES AND SIGNALS. No. of Message

Prefix Code Words	Received.	Sent, or sent out.	Office Stamp.
£ s. d. Charges to collect	From By	At m. To By	
Service Instructions.			

Handed in at [illegible] Office [illegible] m. Received [illegible] m.

TO [illegible]

*Sender's Number	Day of Month	In reply to Number	AAA
[illegible]	9	286	

[illegible]

3.44 pm

FROM
PLACE & TIME CHASE
2.25 pm

* This line should be erased if not required.

(6334). Wt. W7496/M857. 500,000 Pads. 10/16. D. D. & L. (E 489). Forms C/2123/3.

72

Army Form C. 2123.
(In books of 100).

"C" Form.

MESSAGES AND SIGNALS.

No. of Message ....

Prefix ..... Code ..... Words 84	Received. From [illegible] By [illegible]	Sent, or sent out. At ..... m. To ..... By	Office Stamp.
£ s. d. Charges to collect			ARMY SIGNALS IV.17
Service Instructions.			

Handed in at R.C.O. Office 3 p.m. Received 3 2 p m.

TO 9th Divn 274

*Sender's Number	Day of Month	In reply to Number	AAA
GB 899	9/4		

Following	wire	from	GOCRA	17th
Corps	To	9th	34th	and
51st	Divn	artillery	begins	aaa
All	remaining	firing	battery	and
first	line	wagons	will	move
forward	at	once	to	wagon
lines	EAST	of	ANZIN	aaa
Routes	and	orders	of	march
as	given	in	17	Corps
march	Table	issued	with	GS 39/13
of	3rd	April	aaa	DA
COLUMNS	and	BA	Columns	will
not	move	until	further	orders
aaa	Ends	aaa	Added	9th
34th	51st	Divns	repeated	GOCRA
			3 44 pm	

FROM 17 Corps
PLACE & TIME 2-30 pm

* This line should be erased if not required.

(6334). Wt. W7495/M857. 500,000 Pads. 10/16. D. D. & L. (E 489). Forms C/2123/3.

To.

15th Division.
34th Division.

No.G.432. 9/4.

Troops of 4th Division having passed through troops of 9th Division on BROWN LINE G.O.C., 9th Division has handed over Command to G.O.C, 4th Division.

4.26 p.m. 9th Division.

Army Form C. 2123.
(In books of 100).

"C" Form.
MESSAGES AND SIGNALS.

No. of Message..........

Prefix.......... Code.......... Words.......... £ s. d. Charges to collect	Received. From.......... By..........	Sent, or sent out. At..........m. To.......... By..........
Service Instructions.		Office Stamp. ARMY TELEGRAPHS 17.9.IV.17.

Handed in at.......... Office..........m. Received..........m.

TO [illegible]

295

*Sender's Number	Day of Month	In reply to Number	AAA
[illegible]	[illegible]		

[illegible] ERACK [illegible] BLUE [illegible] NOT [illegible]

5.40pm

FROM 17 [illegible]

PLACE & TIME [illegible]

* This line should be erased if not required.

(6334). Wt. W7495/M857. 500,000 Pads. 10/16. D. D. & L. (E 489). Forms C/2123/3.

45

(3)

To.

26th Brigade.
27th Brigade.
S.A. Brigade.
"Q".

No.G.432. 9/4.

On Relief by 4th Division 26th, 27th, and S.A. Brigades will withdraw to the BLUE and BLACK Line.a.a.a. Location of Brigade H.Q. to be notified as early as possible. Boundaries between Brigades will remain as at present a.a.a. Acknowledge.

4.50 p.m. 9th Division

76

Army Form C. 2123.
(In books of 100).

"C" Form.

MESSAGES AND SIGNALS.

No. of Message..........

Prefix ...... Code ...... Words	Received.	Sent, or sent out.	Office Stamp.
£ s. d.	From	At	Y1 9.IV.17. TELEGRAPHS
Charges to collect	By	To	
Service Instructions.		By	

Handed in at .... Office ...... m. Received ...... m.

TO [illegible]

698

*Sender's Number	Day of Month	In reply to Number	AAA
[illegible]			

[illegible] report situation as follows aaa [illegible] line from B.27.c.5.0 to B.27.a.5.5 and on [illegible] holds [illegible] from [illegible] and have [illegible] of [illegible] further information [illegible]

FROM

PLACE & TIME

* This line should be erased if not required.

(6334). Wt. W7496/M857. 500,000 Pads. 10/16. D. D. & L. (E 489). Forms C/2123/3.

"C" Form.

Army Form C. 2123.
(In books of 100).

MESSAGES AND SIGNALS.

No. of Message

Prefix ...... Code ...... Words	Received.	Sent, or sent out.	Office Stamp.
£ s. d.	From	At ...... m.	ARMY TELEGRAPHS YI 9 IV 17
Charges to collect	By	To	
Service Instructions.		By	

Handed in at ...... Office ...... m. Received ...... m.

TO [illegible]

298

*Sender's Number	Day of Month	In reply to Number	AAA
[illegible]			

[illegible handwritten message]

FROM [illegible]
PLACE & TIME

* This line should be erased if not required.

(6334). Wt. W7496/M857. 500,000 Pads. 10/16. D. D. & L. (E 489). Forms C/2123/3.

77

"C" Form (Duplicate).
(In books of 50's in duplicate.)

MESSAGES AND SIGNALS.

No. of Message……………

Prefix / Code / Words	Charges to Pay.	Office Stamp.
[illegible]	£	YI -9 IV.17. TELEGRAPHS

Service Instructions.

Handed in at…………Office………m. Received………m.

TO 9th Div

299

Sender's Number	Day of Month	In reply to Number	AAA

[illegible]

6.25

FROM
PLACE & TIME 12th Div. 5.45 pm

Wt. 432—M437 500,000 Pads. H W V 5/16 Forms C.2123.

78

"C" Form.

Army Form C. 2123.
(In books of 100).

MESSAGES AND SIGNALS.

No. of Message..................

Prefix SB Code [illegible] Words [illegible]	Received.	Sent, or sent out. Office Stamp.
£ s. d.	From [illegible]	At .... m.
Charges to collect	By [illegible]	To ....
Service Instructions.		By ....

ARMY TELEGRAPHS
Y1 -9.IV.17.

Handed in at [illegible] Office .... m. Received [illegible] m.

TO [illegible]

300

*Sender's Number	Day of Month	In reply to Number	AAA
G[illegible]	9		

Report [illegible] all
the objectives including HYDERABAD
redoubt [illegible] over 100 prisoners
taken [illegible] being consolidated
by 2 Battns [illegible] direction
of GAVRELLE [illegible]
[illegible]
[illegible] eastern
edge of FAMPOUX [illegible] Cavalry
reported [illegible] seen
at [illegible]

6-25

FROM 4th Divn

PLACE & TIME 5.25 pm

* This line should be erased if not required.

(6334). Wt. W7496/M857. 500,000 Pads. 10/16. D. D. & L. (E 489). Forms C/2123/3.

79

To.

26th Brigade.
27th Brigade.
S.A. Brigade.

No.G.437. 9/4.

Brigades will report as early as possible when they are re-organised and what their approximate fighting strength is in view of the possibility of being required to assist in re-pelling a Counter-attack.

6.25 p.m. 9th Division.

Army Form C. 2123.
(In books of 100).

"C" Form.
MESSAGES AND SIGNALS.

No. of Message

Prefix SB Code [illegible] Words [illegible]	Received.	Sent, or sent out.	Office Stamp.
£ s. d.	From [illegible]	At m.	
Charges to collect	By [illegible]	To	
Service Instructions.		By	

Handed in at [illegible] Office m. Received [illegible] m.

TO [illegible]

302

*Sender's Number	Day of Month	In reply to Number	AAA
G 13	9		

57th [illegible] FOO at H16 c83
reports [illegible] our
infantry [illegible] FAMPOUX [illegible]
[illegible]
[illegible]
[illegible]

6.42 pm

FROM [illegible]
PLACE & TIME

* This line should be erased if not required.

(6334). Wt. W7496/M857. 500,000 Pads. 10/16. D. D. & L. (E 489). Forms C/2123/3.

81

"C" Form.

(In books of 100).

MESSAGES AND SIGNALS.

No. of Message

Prefix Code Words	Received.	Sent, or sent out.	Office Stamp.
£ s. d.	From [illegible]	At	ARMY TELEGRAPHS Y1 -9.IV.17.
Charges to collect	By [illegible]	To	
Service Instructions.		By	

Handed in at [illegible] Office 7.[illegible] m. Received 7.[illegible] m.

TO [illegible] 9th [illegible]

*Sender's Number	Day of Month	In reply to Number	AAA
G.B.9.[illegible]	9/4	(511)	

Contact aeroplane out. Few reports flares shown from H.16.d central to H.11.a central area. Our men are in [illegible] FAMPOUX and [illegible] established east end of FAMPOUX. [illegible] of [illegible] seen [illegible] after [illegible] H.12.a and H.12.b [illegible] flares [illegible] of air [illegible] front [illegible] of [illegible] FAMPOUX

[illegible] (signature)

FROM 17th Corps

PLACE & TIME 7.0 pm

* This line should be erased if not required.

(6334). Wt. W7496/M857. 500,000 Pads. 10/16. D. D. & L. (E 489). Forms C/2123/3.

82

To.

26th Brigade.
27th Brigade.
S.A. Brigade.

No.G.440. 9/4.

11th Brigade report HYDERABAD Redoubt now definitely held a.a.a. Counter attacks have ceased a.a.a. They are not in touch with the 12th Brigade on the GREEN Line, but have formed a defensive flank facing South. a.a.a. They have received report from Battalion of 12th Brigade that FAMPOUX has not been taken a.a.a. Enemy reported to be entrenched South of GAVRELLE road from H.3.d.7.3. to H.4.d.0.1. and thence in Trench running due East a.a.a. Also report enemy entrenching

83

"A" Form
MESSAGES AND SIGNALS.

Army Form C. 2121

No. of Message..............

Prefix.........Code.........m. Office of Origin and Service Instructions.	Words	Charge.	This message is on a/c of: ....Service. (Signature of "Franking Officer.")	Recd. at ......m. Date...... From...... By......
	Sent At.......m. To....... By.......			

TO 9th Division

Sender's Number.	Day of Month.	In reply to Number.	AAA
* J.C. 56	9th		

Bde H.Q. established FORESTIER REDOUBT

From 26th Bde
Place
Time 9pm.

The above may be forwarded as now corrected. (Z)

Censor. Signature of Addressor or person authorised to telegraph in his name.

* This line should be erased if not required.

(S.O. 1019). Wt. W 5148/M 701 50,000 Pads. 8/16. McC. & Co., Ltd., London.

84

MESSAGES AND SIGNALS.

No. of Message

Prefix SM Code [illegible] Words 34

£ s. d.

Charges to collect

Service Instructions.

Received. From [illegible] By [illegible]

Sent, or sent out. At m. To By

Office Stamp.

Handed in at RB Office 9.5 m. Received 9.35 m.

TO Hunt

*Sender's Number	Day of Month	In reply to Number	AAA
BM 963	9		

Bde Hd Qrs established at No 23 Dugout in our original front line o.c.n. Map reference Sheet ARRAS 51 B N W 3 G 11 d 9 2 and [illegible] reports meet [illegible]

9.35 pm 320

FROM

PLACE & TIME [illegible] 9.5 pm

* This line should be erased if not required.

(6334). Wt. W7496/M857. 500,000 Pads. 10/16. D. D. & L. (E 489). Forms C/2123/3.

APPENDICES

12 - 4 - 17

85

"A" Form
MESSAGES AND SIGNALS.

Army Form C. 2121

No. of Message

Prefix ... Code ... m. | Words | Charge.

Office of Origin and Service Instructions.

Copy

Sent
At ... m.
To ...
By ...

This message is on a/c of:
... Service.
(Signature of "Franking Officer.")

Recd. at ... m.
Date
From
By

TO 9th Division

Sender's Number.	Day of Month.	In reply to Number.	AAA
* G.B. 25	11th		

4th Division will place one infantry Brigade at disposal of 9th Division for tomorrows operations aaa Selected Bde to be reported to Corps H.Q. aaa Arrangements to be made between 4th and 9th Divisions aaa addsd 4th and 9th Divs repeated G.O.C. RA.

Recd 12.5 am.

From 14th Corps
Place
Time 11.40 pm

The above may be forwarded as now corrected.

(Z)

Censor. Signature of Addressor or person authorised to telegraph in his name.

* This line should be erased if not required.

(S.O. 1019). Wt.- W 5148/M 701 50,000 Pads. 8/16. McC. & Co., Ltd., London.

89

"A" Form

MESSAGES AND SIGNALS.

Army Form C. 2121

No. of Message ....

Prefix............Code............m. Office of Origin and Service Instructions.	Words	Charge.	This message is on a/c of:	Recd. at ....m.
Copy		Sent At............m. To............ By............	............Service. (Signature of "Franking Officer.")	Date .... From............ By............

TO 9th Divn

Sender's Number.	Day of Month.	In reply to Number.	AAA
* G.B. 32	12th		

One Field Coy R.E. 9th Divn at present working on Blangy Road under orders of CRE 9th Divn will be available for 9th Divn operations today if required aaa Addressed 9th Divn repeated CE 17th Corps

Recd 11 am.

From 17th Corps

Place

Time 10 40 am

The above may be forwarded as now corrected. (Z)

Censor. Signature of Addressor or person authorised to telegraph in his name.

* This line should be erased if not required.

(S.O. 1019). Wt. W 5148/M 701 50,000 Pads. 8/16. McC. & Co., Ltd., London.

88

MESSAGES AND SIGNALS. No. of Message..................

Prefix.......... Code.......... Words..........	Received.	Sent, or sent out.	Office Stamp.
£ s. d.	From SX	At..........m.	[illegible] 12
Charges to collect	By..........	To..........	
Service Instructions. Priority		By..........	

Handed in at R B Office 11 35 am. Received 11 44 am.

TO Hunt

*Sender's Number	Day of Month	In reply to Number	AAA
Bm 39	12		

Battalion Commanders state men have had no sleep for four nights and no hot food since night of 8th aaa Many were stiff with cold this morning and had to be lifted out of the trenches and rubbed aaa There is no doubt men not in a fit condition for severe operations

FROM
PLACE & TIME Chase 11-30 am

* This line should be erased if not required.

(6334). Wt. W7496/M857. 500,000 Pads. 10/16. D. D. & L. (E 489). Forms C/2123/3.

89

"A" Form

Army Form C. 2121

MESSAGES AND SIGNALS.

No. of Message..............

Prefix.............. Code.............. m. | Words | Charge. | This message is on a/c of: .... Service. (Signature of "Franking Officer.") | Recd. at .... m. Date .... From .... By ....

Office of Origin and Service Instructions. Copy

Sent At.............. m. To.............. By..............

TO 9th Divn

Sender's Number.	Day of Month.	In reply to Number.	AAA
* G.B. 43	12		

14th Corps ultimate objective GREENLAND HILL and the Spur SW. of PLOUVAIN aaa If after capture of todays objective it appears possible to secure further objectives it is important that you should do so as otherwise they will have to be attacked the next day aaa Addressed aaa Addsd 9th Divn repeated GOCRA 4th Divn 34th Divn 6th Corps

Recd 2 10 pm

From 14th Corps

Place

Time 12 50 pm.

The above may be forwarded as now corrected. (Z)

Censor. Signature of Addressor or person authorised to telegraph in his name.

* This line should be erased if not required.

(S.O. 1019). Wt. W 5148/M 701 50,000 Pads. 8/16. McC. & Co., Ltd., London.

90

"A" Form

Army Form C. 2121

MESSAGES AND SIGNALS.

No. of Message ....

Prefix..........Code..........m. Office of Origin and Service Instructions.	Words	Charge.	This message is on a/c of:	Recd. at ....m.
	Sent At..........m. To.......... By..........		..........Service. (Signature of "Franking Officer.")	Date .... From.......... By..........

TO 9th Divn

Sender's Number.	Day of Month.	In reply to Number.	AAA
* G105	12		

Herewith the following information received from aeroplane reconnaissance today aaa H.6.b.5.5 – H.6.a.0.7 – H.6.a.5.0 – H.12.b.6.5 – H.12.b.7.0 – H.12.a.7.5 – H.12.a.9.4 – H.12.a.4.4 – H.12.a.6.0 joining up with existing trenches H.15.b.5.7 to H.18.b.7.3 trench H.12.b.7.0 to H.12.b.2.9 aaa Trench from I.13.b.6.2 to I.15.b.2.8 and from I.13.b.6.2 behind CHEMICAL WORKS to N.E. corner of Cemetery aaa Trenches connecting Chateau with I.14.b.5.7 – N.W. corner of CEMETERY – MOUNT PLEASANT wood road at H.24.a.9.6. aaa Work appears to have been done in cutting from I.14.a.6.5 to I.13.b.7.2

From H.Q. Division
Place
Time 2.43pm

The above may be forwarded as now corrected. (Z)

Censor. Signature of Addressor or person authorised to telegraph in his name.

* This line should be erased if not required.

(S.O. 1019). Wt. W 5148/M 701 50,000 Pads. 8/16. McC. & Co., Ltd., London.

91

"A" Form

Army Form C. 2121

MESSAGES AND SIGNALS.

No. of Message ....

Prefix......... Code.........m. Office of Origin and Service Instructions.	Words / Charge. Sent At.........m. To......... By.........	This message is on a/c of: .... Service. (Signature of "Franking Officer.")	Recd. at ....m. Date .... From......... By.........
Copy			

TO 9th Division

Sender's Number.	Day of Month.	In reply to Number.	AAA
* BM 200	12		

We have to advance 1480 yards in full view before we get up to opening line of barrage aaa Can objective be smoked from Zero minus 45 min onwards until objective is reached aaa Ref G486 instructions contained therein only possible if protective barrage beyond objective is withheld which I hope will be permitted aaa Have asked SA Bde and SA Bde agrees

From 26th Bde

Place

Time 3 10 pm

The above may be forwarded as now corrected. (Z)

Censor. Signature of Addressor or person authorised to telegraph in his name.

* This line should be erased if not required.

(S.O. 1019). Wt. W 5148/M 701 50,000 Pads. 8/16. McC. & Co., Ltd., London.

92

"C" Form

Army Form C. 2123.
(In books of 100.)

MESSAGES AND SIGNALS. No. of Message..................

Prefix ...... Code ...... Words ...... £ s. d. Charges to collect	Received From ...... By	Sent, or sent out At ......m. To ...... By	Office Stamp.
Service Instructions.			

Handed in at ...... Office ......m. Received ......m.

TO ......

*Sender's Number	Day of Month	In reply to Number	AAA
	12		

A german ... to gun Bty are in action on the Road from E28d70 to I4a75 please inform Artillery

Corps HQ informed
5 ...

FROM
PLACE & TIME

100 Bde
4.5 pm

* This line should be erased if not required.

(D 8188) Wt. w. 7496–M857 250,000 Pads. 1/17 H & S (E489.) Forms/C.2123/3.

92

MESSAGES AND SIGNALS. No. of Message..................

Prefix......Code......Words......	Received	Sent, or sent out	Office Stamp.
£ s. d.	From [illegible]	At..........m.	TELEGRAPHS
Charges to collect	By [illegible]	To..........	
Service Instructions.		By..........	

Handed in at [illegible] Office [illegible] m. Received..........m.

TO [illegible]

*Sender's Number	Day of Month	In reply to Number	AAA
	12		

[illegible]	400	reports	as	follows
[illegible]	[illegible]	at	9	[illegible]
our	[illegible]	infantry	have	all
come	back	aaa	[illegible]	aaa
Time	5.20	pm		

FROM
PLACE & TIME [illegible] 5.30 pm

* This line should be erased if not required.

(B 8188) Wt. w. 7496—M857 250,000 Pads. 1/17 H & S (E489.) Forms/C.2123/3.

9H

To.

17th Corps.

No.G.492. 12/4.

Følloving report from F.O.O. 51st Brigade a.a.a. As far as I can see our Infantry have all come back ends a.a.a. Timed 5.20p.m. a.a.a.

6.7.p.m. 9th Division.

95

To.

27th Brigade.
S.A. Brigade.

No.G.499. 12/4.

The following reports from Observers of 17th Division South of the River have been received a.a.a. 6.20 p.m. troops on North reached GAVRELLE - ROEUX road between CHEMICAL WORKS and cross Roads I.7.a.4.4. still advancing a.a.a. White lights sent up Northern edge of ROEUX a.a.a. 7.10 p.m. Prisoners coming in from direction GAVRELLE - ROEUX Road a.a.a. Red flares seen at I.7.d.6.5. a.a.a. 11th Brigade also reported attack of 9th Division appeared to have progressed on the right and it is probable they have reached ROEUX - GAVRELLE road a.a.a. G.O.C's Brigades will report whether there can have been any foundation for such reports a.a.a. Corps wants early information as to whether there is any possibility of the reports having any foundation as it may affect the locality of the bombardment which will take place during tomorrow.

9th Division.

11.55 p.m.

96

"C" Form
Army Form C. 2123.
(In books of 100.)

MESSAGES AND SIGNALS.

No. of Message..........

Prefix .... Code .... Words ....
£ s. d.
Charges to collect
Service Instructions.
Priority

Received
From ....
By ....

Sent, or sent out
At .... m.
To ....
By ....

Office Stamp.
ARMY TELEGRAPHS 12 IV 17

Handed in at .... Office 6.35 p m. Received .... m.

TO Hant

*Sender's Number	Day of Month	In reply to Number	AAA
BM 311	12th		

attack has not progressed
beyond the bottom of the
valley enemy are firing lights
from the [illegible] trench the
position of which reached [illegible]
20 minutes ago enemy's barrage
is good but my line
appears to be holding [illegible]
[illegible] do not know what
progress the [illegible] are making
but think that they have
not succeeded as enemy lights
can be seen [illegible] from
[illegible] [illegible] [illegible] [illegible] front
of [illegible] X

FROM Cove
PLACE & TIME 6.35 pm

* This line should be erased if not required.

(B 8188) Wt. w. 7496–M857 250,000 Pads. 1/17 H & S (E489.) Forms/C.2123/3.

94

To.

XVII Corps.
26th Brigade.
S.A. Brigade.
C.R.A.

No.G.494. 12/4/17.

Message from 27th Brigade timed 6.30 states attack has not progressed beyond the bottom of the Valley and enemy are firing lights from the New Trench reported by R.F.C. observer a.a.a. Enemy's barrage is good, but Machine Gun Fire appears to be holding us up a.a.a. 27th Brigade does not know what progress S.A. Brigade is making but thinks they have not succeeded as enemy's lights can be seen fired from a short way in front of FAMPOUX. Should you require the two Battalions referred to they will be replaced by two Battalions of 10th Brigade which is in Divisional Reserve.

7.20p.m. 9th Division.

"C" Form

Army Form C. 2123.
(In books of 100.)

MESSAGES AND SIGNALS. No. of Message.........

Prefix AB Code HS Words 74

Received From KT By [illegible]

Sent, or sent out At.........m. To......... By.........

Office Stamp.

Charges to collect £ s. d.

Service Instructions. Priority Operation

Handed in at RB Office 8.25 m. Received 8.28 m.

TO Hunt

(14)

*Sender's Number	Day of Month	In reply to Number	AAA
Bm 453	12		

attack has failed aaa very many casualties caused by machine gun fire from CHEMICAL WORKS and direction of MOUNT PLEASANT WOOD aaa attacking troops reached a point slightly in advance of that reached yesterday but no movement of any kind could be seen at 7.30 pm aaa RANK approximate strength 260 still intact and in western end of FAMPOUX aaa advise what action to be taken.

8.20 pm

FROM Chase

PLACE & TIME 7 pm

* This line should be erased if not required.

(B 8188) Wt. w. 7426—M857 250,000 Pads. 1/17 H & S (E489.) Forms/C.2123/3.

To.

26th Brigade.
S.A. Brigade.

No.G.495. 12/4.

Division on our right are sending out patrols to try and gain touch with our right flank a.a.a. They will cross railway Bridge H.24 A. a.a.a.

10.40 am. 9th Division.

100

To.

26th Brigade.
27th Brigade.
S.A. Brigade.
197 M. G. Coy.
C.R.A.
C.R.E.
4th Division.
17th Corps.

No.G.496. 12/4.

26th Brigade will take over tonight the front line from River SCARPE to HYDERABAD Redoubt (exclusive) a.a.a. The 4th. Division will continue to hold the line from HYDERABAD Redoubt (inclusive) to H.4.b.3.5. a.a.a. Boundary between 4th and 9th Division will be HOARY and HECTIC Trenches (inclusive to 4th. Division) thence a line to cross roads at H.15.a.9.9. thence the ATHIES ST LAURENT BLANGY Road a.a.a. The S.A. Brigade on relief will be withdrawn to FAMPOUX and the German fourth line system South of the FAMPOUX - ATHIES Road a.a.a. The 27th Brigade on relief will be withdrawn to the German fourth line system North of the FAMPOUX - ATHIES Road and to ATHIES a.a.a. Where ground has been gained in front of the original front line the new line will be consolidated provided the troops holding it are not isolated a.a.a. In cases where troops are isolated they should be withdrawn to the best line which will enable connection to be maintained with troops on the flanks a.a.a. Details of reliefs will be arranged between G.O.C. 26th Brigade and G.O.C. 27th, S.A., 10th and 12th. Brigades a.a.a. Completion of relief to be reported to DivisionalHeadquarters a.a.a. The 26th Brigade will arrange to place a proportion of Vickers Guns in the front line to meet and break up any possible counter attack a.a.a. Great care is to be taken in the selection of suitable positions so as to ensure that the fire of adjacent pairs of Guns crosses and that no intervening ground is unswept by Machine Gun fire a.a.a. Machine Gun Fire will be employed during the night to prevent the enemy from consolidating his line a.a.a. The 197th Machine Gun Company is placed at the disposal of the 26th Brigade a.a.a. An Officer of the Company will report to G.O.C. 26th Brigade for orders as to disposal a.a.a. ACKNOWLEDGE a.a.a.

Addressed 26th, 27th and S.A. Brigades and 197th Machine Gun Company. Repeated C.R.A, C.R.E, 4th Division and 17th Corps.

11 p.m. 9th Division.

102

"C" Form

Army Form C. 2123.
(In books of 100.)

MESSAGES AND SIGNALS. No. of Message..........

Prefix Sm Code KB Words 43 £ s. d. Charges to collect Service Instructions.	Received From ROO By	Sent, or sent out At..........m. To.......... By..........	Office Stamp. ARMY TELEGRAPHS 12.IV.17.

Handed in at RCO Office 10.27 pm. Received 11.07 pm.

TO 9 Divn

*Sender's Number	Day of Month	In reply to Number	AAA
G.1356	12/4		

Divns will arrange to harass Germans with incessant machine gun and Rifle fire and will interfere with enemy consolidation by every means in their power and assist 4th 9th and 34th Divns and [illegible]

58

11-20 p

FROM PLACE & TIME 17 Corps 9-55 pm

* This line should be erased if not required.

(B 8070) Wt. w. 7496—M857 250,000 Pads. 10/16 H & S (E436.) Forms/C.2123/3.

www.ingramcontent.com/pod-product-compliance
Lightning Source LLC
Chambersburg PA
CBHW081427300426
44108CB00016BA/2320
* 9 7 8 1 4 7 4 5 0 7 3 4 9 *